Healthcare Reform in China

Carine Milcent

Healthcare Reform in China

From Violence To Digital Healthcare

Carine Milcent
CNRS and Paris School of Economics (PSE)
Paris, France

ISBN 978-3-319-69735-2   ISBN 978-3-319-69736-9   (eBook)
https://doi.org/10.1007/978-3-319-69736-9

Library of Congress Control Number: 2017958008

This Palgrave Pivot imprint is published by Springer Nature
The registered company is Springer International Publishing AG
The registered company address is: Gewerbestrasse 11, 6330 Cham, Switzerland

To Béatrice, Johanne, Léonie et Alexandre….

And, to Thomas

ACKNOWLEDGEMENTS

I would like to thank Thomas Serrurier for his active involvement in this book, helping me get results of better quality. I am really grateful to him for his patience and support in overcoming numerous obstacles I have been facing through the research and writing.

I would like to thank relatives such as Celia for their feedback, cooperation and of course friendship.

I would like to thank my friends for accepting nothing less than excellence from me. Last but not the least, I would like to thank my family: my kids and husband for supporting me spiritually throughout writing this book and my life in general.

Opinions expressed in this book are the author's.

This book is divided into 10 chapters that can be read separately, even though knowing the background and overlays of reforms that have built up current situation is definitely beneficial to understand the current challenges of the healthcare system and the next round of changes likely to happen.

This research is supported by the Projet International de Coopération Scientifique (PICS) research grant No. 263008 to the French National Center for Scientific Research (CNRS).

CONTENTS

LIST OF FIGURES

LIST OF TABLES

CHAPTER 1

Introduction

Abstract This book aims at presenting the Chinese healthcare system and its latest reforms. Chapter 2 presents the specific definition of a health good and its implications. Then, in Chap. 3, the general landscape of healthcare in China is described. Chapter 4 focuses on public hospitals and their evolution, while Chap. 5 analyzes the status and actual situation of medical staff. As a thread throughout these chapters, inefficiencies in the system tend to appear, as do the current reforms aimed at dealing with them. Public insurance plans implemented over the past two decades are discussed in Chap. 6. The medical drug market is presented in Chap. 7 and the determinants of the phenomenon of violence affecting Chinese hospitals are described, through the relationship between the patient or patient's relatives and medical staff, in Chap. 8. Chapter 9 delves deeply into the development of digital healthcare in China and how it can solve inefficiencies in the hospital system. The concluding chapter (Chap. 10) offers a vision of the future directions that the Chinese social model could take, based on the observations in previous chapters of current reforms and experiments.

Keywords Healthcare in China • Insurance • Medical staff • Public hospitals • Medical drug market • Digital healthcare

© The Author(s) 2018   1
C. Milcent, *Healthcare Reform in China*,
https://doi.org/10.1007/978-3-319-69736-9_1

The healthcare industry in China is experiencing a period of high-speed development—it had grown to RMB 2 trillion in 2014 and was set to reach nearly RMB 3 trillion in 2016.[1] At the heart of this industry stand public hospitals. Indeed, China's public hospitals manage 90% of consultations for ambulatory care or outpatient care, and 90% of hospital inpatient admissions.[2] As such, public hospitals deal with requests for outpatient treatment just as they must deal with inpatient treatment.

Access to healthcare is at the intersection of many challenges faced by China today. Aware of the stakes, the government has been engaged in a series of reforms in which two apparently opposite philosophies co-exist: a highly regulated market and incentive for competition in healthcare through the development of the private market. 2009[3] marked a turning point. Given the need to establish basic access for all, the State Council announced the introduction of universal and comprehensive health coverage by 2020. This objective was pursued during the 12th Five Year Plan (2012–2016).

The 12th Five Year National Healthcare Service System Plan 2015–2010 announced a universal "safe, effective and affordable basic healthcare services" by 2020. Five major issues were pinpointed:

- Expand basic medical-insurance programmes
- Establish a national essential drug system
- Develop a primary healthcare service system
- Provide equal access to urban and rural residents
- Continue the reforms of public hospitals.

The 13th Five Year Plan (2016–2020) pursues the same objective with some new directions. The "Healthy China Action Plan" focuses on deepening healthcare reform through:

- Strong efforts to develop advanced medical equipment
- The development of traditional Chinese medicine (TCM) healthcare services
- The implementation of a "fitness for all" strategy
- The encouragement of non-governmental participation in the healthcare services industry
- Granting non-profit private hospitals the same status as public hospitals.

Before examining the healthcare system in all its various incarnations, I first offer a brief overview of the current state of the population's health and healthcare. In 2015, mainland China had a natural population growth of 5.21 per thousand, with a gross birth rate of 12.37% and a gross death rate of 7.16%. Urban residents now account for 54.8% of the total population (or 1.4 billion people). The population is 51.2% male and 48.8% female.[4] Life expectancy has improved considerably over the years: while in 1990 it was 67 years for men and 70 for women, by 2010 it had risen to 72.5 for men and 76.8 for women. Likewise, the mortality rate for children under five and the maternal mortality rate have seen distinct improvements. However, it is also apparent that medication (especially antibiotics) is currently being over-consumed. It is acknowledged that 70% of prescription medicines contain antibiotics.[5] One consequence of this inappropriate use of medication is an increase in morbidity and mortality. Lianping Yang et al.[6] estimate that each year, 2.5 million patients are admitted to hospital suffering from unwelcome medicinal side-effects.[7] On the economic front, China's gross domestic product (GDP) is not far behind that of the United States.[8] While the growth rate appears to be slowing,[9] it was nonetheless estimated to reach 6.9% for 2016.[10] Overall, the general level of wealth among the population is on the rise. In 1990 per capita GDP was RMB 1644, whereas by 2012 it had reached RMB 38,420.

Access to healthcare in China today poses a completely different challenge to that of 30 years ago, mainly because of rapid ageing of the population, a result of the one-child policy, which led to a low birth rate, and an increase in life expectancy made possible by the organization of the health system set up during the Maoist period, and finally by the economic growth of the past three decades (Fig. 1.1). In this new demographic context, the system of access to healthcare needs to be reorganized in order to treat patients in long-term care or in situations of dependence. The creation of reception structures is under discussion, and pilot experiments have been put in place. Although the third plenum of the 18th Party Congress in November 2013 decided to progressively relax the one-child policy, with the possibility of a second child in a specified number of cases,[11] demographic inertia makes the impact of ageing inevitable.

Alongside these developments, the demand for healthcare has also undergone a transformation due to the drastic reduction of poverty.[12] However, the distribution of the fruits of growth is far from homogeneous. Central and provincial government spending is much higher in rich

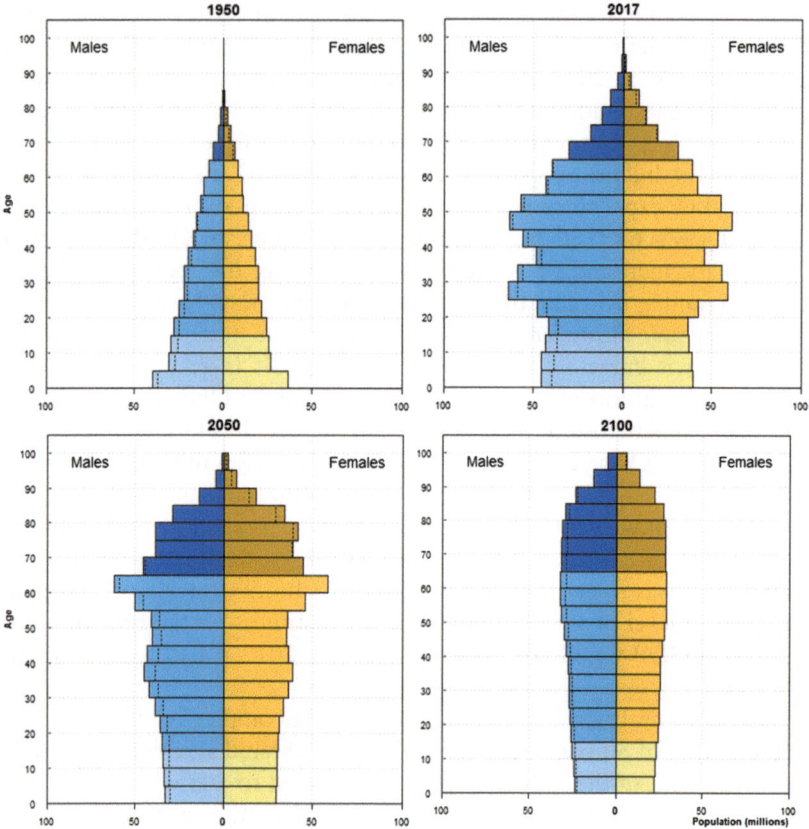

Fig. 1.1 Ageing population, the demographic shift. The dotted line indicates the excess male or female population in certain age groups. The data are in thousands or millions. Source: United Nations, Department of Economic and Social Affairs, Population Division (2017). World Population Prospects: The 2017. https://esa.un.org/unpd/wpp/Graphs/DemographicProfiles/

and urban areas than in poor and rural areas.[13] Thus, the Chinese health system is now confronted with a highly segmented population in terms of income and expectations.

As a result, the Chinese healthcare system has been forced to adapt, not only to demographic changes but also to a demand for new treatments: from dealing with a low-income population with high birth and death rates, primarily requiring basic care, it has moved to looking after a comparatively older population with a low birth rate and higher income, demanding ever-more-effective healthcare treatment. Since the economic reforms, the expected level of treatment quality has risen considerably, which *de facto* reduces the number of establishments able to meet these expectations to only the very best urban hospitals, thus creating high demand and low supply for such treatment, while less reliable healthcare establishments have found themselves in a situation where there is too much supply, but insufficient demand.

Beyond the external shocks associated with demographic, economic, and social transition, China's healthcare system faces particular challenges due to the specific role played by public hospitals. The quality of care now expected by a growing proportion of the population is only accessible in some public hospitals, mainly those with a high level of care, referred to as Level 3 (*sanji* 三级), and which are therefore at the heart of the Chinese health system. Contrary to practice in the West where the patient consults a general practitioner in a healthcare practice for problems that are considered minor, China's public hospitals, especially those referred to as "excellent" (*sanji tedeng* 三级特等), deal with both outpatient consultations and hospital admissions on a massive scale, resulting in severe congestion.

This situation is the result of a three-stage evolution in healthcare supply.

- *From the 1950s to the economic reforms*, the provision of healthcare was structured by local care and primary level hospitals (Level 1). In rural areas, medicine was practised by agricultural workers who had undergone rapid medical training (called "barefoot doctors"). Depending on the severity of the condition, the patient was then redirected to better-equipped facilities with more qualified staff. The higher the population density, the bigger the hospital in terms of number of beds and medical staff: this was the intermediate level (Level 2). Then, at the top of the pyramid, came high-level health-care (Level 3). Administratively, the population had no other choice but to follow this funnel-shaped care pathway.
- *Beginning in the 1980s*, the provision of healthcare was disorganized under the influence of several factors, leading to the disappearance and subsequent redefinition of local care provision. The cost of healthcare, hitherto virtually free, increased dramatically as a result of the state's financial disengagement, enabling hospitals to generate

profits and use them as they saw fit. At the same time, the level of quality also improved. The result was a fragmentation of the population in its access to healthcare according to income, geographical area of residence, and residence permit (*hukou* 户口): rural or urban.

- *The third phase of the evolution* of the health system corresponds to a greater openness, both geographical (with a more mobile population and improved transport) and administrative. At the same time, hospitals have acquired sophisticated equipment, greatly improving the quality of care, but with significant inequalities depending on the size of healthcare facilities and on geographical area. The effect of these developments is a greater incentive to attend hospitals offering a high level of quality of care, resulting in massive concentration in some areas and neglect in the provision of care elsewhere. Healthcare demand is no longer defined solely by the financial accessibility of the population, but also by the levels of quality offered by the health structures. Today, some localities have empty public health facilities with low-grade equipment co-existing with high-tech public health facilities besieged by thousands of patients prepared to wait hours or even days for a medical consultation. This demand for healthcare provided by "trained and qualified" medical staff has led to a decrease in the supply available to meet the demand, and therefore to ever-longer waiting times and ever-shorter consultations. Treatment prices have shot up, which can be explained in part by the lack of qualified staff, but also by the state's withdrawal of funding from public hospitals. Moreover, doctors with a financial stake in the profitability of their establishment tend to over-prescribe and over-diagnose, and the cost of medication has also shot up, all against a backdrop of corruption.

The doctor–patient relationship has therefore been transformed into a dynamic of conflict in the face of exorbitant treatment costs, extremely long waiting times, ever-shorter consultation appointments, and the increasingly widespread practice of bribery. Paying money "under the table" helps to reduce the waiting time and ensure better medical care for the patient.

In recent years, different forms of violence have appeared throughout Chinese hospitals. This might be a comparatively non-aggressive form of blame, such as families displaying the dead body of a loved one outside a hospital; but can also take a more active form, ranging from fights and damage to premises to extremely violent acts inflicted on medical personnel, sometimes even involving help from organized gangs.[14] When entered into the usual search engines, the keywords "hospital, violence" bring up hundreds of news articles relating stories of doctors who have been injured or killed by patients.[15]

To curb this phenomenon, the central government aims to regain control over the treatment path of patients by increasing the number of medical consultations, particularly high-quality medical consultations, and by putting in place family doctors or referring doctors. Owing to these objectives, the health sector is booming. The number of medical and healthcare establishments continues to increase, with growth occurring in cities as well as rural areas, and in the public as well as in the private sector, accompanying the demographic changes within Chinese society.[16] Consequently, this sector employs an increasing number of people.[17] In 2015, it accounted for 7.39 million workers.[18] Nonetheless, this development is not linear in every layer of Chinese society and comes with considerable heterogeneities.[19]

The economic reforms of the 1980s have introduced market mechanisms to varying degrees, leading to extreme disparities in access to healthcare, not only between rural and urban areas, but also within the areas themselves. After that, it became necessary to ensure that basic healthcare was accessible to all. There were two co-existing philosophies: universal access to basic treatment thanks to a tightly-regulated market, while for other forms of treatment, competition would be encouraged within the private sector. A range of instruments has also been tested through public health insurance mechanisms: the establishment of a healthcare market through incentives for the creation of private institutions, the transformation of public institutions into private institutions, and the establishment of community health centres for medical consultations to act as a "gateway" to all care pathways. However, these measures are currently yielding mixed results.

One obstacle to these attempts at reform is the lack of mobility among medical personnel. Due to their status (equivalent to that of a civil servant, with a certain number of additional privileges), medical personnel display a strong preference for working within a public organization. For reasons that will be explained in this book, medical personnel that meet the new standards of demand for "trained and qualified" staff are only found in the largest, highest-performing public establishments. As a result, while supply is diversifying, demand remains vastly centred on the highest-quality public establishments.

To face the structural difficulties of China's healthcare system, digital tools finally appear as a pragmatic way to limit, if not solve, the problems of congestion. These solutions, grouped under the term "digital health" or "e-health", are experiencing exponential growth, especially in recent years.

In Chap. 9, I will explain the role the internet plays in easing pressure thanks to its potential as a telemedicine tool, but also a tool for remote advice and consultation.[20] The result is that public hospitals appear more accessible, owing to the fact that patients no longer need to queue in a waiting room, and demand is more manageable. Similarly, if the demand for consultations that would usually be held at a public establishment can be partially met via the internet, this could also lead to a reduction in demand for treatment. If the pressure of demand is somewhat eased, it should make it possible to lengthen consultation times, thereby improving dialogue between medical staff and patients. Furthermore, this also introduces a form of competition between physical consultations and virtual consultations, which may allow for the cost of physical consultations to decrease. I also detail the growing use of digital technology such as mobile phone applications (whether online medical advice or payment methods for hospitals), Big Data containing patient medical information accompanied by socio-economic variables, and their virtual storage on remote servers or clouds. A number of services offered by e-health are mentioned, such as the construction of databases on the history of patient care, telemedicine, teleconsultation, online sales of medical drugs, queue management, and payment methods via applications for mobile phones. Moreover, the use of apps like WeChat for making appointments and managing medical records, as well as the possibility of semi-private forums or discussion groups that enable space for criticism, giving at least the appearance of anonymity, contribute to transforming healthcare demand and thus the health system as a whole.

However, the solutions offered by the internet are not without drawbacks, raising issues such as data confidentiality, responsibility in the event of medical wrongdoing, and the question of standardizing and supervising the quality of service on offer.

This book highlights the evolution of the Chinese health system and the issues of access to care for the population. The health system is constantly changing to adapt to this new reality, torn between its opening up to the market and strong administrative management. Chapter 2 gives a general presentation of what is called "public good" and specifically when applied to the healthcare field. In Chap. 3, I outline the evolution of the Chinese health system, from its inception in the post-Mao era to the present day, while also touching upon the effects of economic reforms. In Chap. 4, I analyze the Chinese institutional context as far as the hospital healthcare system is concerned. I also introduce the DRG-based payment system that involves Big Data analysis. Chapter 5 presents medical staff and their specificities. It explains what it means to be a doctor in China and presents the current reforms affecting medical professionals. Chapter 6 describes public healthcare insurance and the emergence of private insurance companies. Chapter 7 presents the policy on medical drugs, and the evolution of drug sale regulation. In Chap. 8, I focus on describing the key factors that have led to the rise in violence between medical staff and patients, and the government's attempts to introduce primary care centres as a new point of entry for the treatment process to curb this phenomenon. In Chap. 9, I present the effects of the most recent reforms, as well as the solutions offered by the use of e-health, as well as its limits and shortcomings; in other words, how internet and digital e-health may appear as the solution or a part of the solution to solving Chinese healthcare inefficiency.

This book draws on materials such as press articles and official statements, regulatory texts, official websites, and scientific articles published in both English and Chinese. It also makes reference to interviews conducted within hospitals and health authorities. These interviews were carried out in Shanghai and Beijing between March and December 2015. Among those interviewed were doctors at Level 1, 2, and 3 hospitals, health centres, hospital financial directors, hospital information systems directors, nurses, researchers at the Chinese Academy of Social Sciences (CASS) and Fudan University, and managers at consulting firms. It also refers to academic literature mainly but not only in economics, and medical and sociology literature.

This book's contribution is to provide a wider overview of the Chinese health system, its access, reforms and current developments. It illuminates and analyzes the changes in the Chinese health system from the Maoist period to the present day. The tensions between the pro-market and pro-welfare components of the reforms are detailed, as is the growing use of digital technology: mobile phone applications (whether online medical advice or payment methods for hospitals) and Big Data containing patient medical information. A number of services offered by e-health are mentioned, such as the construction of databases on the history of patient care, telemedicine, teleconsultation, online sales of medicines, queue management and payment methods via applications for mobile phones.

The literature on the Chinese healthcare system describes its development, its reforms and the effects of these reforms,[21] in particular the effect of introducing health insurance. However, very little has been written so far on the topic of violence[22] and even less on the emergence of digital technology as a solution to the inefficiencies of the Chinese health system.

NOTES

1. "The Scale of China's Healthcare Industry has Already Reached RMB 2 Trillion," Xinhua News, 28 July 2015. http://news.xinhuanet.com/local/2015-07/28/c_128064713.htm
2. Jeffrey Moe, Shu Chen, and Andrea Taylor, "Initial Findings in a Landscaping Study of Healthcare Delivery Innovation in China," IPIHD (International Partnership for Innovative Healthcare Delivery) research Report 14-01, 2014; Xuezheng Qin, Lixing Li, and Chee-Ruey Hsieh, "Too Few Doctors or Too Low Wages? Labor Supply of Healthcare Professionals in China," China Economic Review, Vol. 24, No. 1, 2013.
3. For some observers, the turning point of the reforms towards a more social society was marked by the speech of Hu Jintao, Secretary General of the Party in 2006, when he introduced the notion of a "harmonious society." Joe C.B. Leung and Yuebin Xui, China's Social Welfare, Cambridge, UK, Malden, MA, Polity Press, 2015.
4. National Bureau of Statistics of China, "Statistical Communiqué of the People's Republic of China on the 2014 National Economic and Social Development," 26 February 2015, www.stats.gov.cn/english/PressRelease/201502/t20150228_687439.html. Accessed September 2017. The figures presented here do not include Hong Kong, Macao or Taiwan.
5. Lucy Reynolds and Martin McKee, "Factors Influencing Antibiotic Prescribing in China: An Exploratory Analysis," Health Policy, Vol. 90, No. 1, 2009, pp. 32–36.
6. Lianping Yang, Chaojie Liu, J. Adamm Ferrier, Wei Zhou, and Xinping Zhang, "The Impact of the National Medicines Policy on Prescribing Behaviours in Primary Care Facilities in Hubei Province of China," Health Policy Plan, Vol. 28, No. 7, 2013, pp. 750–760.
7. It is thought that the excessive use of antibiotics, and particularly ototoxic medicines, accounts for 60% of hearing loss among children.
8. According to figures from the International Monetary Fund (IMF), in 2014 China's GDP was slightly higher than that of the United States.
9. The rate of growth was 10.6% in 2010.

10. "China Economic Outlook," FocusEconomics, 18 October 2016. Source: People's Bank of China, 2017.

11. Deng Shouqiang, "'Dandu er tai' fang kai: Pinglun cheng houxu gonggong fuwu ying gen shang" (Relaxing the One-child Policy: Comments say Public Services Should Follow Up), Zhongwenwang xinwen zhongxin, 18 November 2013, http://news.china.com.cn/2013-11/18/content_30628501.htm. Accessed 18 November 2016.

12. S. Wang, "Conquering Poverty while in the Midst of Developing the Nation," In M. Wang (ed.), Thirty Years of China's Reform, London: Routledge, 2012, pp. 476–512.

13. Li Shi, Hiroshi Sato, and Terry Sicular (eds.), Rising Inequality in China: Challenges to a Harmonious Society, Cambridge: Cambridge University Press, 2015.

14. Jiong Tu, "Yinao: Protest and Violence in China's Medical Sector," Berkeley Journal of Sociology, 11 December 2014, http://berkeleyjournal.org/2014/12/yinao-protest-and-violence-in-chinas-medical-sector. Accessed September 2017.

15. A recent example: Xinhua, "Doctor Dies after Stabbing Attack in Guangzhou," China Daily Asia, 7 May 2016. www.chinadailyasia.com/nation/2016-05/07/content_15429118.html. Accessed September 2017.

16. In 2015, there were 5.9 million beds, of which 5.5 million were allocated for elderly people. In total, there are 2.8 million elderly people staying at these establishments. National Bureau of Statistics of China, "Statistical Communiqué of the People's Republic of China on the 2014 National Economic and Social Development," op. cit. Care for the elderly will not be explored further in this chapter.

17. In 2015 there were 5.9 million beds, of which more than 5.5 million were for the care of the elderly. In total, 2.8 million seniors are residents of an institution. Source: National Bureau of Statistics of China, "Statistical Communiqué of the People's Republic of China on the 2014 National Economic and Social Development," op. cit.

18. This figure includes 2.82 million doctors and assistants, and 2.92 million accredited nurses. The official number of beds is 6.52 million, of which 4.84 million are in hospitals and 1.17 million are in health centres.

19. In 2015, there were 982,443 such institutions. This figure includes 25,865 hospitals, 36,899 cantonal township health centres, 34,264 health centres at village or village agglomeration level, 646,044 clinics at village or village agglomeration level, 3491 centres for the prevention of epidemic diseases, and health surveillance centres. Source: National Bureau of Statistics of China, "Statistical Communiqué of the People's Republic of China on the 2014 National Economic and Social Development," 26 February 2015, www.stats.gov.cn/english/PressRelease/201502/t20150228_687439.html. Accessed September 2017.

20. These terms will be more precisely defined later in the book.
21. John S. Akin, William H. Dow, Peter M. Lance, and Chung-Ping A, Loh, "Changes in Access to Health Care in China, 1989–1997," Health Policy and Planning, Vol. 20, No. 2, 2005, pp. 80–89; Sarah L. Barber and Lan Yao, "Development and Status of Health Insurance Systems in China," The International Journal of Health Planning and Management, Vol. 26, No. 4, 2011, pp. 339–356; Meng Qingyue and Tang Shenglan, "Universal Health Care Coverage in China: Challenges and Opportunities," Procedia—Social and Behavioral Sciences, Vol. 77, 2013, pp. 330–340; Hufeng Wang, "A Dilemma of Chinese Healthcare Reform: How to Re-define Government Roles?" China Economic Review, Vol. 20, No. 4, 2009, pp. 598–604; Hufeng Wang, Michael K. Gusmano, and Qi Cao, "An Evaluation of the Policy on Community Health Organizations in China: Will the Priority of New Healthcare Reform in China be a Success?" Health Policy, Vol. 99, No. 1, 2011, pp. 37–43; Hong Liu, Song Gao, and John A. Rizzo, "The Expansion of Public Health Insurance and the Demand for Private Health Insurance in Rural China," China Economic Review, Vol. 22, No. 1, 2011, pp. 28–41.
22. Xinqing Zhang and Margaret Sleeboom-Faulkner, "Tensions between Medical Professionals and Patients in Mainland China," Cambridge Quarterly of Healthcare Ethics, Vol. 20, No. 3, 2011, pp. 458–465; Xin Xu and Rongrong Lu, "Baoli yu buxinren: zhuanxing Zhongguo de yiliao baoli yanjiu: 2000–2006" (Violence and Mistrust: Research on Violence in Medical Treatment in Transforming China [2000–2006]), Fazhi yu shehui fazhan (Law and Social Development), No. 1, 2008, pp. 82–101; Therese Hesketh, Dan Wu, Linan Mao, and Nan Ma, "Violence Against Doctors in China," The British Medical Journal Clinical Research, No. 345, 2012, pp. 1–5.

BIBLIOGRAPHY

Akin, John S., William H. Dow, Peter M. Lance, and Chung-Ping A. Loh, "Changes in Access to Health Care in China, 1989–1997," Health Policy and Planning, Vol. 20, No. 2, 2005, pp. 80–89.

Barber, Sarah L., and Lan Yao, "Development and Status of Health Insurance Systems in China," The International Journal of Health Planning and Management, Vol. 26, No. 4, 2011, pp. 339–356.

Hesketh, Therese, Dan Wu, Linan Mao, and Nan Ma, "Violence Against Doctors in China," The British Medical Journal Clinical Research, No. 345, 2012, pp. 1–5.

Leung, Joe C.B., and Yuebin Xui, China's Social Welfare, Cambridge, UK and Malden, MA: Polity Press, 2015.

Liu, Hong, Song Gao, and John A. Rizzo, "The Expansion of Public Health Insurance and the Demand for Private Health Insurance in Rural China," China Economic Review, Vol. 22, No. 1, 2011, pp. 28–41.

Moe, Jeffrey, Shu Chen, and Andrea Taylor, "Initial Findings in a Landscaping Study of Healthcare Delivery Innovation in China," IPIHD (International Partnership for Innovative Healthcare Delivery) Research Report 14-01, 2014.

Qin, Xuezheng, Lixing Li, and Chee-Ruey Hsieh, "Too Few Doctors or Too Low Wages? Labor Supply of Healthcare Professionals in China," China Economic Review, Vol. 24, No. 1, 2013.

Qingyue, Meng, and Tang Shenglan, "Universal Health Care Coverage in China: Challenges and Opportunities," Procedia—Social and Behavioral Sciences, Vol. 77, 2013, pp. 330–340.

Reynolds, Lucy, and Martin McKee, "Factors Influencing Antibiotic Prescribing in China: An Exploratory Analysis," Health Policy, Vol. 90, No. 1, 2009, pp. 32–36.

Shi, Li, Hiroshi Sato, and Terry Sicular (eds.), Rising Inequality in China: Challenges to a Harmonious Society, Cambridge: Cambridge University Press, 2015.

Tu, Jiong, "Yinao: Protest and Violence in China's Medical Sector," Berkeley Journal of Sociology, 11 December 2014, http://berkeleyjournal.org/2014/12/yinao-protest-and-violence-in-chinas-medical-sector. Accessed 26 October 2016.

Wang, Hufeng, "A Dilemma of Chinese Healthcare Reform: How to Re-define Government Roles?" China Economic Review, Vol. 20, No. 4, 2009, pp. 598–604.

Wang, S., "Conquering Poverty while in the Midst of Developing the Nation," In M. Wang (ed.), Thirty Years of China's Reform, London: Routledge, 2012, pp. 476–512.

Wang, Hufeng, Michael K. Gusmano, and Qi Cao, "An Evaluation of the Policy on Community Health Organizations in China: Will the Priority of New Healthcare Reform in China be a Success?" Health Policy, Vol. 99, No. 1, 2011, pp. 37–43.

Xu, Xin, and Rongrong Lu, Baoli yu buxinren: zhuanxing Zhongguo de yiliao baoli yanjiu: 2000–2006 (Violence and Mistrust: Research on Violence in Medical Treatment in Transforming China [2000–2006]). Fazhi yu shehui fazhan (Law and Social Development), No. 1, 2008, pp. 82–101.

Yang, Lianping, Chaojie Liu, J. Adamm Ferrier, Wei Zhou, and Xinping Zhang, "The Impact of the National Medicines Policy on Prescribing Behaviours in Primary Care Facilities in Hubei Province of China," Health Policy Plan, Vol. 28, No. 7, 2013, pp. 750–760.

Zhang, Xinqing, and Margaret Sleeboom-Faulkner, "Tensions between Medical Professionals and Patients in Mainland China," Cambridge Quarterly of Healthcare Ethics, Vol. 20, No. 3, 2011, pp. 458–465.

CHAPTER 2

The Notion of a Health Good in China and Elsewhere

Abstract Is the intervention of the state in the healthcare market legitimate and efficient? To answer this question, a clear definition of a health good and its implications is needed. Can we just apply the general definition of a public good for all health goods? Should we consider different types of health goods? If yes, how do we delimit the frontier between a public good and a private good? With a rapid glance at the diversity of organizations in the healthcare system that exist in the world, it appears there is little consensus on what can and should be defined as a public good. Generally speaking, all countries have a mixed health system, combining pro-market elements with welfare state safeguards, and China is no exception: all reforms of the healthcare system implemented since the 1980s have swung between both. To understand the Chinese health system and its recent evolution, we need to start by defining the global framework in which the "health good" is set.

Keywords Health good • Public good and private good • Competition • Price elasticity • Healthcare

To understand the Chinese health system and its recent evolution, it is necessary to start by defining the global framework in which it is set. All countries have a mixed health system, combining pro-market elements with welfare state safeguards, and China makes no exception. All reforms of the healthcare system implemented since the 1980s have swung between both.[1]

From 2003, and more intensively from 2009, a number of reforms have been implemented to facilitate universal access to basic care. The result is public healthcare coverage, designed for primary care improvement with the emphasis on a basic care basket accessible to all. All these reforms lean toward a pro-welfare state policy. At the end of 2013, following the Third Plenum of the 18th Central Committee of the Communist Party, a new set of reforms were launched, in favour of private hospital investment, including the privatization of some existing public hospitals, showing a clear shift towards a pro-market and competition policy.

In fact, what dominates is a lack of consensus between pro-market and a pro-welfare state policies in hospital management. Pilot experiments were initiated in 2009 in 17 cities. To date, if some of these pilot programmes are still active, no generalization has been launched. Efficiency comparison between these experiments could have helped define a clearer direction, but major differences in the way they were carried out make these comparative studies quite inconclusive.

In reality, depending on the type of health good (primary care, hospital care, medicines, etc.), the direction taken in the reforms of the Chinese system cannot be interpreted in the same way. The goal of this chapter is to briefly present how economics defines the notion of a public good versus a private good. The definitions presented here are those commonly used in economic literature. Amongst the well-known publications covering this, I cite Cornes and Sandler (1986), Leach (2004) and Hess and Ostrom (2006).[2] We then introduce the specificities of a health good in China and take an overview of the healthcare system.

A HEALTH GOOD: DEFINITION AND IMPLICATIONS

Public Good and Private Good: General Definitions

A good is defined as *rival* (or subtractable) when its consumption by an agent implies it cannot be consumed simultaneously by another agent. As an example, the use of a tool by someone prevents others from benefiting from its use at the same time. It is the same for a MRI scan. Going into more detail, the consumption of an apple also falls into this category but it adds finality to the good. For healthcare, medical consumable devices can only be used once for one patient. In contrast, a perfectly non-rival good is a good that can be consumed by everyone at any moment. For example, air or public lighting are non-rival goods.

So far, we have considered rivalry as a binary notion. In reality, many goods have partial rivalry. The notion of rivalry is more a continuum than anything. For instance, the connection to a website is a rival good in the sense that more than one user can be connected at the same time but if too many are, then congestion issues result. It is the same for roads with the occurrence of traffic jams. Hospitals can experience the same phenomenon, creating scarcity or excessively long queues.

Pure free market conditions create a regulation through price, making it possible to solve, or at least reduce, the issue of scarcity and long queues. Yet, such a system implies that wealth is evenly distributed as a starting point. In case of inequalities within the population, such a free market regulation creates a financial roadblock. Choice is no longer a criterion as the financial constraints close access to the good.

A good is called *excludable* if it is possible to prevent consumers that do not pay for this good from benefiting from it. In contrast, a good becomes *non-excludable* if it is not possible to restrain its use to consumers who pay for it. Public lighting for instance is a perfect example of a non-excludable good. Anyone, locals or tourists alike, whether they have paid for it or not can benefit from it. Nonetheless, as for rivalry, the use of a good by all has limits. In our example, it can be the number of people at a given moment in the street. Even though this may seem quite binary in the first place, it is actually a continuous notion: a good has a certain degree of excludability. As far as healthcare is concerned, this degree is high.

Pure private goods are defined as both rival and excludable, whereas pure public goods are both non-rival and non-excludable. Criteria for being non-rival and non-excludable can fluctuate over time, due to natural or political factors.

Some goods are defined as non-excludable but rival. These are called *common pool goods*. Others are non-rival but excludable. They are called *club goods*. To give an example of the former, we can quote non-renewable natural resources. They are to some extent non-excludable, but in their consumption leading to their disappearance, they are rival. For the latter, a typical example is a gym subscription, which makes going to this gym non-rival but excludable.

Is health a public good? The individual is the main beneficiary of health. In that sense, health is a rival and excludable good, making it a private good.

Now, are health goods public goods? Goods and services established to give care to an individual are by definition rival and excludable, defining a private good. Yet, the specificities of these goods can lead the regulator to turn them into public goods. This can be explained by the following:

- The fact that some pathologies are communicable. In such cases, treating the patient has an obvious positive impact for this individual but also for those around, by avoiding the spread of the disease. This is what is called a *positive externality*.

  The effect of the treatment affects the patient but also his or her wider circle, even though only the patient was treated. It can be qualified as non-rival but excludable. The SARS epidemic in China in 2003 is a very good example. The epidemic was controlled by isolating affected people and strictly monitoring the appearance of symptoms. Indeed, each contamination of an individual had a direct impact on his or her health but potentially also on that of the people around. Generally speaking, making vaccines public goods (non-rival through an increase in the number of professionals able to perform vaccinations and non-exclusive through being free or least affordable to all) tends to curb and finally stop the spread of viruses.

- One can consider health as a capital that is being depleted over time (Grossman, 1972). The better each individual maintains this capital, the better his or her productivity at work. Therefore, the sum of individual health goods has a direct impact on the total production at country level. Put another way, individual health goods, in spite of having the characteristics of private goods, have an externality impact close to public goods. The cumulative effect of individual health levels implies, at the macro level, a non-rivalry (a global good health status benefits everyone allowing us all to enjoy a good health environment at all times) and a non-exclusivity (for each individual, a global good health level implies a better individual health level without additional cost: for instance, risks of infection will be lower, whatever the individual behaviour in terms of risk prevention). A 2001 report from CMH-WHO[3] points out that a 10% increase in life expectancy at birth implies a surplus of economic growth by at least 0.3% per year, holding other growth factors constant.

The Health Good and Assumptions of Pure and Perfect Competition

The following assumptions apply to pure and perfect competition theory:

- *Atomicity* (i.e. an infinite number of suppliers and demanders for a same good): "infinite" actually means sufficient to enable full competition between suppliers and between demanders. This implies that the price has not been fixed by one side as a result of market condition. It is said that the price is a "price taker".
- *Homogeneity of product*: health products or services are assumed identical, homogeneous, without differentiation, hence totally substitutable. In such cases, consumers can make trade-offs based on price only. In reality, there are differences amongst health goods. Yet, when these differences do *not* generate a non-substitutability, health goods can still be considered quite homogeneous. On the other hand, when there is non-substitutability, pure competition between health suppliers is no longer possible. This can explain the difficulties the Chinese regulator has in trying to improve the health system by setting up additional local health centres. For customers, being treated in a local centre or in an excellent quality level hospital are indeed non-substitutable. This also explains the congestion in the excellent quality level hospitals (called further Level 3 hospitals).
- *Freedom of entry and exit*: no barrier prevents a producer or consumer from entering the market. Symmetrically, agents can leave the market at any time. This point emphasizes the asymmetry created by taxes imposed on a part of the healthcare market, namely the private sector. The public sector is immune to this financial burden. Besides, the obscurity of land rights regulations when setting up private healthcare centres may also explain the slow growth of a private healthcare institution market.
- *Transparency*: the market delivers comprehensive information to agents on the nature, quality and price of available goods. We will see that this point is key for the establishment of a list of medical drugs considered as essential, including for generic medicine.
- *Mobility of production factors*: labour and capital can move from one market to the other in the pursuit of better profit. Here, the doctor's

status and the medical staff's level of training between the different areas, including rural and urban ones, is one reason for the inefficiency in the Chinese healthcare system.

When at least one of the assumptions of pure and perfect competition is not verified, the regulator must act to re-establish it. Assessing the validity of these assumptions for the actual healthcare market, we can see where the market tends to fail:

• The quality level is not observable or imperfectly observable. Recent reported scandals in Chinese newspapers regarding products widely praised in search engines but which turn out to be hazardous show the fragile level of information available to customers. Another story that made the headlines was about a 21-year-old Chinese student suffering from cancer. To select his treatment and hospital, he searched for information on the quality of the available treatments on Baidu. This is the number one search engine in China and it controls 80% of the search market. Unfortunately, the information he gathered turned out to be wrong. He publicized his distress about this erroneous information in a long post just before he died.[4] This drove Baidu to publishing a number of press releases, maintaining that ethics should come before profit. But is this really the role and responsibility of such a for-profit organization? What role should the regulator have in such cases? Should this kind of information not be distributed by a non-profit or public service organization?

• In addition, there are usually not that many suppliers in the healthcare market. For instance, for drugs or medical devices, patents often ensure a monopoly situation on many products for some years. Likewise, hospitals delivering high quality standards tend to be in a monopoly situation in the area they cater for. They have an autonomous management making it possible for them, to a large extent, to set prices themselves.[5] Healthcare demand then has no choice but to accept the price quoted for the treatment. Depending on the severity of the affliction, two factors come into play. On the one side, demand from patients and their relatives tend to become increasingly price inelastic:[6] the health good is acquired, whatever its cost. Additionally, emergency is often linked to the severity factor of a pathology. Therefore, under the pressure of time, the price variable gets little scrutiny in the decision process, potentially leading to individual bankruptcy. This was a very common phenomenon in China before the implementation of public insurance.[7] These insurance schemes address patient solvency issues, but the market is still failing, as price is not the result of supply and demand but is set by the supplier.

- As far as healthcare is concerned, there is a large gulf between supply and demand. Supply has extensive information about the state of the patient that he or she does not even possess. It is thus possible to generate unnecessary costs through over-diagnosis and over-prescription of drugs and examinations. This phenomenon is called *induced demand*, in other words a surplus in demand caused by the supplier's behaviour and not by the patient's actual health needs. This has been observed in hospitals with high quality standards and has been extensively documented in empirical literature.[8] In the case of China, a "zero mark-up"[9] policy has been implemented for a few years by the government, in order to control the price of medical drugs prescribed to patients, with a very minimal margin rate for a list of drugs considered as essential. Yet, government price control over hospitals that have financial autonomy is tricky, in particular in the case where information is asymmetrical, the regulator having little data feedback from the ground level. For the regulator to actually assess the relevance of all procedures and prescriptions, a comprehensive information feed would be necessary as well adequate administrative resources to process this information.

All the failings in the market for health goods justify intervention from the regulator, be it for public goods or private goods. Nevertheless, we have considered here the health good as a whole, both homogeneous and perfectly defined. In reality, a health good regroups different items that are increasingly diverse, from medical drugs to connected devices used for leisure purposes. They can be actual physical products, like a vaccine dose for instance, but also intangible items such as mobile apps. The latter category is becoming increasingly common. It can also include services involving actual contact, like regular medical consultations for instance, or only digital contact, like online consultations. The severity level also plays a part: should we consider surgery to fix myopia to be at the same level as a heart transplant? Price elasticity is a commonly used tool in economics to sort them apart.

Price Elasticity

When the healthcare supply is not regulated and prices are fixed by the market, how does demand fluctuate with price? This is what price elasticity studies intend to determine.

The elasticity of demand against price measures the variation in demand in reaction to a 1% increase in price, all else being equal. When this variation is below 1%, it means that demand is little affected by a price increase: demand is said to be *inelastic*. Primary necessity goods fall into this category. As far as healthcare is concerned, it is usually considered that for acute pathologies, families are fairly insensitive to the price of the treatment, causing many personal bankruptcies when there is no insurance in place to cover this spending.

In contrast, a good is considered *elastic* when demand goes down by more than 1% for a 1% price increase. The more the demand goes down, the more the good is elastic against price. For healthcare, goods with such characteristics are called *health comfort goods*. These are goods that do not affect the vital prognosis of the agent. Dental care, optical care or cosmetic care are amongst such goods. Still, one can question to what extent these so-called *comfort goods* affect agents, be it their quality of life or even their employability.

In studies on price elasticity of healthcare demand, income is usually considered as a given variable: it is considered as having no impact on the decision to consume in relation to price. In the context of unequal distribution of revenue, elasticity can be observed the other way around, through income elasticity. For a healthcare demand that is considered fixed, there are three types of income elasticity. *Inferior goods* are goods whose consumption increases when income decreases: they are substitution goods to others that are no longer affordable. As an example, take medical drugs bought online: price is often the purchase trigger, as they are usually cheaper, but criticized for their dubious origin and quality. In that sense, they can be considered *inferior goods*. Similarly, online consultations are heavily debated as they have attractive prices but lack guarantees on the quality of diagnosis. Implicitly, what critics of online consultations denounce is their inferiority. They do not enable a comprehensive examination and complete diagnosis to be made and are substitutes for more expensive physical consultations.[10]

Superior goods are goods where demand increases with income. As far as healthcare is concerned, these usually encompass goods that have little impact on vital prognoses. Finally, *normal goods* are goods where demand is not sensitive to income. This category includes the goods that pose a threat of personal bankruptcy, as patients and their families are likely to pay for heath goods until they are in financial difficulties.

Depending on the severity of the affliction and its impact on life expectancy and quality of life, health goods can be considered superior, normal or inferior goods. In the case of a normal or inferior good, the question of a regulated market for healthcare is relevant. The regulator may want to ensure that the population has access to a given level of health or at least to a basic care basket. The bigger the scope of such a basket, the mix between pro-market and pro-welfare state components of the system will tend to lean towards the latter.

SHOULD HEALTH BE A UNIVERSALLY ACCESSIBLE GOOD OR ONE GOVERNED BY SUPPLY AND DEMAND?

Is Health a Good Accessible to All?

The Word Health Organization (WHO) Constitution enshrines "the highest attainable standard of health as a fundamental right of every human being".[11] Nevertheless, the term "standard of health" encompasses both objective measurable indexes (e.g. glycemic level) and more subjective items (e.g. feelings of tiredness or depression). Depending on the criteria chosen to define good health, health policies and programmes can be very different from one country to the next. For example, in some countries such as France, some cosmetic surgery procedures are commonly reimbursed provided the positive psychological effects of the treatment are observed and described by a doctor. In many other countries, such as China, cosmetic surgery is never covered by any public insurance scheme.

Scientific and technological innovations will also create new ways to address health that were previously not considered. The part they are to play in the "health standard" is yet to be defined and is currently very variable from one country to the next. Obviously, internet and connected devices bring about a whole new set of tools that improve information to patients and thus enable them to improve their health. This encompasses apps for smartphones targeted at the general public or devices such as connected watches that can measure sleep cycles, number of steps and calories burnt. But there are also more medically specialized devices such as those supporting patients with diabetes, by measuring glycemic levels through glucose capture in the abdomen or in the eye. They make it possible to identify the optimal timing for an insulin injection. Other devices can help address cardiac emergencies by measuring heart rate. Whether these devices should be covered by public insurance is currently a source of debate, and is dependent, among other things, on the nature of the good—superior, normal or inferior.

The issue of information collection by both public and private bodies is also quite acute. The operators of connected devices, for instance, collect an impressive amount of data coming from their users, which could be very valuable for public health research. For example, the app GlucoSuccess from ResearchKit, targeted at diabetes patients, provides data to researchers from the Massachusetts General Hospital.[12] These data are used to improve knowledge about patients with diabetes and its evolution. Yet, the collection of personal medical data by private companies and its potential abuse is not without controversy. Legal frameworks and jurisprudence are still constantly evolving in this area.

On social networks or discussion forums, many people reckon that these connected devices should be covered by health insurance policies. Yet, so far there does not appear to be any country reimbursing the cost of any connected device or health app. Is that a limitation to the spread of these connected objects? If the answer is negative then this implies that the acquisition of connected devices is possible without any discrimination, as defined by the WHO, meaning that:

- These devices must be physically available to all. This is probably generally the case thanks to online distribution.
- They must be financially affordable. The price of the device and app must be set so as to satisfy demand.
- Finally, the regulator must ensure that information regarding the existence of such connected devices, their characteristics, medical use and limits, is widely available.

Moreover, the mass of collected data could lead to a screening of the population and to discrimination in access to health insurance. People with a higher risk of suffering from certain pathologies would then have to pay higher insurance premiums. The regulator then has to intervene to provide accessibility to health insurance (public or private) or accessibility to healthcare for, at least, those excluded.

Health as a Private Good and the Healthcare Market

Affordability of care can be secured through one or various public insurance schemes. This does not necessarily imply that health providers, goods and services should themselves be public. For instance, in the United States, health supply is mostly private.[13] Affordability is ensured by insurance policies subscribed to by individuals or through employers. Yet, for those with higher risks, public insurance has been set up to secure the affordability of a predefined basket of care.

In many countries, the healthcare market is highly regulated, as is the case in Europe. However, there are many other countries where the healthcare market is much less regulated and follows the law of supply and demand for many health goods. The notion of healthcare accessibility is then limited to a certain predefined category of goods. These goods are included in what is commonly called a basic care basket. These are health goods whose universal accessibility is considered mandatory, without any discrimination whatsoever, and accessibility must be both physical and financial.

This financial affordability is ensured through the implementation of public health insurance policies or through free care, as it is the case in countries, such as the United Kingdom, that have set up a National Health Service (NHS). The price of care can be either market-based or regulated. In a context where health spending is strongly monitored, the price of a basic care basket is most commonly regulated. For instance, in the United States, patients over 65 years of age are eligible for a public insurance scheme (Medicare). A payment mechanism has been set up to regulate hospital costs. This consists of a lump sum payment per diagnoses related group (DRG) referring to both the pathology and the procedures used to treat it. The validity of this type of system is based on various factors. Among others, it implies that the lump sum is high enough to avoid private health suppliers voluntarily withdrawing from the procedure, creating offer disruption and physical non-accessibility for the patient. In a less extreme scenario, a lump sum that is not attractive enough tends to lead to a phenomenon of patient screening and skimming.

DIFFERENTIATED ACCESS ACCORDING TO TYPE OF GOOD

As has been already mentioned, access to care can be differentiated according to the type of health good. When public health insurance covers mainly a basic care basket, then accessibility to other health goods will be totally different, with often unregulated prices.

Cases According to the Vital Prognosis (Engaged or Not)

Recent evolutions in the health systems of Organisation for Economic Co-operation and Development (OECD) countries tend to converge towards some kind of coverage for the costliest and most vital care through different types of mechanism. In European countries, whether the organization is Beveridgian or Bismarckian in its inspiration, the care basket that is fully covered by the community is being reduced in terms of number of pathologies, but the most severe cases are better covered. Acute pathologies, strongly affecting the life expectancy of the patient and generating costly procedures are not only covered through well-established procedures but also those using technical innovation.

In countries where the health goods market is competition-oriented, public insurance schemes have been set up, covering an increasing share of the population. For instance, in the United States, the Medicare programme has been supplemented with "Obamacare", covering not only the elderly but also the least well-off.

In cases which are not diagnosed as vital, public regulator intervention varies widely from one country to another.

Medical Consultations: From Physical to Online

A health good, in its wider sense, includes health services. The professionals performing these services can be either self-employed or hired by an organization. Depending on status, they are differently incentivized to influence the number of consultations they perform. For instance, if the practitioner is salaried without any bonus scheme, he or she will have no incentive to increase production. In contrast, if he or she is self-employed with a per-consultation fee, then there is a financial incentive to perform as many consultations as possible. This is what economists call *induced demand*. The supplier influences demand in order to increase it, even if this is not medically necessary.

These differences in supplier status do not necessarily have implications for market regulation. For instance, in France, practitioners can be either salaried or self-employed, but the price of consultation is regulated in both cases, being fixed by decree.[14] Suppliers in the private sector can, in some cases, fix their own prices, above that of the decree, but in such cases public insurance just covers the part of the cost equal to the official price, the surplus being paid by the patient. In the United Kingdom, the price of health services is also regulated. For some years, a private healthcare market has been developing fast, but patients using such services are not covered by the NHS.

Online health goods have been appearing over the past decade and have changed the landscape of health supply. To a large extent, they help in solving the issue of physical accessibility.

As far as financial accessibility is concerned, two factors come into play: price itself and insurance coverage. If the price is low, patients will be able to acquire the health good, whether or not it is covered by insurance. On the other hand, if the price is borderline with the patient's ability to pay, its financial accessibility can only by granted through health insurance, even if only partially.

Among health goods available over the internet, online medical consultations are now authorized in an increasing number of markets, for example, Switzerland, Sweden, Finland, the United Kingdom or France (since the end of 2010). One of the main arguments of the supporters of such a development is that it improves financial accessibility but also eases monitoring of suppliers' shortages. Nevertheless, many countries strictly regulate this market to control its development. In France, for instance, the possibility of a practitioner or a group of practitioners offering online consultations is bound by a formal authorization from the regional health regulatory agency (ARS, Agence de Santé Régionale). The project will only be accepted if there is a recognized lack of healthcare supply in the region. Online consultations are thus only seen as a way to mitigate the lack of physicians in certain, mostly rural, areas. The flip side of this rigidity is that the cost of online consultations is fully covered by the public health insurance system in these European countries.

Online consultations are to be differentiated from online medical advice that does not lead to an official medical diagnosis and prescription. Online medical advice services also develop quickly, even faster than online consultations. One of the reasons is the very loose regulatory framework in which they operate. In addition to this, online medical services also include monitoring. They help develop home-based care replacing hospitalization. Physicians can analyze data collected via connected devices, a visiting nurse or directly sent by the patient. This type of monitoring can appear particularly well suited for chronic diseases and care of the elderly.

Another sector of use of online health services is physician to physician (P2P), be it online coaching/tele-expertise or online assistance/telehealth monitoring. *Tele-expertise* means asking for advice about a particular case from a fellow physician with a rare or locally unavailable skill. For instance, an emergency physician can ask for a neurologist's advice when treating a stroke. Progress in medicine often implies the need to increase specialized advanced knowledge. The internet is then a very precious tool to pool this knowledge as much as possible. *Online assistance* or *telehealth monitoring* is more intrusive in the support given by the fellow practitioner, with direct intervention in the medical procedure. A famous example of such assistance is the collaboration between Shenzhen No. 2 People's Hospital in China and two physicians from the University of California in San Francisco (UCSF), in which they have remotely supported the surgery on a brain tumor.[15]

In a totally free healthcare market, the price of such acts should be defined only by supply and demand. On the other hand, in the case of a regulated healthcare market, such co-operation is handicapped by unstandardized reimbursement schemes.

Prescription and Non-prescription Drugs

The issue of accessibility to medicine is quite acute on a global scale. Prices for drugs not only depend on the price set by the pharmaceutical companies but also on the margin applied by all intermediaries in the distribution chain right up to the patient. Drug prices can be regulated in cases where they are covered by a public insurance scheme. The more a drug is reimbursed, the more actual demand will tend to converge towards potential demand levels (numbers of patients that would use this drug for medical reasons, independently of financial considerations).

When a new innovative drug is developed and patented, its price is set by the pharmaceutical company. If the cost of this drug is reimbursed through public health insurance, its price will then be the outcome of a negotiation between the regulatory body and the pharmaceutical company. When this drug reaches a certain age it is no longer under patent and other companies can start producing it. These newcomers are called generics. Logically, they can sell only if their price is set below that of the original drug using the same composition and having same mode of intake. As barriers to entry have supposedly fallen, the equilibrium price is, in theory, equal to the marginal cost to produce the drug. As a consequence, the price of generics, when they exist, is considered the lowest possible for a determined compound.

A vast majority of OECD countries have defined a basic basket of drugs to be covered by the community. China is in a similar situation. The National Essential Drug List was established in 2012, with competition organized at provincial level and a zero mark-up policy for all primary care providers. These basic baskets vary from one market to the other but usually give priority to generics, in order to minimize cost.

In parallel, competition in the drug market can be increased through the use of the internet, the online market for healthcare products being *de facto* open to anyone connected. From the supply side, this online market raises various questions. Which kind of medicine should be sold online? Only non-prescription drugs or any drug? Should there be any specific procedure or should they be treated as traditionally distributed drugs? Behind all this lies the lingering issue of the quality of drugs sold online. How can quality be controlled? How do we prevent counterfeit drugs from entering the market? In Europe, online sales of medical drugs are soaring. In Spain, Belgium, France and Italy, this is only allowed for non-prescription drugs. In other markets, such as the United Kingdom, Germany, Switzerland, Sweden, Norway or Portugal, online sales are legal for any kind of medicine, be it (under restrictive rules) prescription or non-prescription. The same situation applies in the United States. According to the Food and Drug Administration (FDA), only 3% of online pharmacies are fully safe, from medical and legal standpoints.[16] To improve such a situation, some countries have established a comprehensive list of websites allowed to sell medical drugs. This is the case in France, where its custodian is the National Orders of Pharmacists. Other attempts to improve buyers' safety include the establishment of a logo by the European Union allowing customers to quickly check the legality of the online purchase they intend to make.

SPECIFICITIES OF THE HEALTH GOOD IN CHINA

Defining the health good in China requires a description of the Chinese healthcare system and its specificities, bearing in mind that the structure of the healthcare market is complex.

The first specificity is that today, most patients go to public hospitals for treatment. This is true for inpatient care but in China this is also the case for outpatient care. Major public hospitals account for more than 90% of inpatient admissions and more than 50% of outpatient consultations, with between 60 and 80 consultations per day per physician.[17]

Then, the "consultation and prescription phase" is merged with the "medical act and medical drug acquisition" phase. After the consultation itself, a patient will go the pharmacy counter to be given the prescribed medicine. Whenever the structure makes it possible, all tests such as blood sampling and analysis or radiography will also be performed on site. Finally, the patient will proceed to check out to pay for the total amount of the whole process, in one single invoice. The patient cannot cherry-pick from the analysis and medicine prescribed by the practitioner. This is commonly accepted by Chinese patients, when most Westerners would probably have a hard time complying with such methods.

Last, the structure of public hospitals is also very specific to China. On the one hand, they are very much like a public administration. For instance, in terms of personnel, salary scale and career development are managed by the Ministry of Social Security and Human Resources. On the other hand, hospitals have a wide financial autonomy. Direct funding by the central or provincial government accounts for a very marginal part (less than 10%). In parallel, hospitals have been incentivized to modernize their equipment and improve their quality. As a consequence of this, public hospitals can make profit. They usually enjoy a monopoly situation in their area of influence (except maybe in public healthcare facilities with low level quality (defined later as Tier 1 hospitals and part of Tier 2 hospitals) metropolises) while acting very much like private companies.

Physicians and other medical staff receive bonuses indexed to the profit made by the hospital. This can lead to a behaviour aimed at maximizing profit through over-diagnosis and over-prescription. The health good when it concerns health services is then governed by market rules, and this generates an accessibility issue for many. As a countermeasure, public insurance schemes were implemented in the first decade of 2000, as a pro-welfare state policy tool (New Co-operative Medical Scheme—NCMS—for rural zones, Urban Employee Basic Medical Insurance—UEBMI—for employees in urban zones and Urban Resident Basic Medical Insurance—URBMI—for urban residents who are not covered by UEBMI).

A new round of reforms started in 2009.[18] One of the objectives was the implementation of a free market, in particular for primary care, in order to ease the congestion in public hospitals. This has encountered mixed results as patients have so far little trust in the level of quality offered by these newly set-up centres. In parallel, public health insurance schemes for both rural and urban areas have been upgraded to include a wider range of care and better coverage rate. Financial accessibility to medical drugs was the aim. A *zero mark-up* policy for a predefined basket of drugs has been implemented in primary care centres. Finally, the profit sources of hospitals have been more closely monitored.

Since 2013, the latest set of reforms has fostered private investors in the hospital market. In parallel, a policy incentivizing the development of private insurance schemes was implemented. A more concentrated organization, modelled on the Health Maintenance Organizations (HMOs) in the United States, is one of the model encouraged, either through acquisition of existing facilities or creation of new hospitals. In such a model, private insurance would take care of both primary care and hospital admissions, as part of a bundled package. As in the case of the US Medicare federal programme, financial transfers between public and private insurance funds would compensate insurance companies for patients eligible for public programmes (i.e. NCMS, URBMI and UEBMI).

The 13th Five Year Plan (2016–2020) showcases the concept of "competition" but also those of "fairness, equity and justice", leaving some ambiguity about the finality of reforms. As explained by Yip and Hsiao (2015)[19], "the market does not address issues of equity or fairness. It assumes that the income/wealth of the society is already equitably distributed".

This shows that in China today the health good cannot be defined as the public good it was considered to be before the start of economic reforms. Yet, it cannot be considered a 100% private good, as it largely was at the beginning of 2000, with a few exceptions.

What with the fragmented nature of the initial Chinese healthcare system, the co-existence of various insurance schemes and the economic and social inequalities throughout the vast Chinese territory, one can only wonder whether the country is heading towards a single homogeneous definition of the "health good" or toward a multiplicity of definitions, depending on local and other specificities.

To start addressing this issue, the next chapter focuses on the history and evolution of healthcare supply in China.

Notes

1. W. Yip and W. Hsiao, "What Drove the Cycles of Chinese Health System Reforms?" Health Systems & Reform, Vol. 1, No. 1, 2015, pp. 52–61.
2. C. Hess and E. Ostrom, "Introduction," In C. Hess and E. Ostrom (eds.), Understanding Knowledge as a Commons: From Theory to Practice, Cambridge, MA: The MIT Press, 2006; R. Cornes and T. Sandler, The

Theory of Externalities, Public Goods, and Club Goods, Cambridge University Press, 1986; J. Leach, A Course in Public Economics, Cambridge University Press, 2004, pp. 155–156.

3. Commission on Macroeconomics and Health _ CMH, WHO, 2001 http://www.who.int/macrohealth/infocentre/advocacy/en/investinginhealth02052003.pdf. Accessed September 2017.

4. http://www.reuters.com/article/us-baidu-regulations-idUSKC-N0Y203N; http://www.cnbc.com/2016/05/10/baidu-ceo-tells-staff-to-put-values-before-profit-after-cancer-death-scandal.html; http://www.nytimes.com/2016/05/04/world/asia/china-baidu-investigation-student-cancer.html?_r=0; http://www.scmp.com/news/china/policies-politics/article/1940511/china-launches-probe-baidu-over-paid-search-listings; http://www.scmp.com/news/china/policies-politics/article/1940668/baidu-scandal-spotlight-china-military-hospitals; http://searchengineland.com/chinese-scrutiny-baidu-ads-bogus-cancer-treatment-causes-death-249189; Accessed September 2017.

5. The situation is actually more complex. This will be explained in more detail in later chapters.

6. See next paragraph on price elasticity in the context of health goods.

7. Y. Liu and K. Rao, "Providing Health Insurance in Rural China: From Research to Policy," Journal of Health Politics, Policy and Law, Vol. 31, No. 1, 2006, pp. 71–92.

8. Karen Eggleston, Ling Li, Qingyue Meng, Lindelow Magnus, and Wagstaff Adam, "Health Service Delivery in China: A Literature Review," Health Economics, Vol. 17, No. 2, 2008, pp. 149–165; William C. Hsiao and Yuanli Liu, "Economic Reform and Health—Lessons from China," The New England Journal of Medicine, Vol. 335, 1996, pp. 430–432.

9. This policy will be explained in more detail later.

10. http://www.forbes.com/sites/brucejapsen/2015/08/09/as-telehealth-booms-doctor-video-consults-to-double-by-2020/#520077035d66. Accessed September 2017.

11. http://www.who.int/mediacentre/factsheets/fs323/en/. Accessed September 2017.

12. http://www.stuffi.fr/objets-connectes-luttent-contre-diabete/. Accessed September 2017 (in French).

13. With the exception of public dispensaries, a limited number of public hospitals, and health centres for war veterans.

14. Most of the French medical doctors belong to the group of practitioners called "secteur I".

15. http://www.szdaily.com/content/2016-06/29/content_13540312.htm. Accessed September 2017.

16. http://abcnews.go.com/US/order-prescription-drugs-safely-online/
    story?id=31047387. Accessed September 2017.
17. W. Yip and W.C. Hsiao, "What Drove the Cycles of Chinese Health System
    Reforms?" Health Systems & Reform, Vol. 1, No. 1, 2015 Feb 25,
    pp. 52–61.
18. D. Thompson, China's Health Care Reform Redux, 2009.
19. Ibid.: W. Yip and W.C. Hsiao, "What Drove the Cycles of Chinese Health
    System Reforms?" Health Systems & Reform, Vol. 1, No. 1, 2015 Feb 25,
    pp. 52–61.

BIBLIOGRAPHY

Commission on Macroeconomics and Health _ CMH, WHO, 2001. http://
    www.who.int/macrohealth/infocentre/advocacy/en/investingin-
    health02052003.pdf. Accessed September 2017.
Cornes, R., and T. Sandler, The Theory of Externalities, Public Goods, and Club
    Goods, Cambridge University Press, 1986.
Eggleston, Karen, Ling Li, Qingyue Meng, Lindelow Magnus, and Wagstaff
    Adam, "Health Service Delivery in China: A Literature Review," Health
    Economics, Vol. 17, No. 2, 2008, pp. 149–165
Grossman, Michael, "On the Concept of Health Capital and the Demand for
    Health," The Journal of Political Economy, Vol. 80, No. 2, 1972.
Hess, C., and E. Ostrom, "Introduction," In C. Hess and E. Ostrom (eds.),
    Understanding Knowledge as a Commons: From Theory to Practice,
    Cambridge, MA: The MIT Press, 2006.
Hsiao, William C., and Yuanli Liu, "Economic Reform and Health—Lessons from
    China," The New England Journal of Medicine, Vol. 335, 1996, pp. 430–432.
Leach, J., A Course in Public Economics. Cambridge University Press, 2004,
    pp. 155–156.
Liu, L., and K. Rao, "Providing Health Insurance in Rural China: From Research
    to Policy," Journal of Health Politics, Policy and Law, Vol. 31, No. 1, 2006,
    pp. 71–92.
Thompson, D., China's Health Care Reform Redux, 2009.
Yip, W., and W. Hsiao, "What Drove the Cycles of Chinese Health System
    Reforms?" Health Systems & Reform, Vol. 1, No. 1, 2015, pp. 52–61.

CHAPTER 3

Organization of Healthcare in China and its Reforms

Abstract The structure of healthcare supply in China is very specific. Indeed, as of 2011, more than 85% of all health personnel worked in public healthcare institutions. In addition, public hospitals provide a very large part of outpatient services on top of their inpatient provision. The goal of this chapter is to explain the reasons behind this very high provision and its consequences. The background presented makes a clear differentiation between rural and urban areas. For each geographical area, a historical and longitudinal reading aims at explaining the current situation. Shortly after the creation of the People's Republic of China in 1949, a healthcare system organized in three tiers, known as the Community Medical System (CMS), was set up in rural locations. Patients had to enter the system through the first tier and were then funnelled into other tiers for the more severe cases. Patients whose affliction required very specific treatment were transferred to urban areas, into provincial or central hospitals. In urban areas, from 1949 to 1980, healthcare access was organized at company level. If, today, the general organization of the healthcare system remains in rural areas, economic as well as administrative reforms have deeply reshaped access to healthcare in these structures.

Keywords Healthcare organization • Ownership • Three tiers • Rural areas versus urban areas • *Hukou*

© The Author(s) 2018   35
C. Milcent, *Healthcare Reform in China*,
https://doi.org/10.1007/978-3-319-69736-9_3

Structure of Healthcare in China and its Evolution

The Chinese healthcare supply structure is very specific. Indeed, as of 2011, 85.19% of all health personnel and 82.80% of all practising medical doctors worked in public healthcare institutions. In addition, public hospitals provided 89.78% of all outpatient services and 87.92% of all inpatient services.[1] The goal of this section is to explain the reasons behind this very high proportion and its consequences.

In the following chapters of this book, I focus on the hospital as the inner centre of the healthcare system in China. However, the recent series of reforms, largely initiated from 2009, tends to decentralize healthcare suppliers. These reforms aim to offer an alternative to hospitals for patients. In the countryside, the alternative healthcare institution is mainly privately run. As a consequence, private providers play a major role in rural China that may be intensified in the future, depending on the ability of private healthcare centres to replace hospitals as the primary care provider in the healthcare system. In other words, how the healthcare centre performs as a "gateway" to all care pathways. So far, as we will see, this series of reforms has not reached its goal, yet.

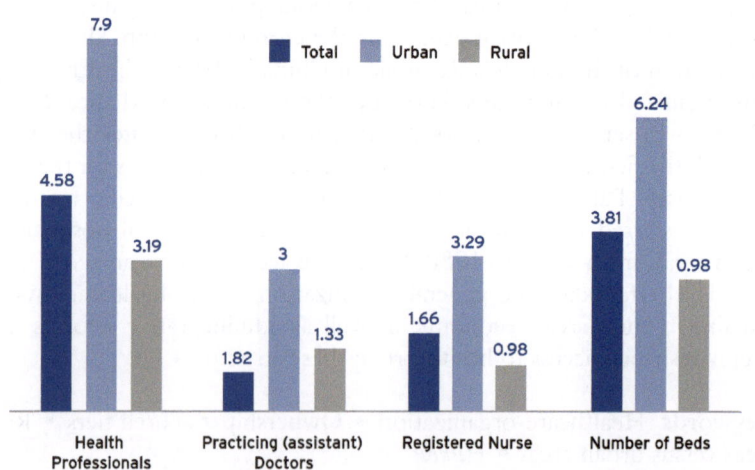

Fig. 3.1 Medical personnel and number of beds in China in 2011 (per 1000 inhabitants). Source: China Health Statistics Yearbook, 2012

Healthcare Footprint in Rural Zones

Shortly after the creation of the People's Republic of China in 1949, a healthcare system organized in three tiers was set up, known as the Community Medical System (CMS).[2,3] Patients had to enter the system through the first tier and were then funnelled into other tiers for the more severe cases. The first tier were "Village Clinics", the second tier "Township Health Centres" (THC) and the third tier "County Hospitals". Patients whose affliction required very specific treatment were transferred to provincial hospitals or central hospitals, in urban areas.

Healthcare in rural areas came at almost no cost to patients but the quality level was quite low. For non-free care, prices were fully regulated. This system was fully financed by the government. Health stations at different levels (province, prefecture and district) were in charge of the prevention of epidemics and other contagious diseases such a leprosy.

- Tier I: after the implementation of this tier, dispensaries were offering care provided by local people with very little training (a couple of weeks was the norm). They were called "barefoot doctors" and were tasked with addressing prevention, ambulatory care and first aid. Their dispensaries were financed by the entities managing the collectivized land.
- Tier II: township hospitals had better equipment than Tier I dispensaries. They took care of patients with more severe pathologies and were usually located in semi-urban areas. They were co-financed by the different administrative levels, from municipality to central state. Any citizen with a rural residence permit was directed toward this type of facility, according to health needs. These structures could handle both in- and outpatients but were not able to deal with emergencies or surgery patients.
- Tier III: also called "county hospitals", catered for the needs of all inhabitants in the district for the most severe cases. Their equipment level was the highest of all and staff were more senior than in other categories. The biggest hospitals were called provincial hospitals or central hospitals.

If today the general organization of the healthcare system remains, economic as well as administrative reforms have deeply reshaped access to healthcare in these structures. We will come back to this point in more detail later in this chapter.

Between 1966 and the early 1980s, all communities had a dispensary. The healthcare system was generally managed at this local level, with each village or village community managing its own dispensary. Land collectivization and free basic healthcare went together. As pointed by Hesketh and Wei. (1997)[4], Yip and Hsiao (2015)[5] and Milcent (2016)[6], from the late 1950s to the 1980s, this organization of the Chinese healthcare system led to a striking improvement in the health of the population. The indicators presented in the introduction show this clearly. Yet, the level of quality remained quite low and equipment mediocre.

With the economic reforms and decollectivization of agriculture, rural inhabitants were no longer obliged to contribute to the community medical system. In parallel, health providers (of Tiers II and III) acquired increasing autonomy, including how their profits were used. This enabled them to develop their facilities and invest in new medical equipment and technologies.

On the flip side, the government in parallel quickly reduced its financial support, leaving the burden of these infrastructures to provincial authorities. The reduction in subsidies has been fast and severe, reaching only 10% of the total budget of hospitals by the early 1990s.[7,8] This model of hospital autonomy can be seen as quite close to the UK system set up with the 2002 to 2006 reforms. Hospitals in the United Kingdom were, until then, totally regulated by the government and acquired autonomy both in terms of financial management and human resources management. One of the main differences between the United Kingdom and China is the existence of the UK National Health Service (NHS), implying a coverage of hospital costs for patients by a public body; whereas in China, for Tier II and Tier III hospitals, access to healthcare was universal as long as the government was financing the cost. Its disengagement has meant the end of free healthcare for patients.

With little or no public subsidies, public hospitals were not bound to fulfil public service tasks any more. In addition, healthcare structures started behaving like for-profit structures. Many were in situations close to monopoly in their local market, making it possible for them to apply any price. Without competition, there was no alternative for patients, and the cost of healthcare (consultations and prescription) just rocketed.[9,10] This turmoil in healthcare offer came at the same time as a very strong, but unequally split, increase in income. In other words, healthcare came at a price, now defined by the supply side. The Chinese government gave incentives to set up private facilities. These eventually replaced already existing public dispensaries or were in competition with them. Services provided by newly set-up private structures had, on average, better quality than those provided until then by public healthcare centres.

In parallel, the funnelling of patients from Tier I structures who before-hand had access to Tiers II and III became quite meaningless in the midst of the upheaval in healthcare offer. As a consequence, the rural population became able to choose their healthcare supplier. The now wealthier part of the population quickly turned to better quality, private hospitals, whose fees they could afford. This led to the three-tier public sector first shaking and finally collapsing altogether, leaving rural areas without free access to healthcare.

The amount of public dispensaries has indeed shrunk. If the average distance from the patient to the closest hospital has been reducing, that to a public hospital has increased, as shown by Akin et al. (2005).[11] After witnessing the collapse of the community healthcare system, the Chinese rural population was offered a proximity care supply that was mostly private or public but behaved like for-profit structures, and, as a consequence, was expensive. Yet, its level of quality was above the standards of what previously existed in rural areas.

The decreasing access to healthcare for the least affluent rural inhabitants, and later an increasing proportion of the population, became a major political issue. To solve it, a public insurance system called the New Community Medical System (NCMS) was initiated in 2003. This acted as a shot in the arm, but failed to provide a durable solution.

If we compare the healthcare offer in rural and urban areas, we see that differences in price and quality have been increasing, according to the new, three-level nomenclature (plus sub-levels). This classification followed the policy of government subsidies to hospitals, as well as clarifying the difference between public/private and non-profit/for profit status.[12,13] This lead the rural population to turn to hospitals able to offer the best level of quality, even if located in urban areas.

This change was made possible by a greater mobility of the population. Indeed, the rural agricultural worker population has decreased at a fast pace while an increasing number of people have started commuting from rural areas to cities, either on a daily basis or for longer periods of time. Consequently, the road network improved, reducing transport time to the cities, and more and more rural inhabitants travelled long distances and stood for hours or even days in waiting rooms for an outpatient consultation. The result of this preferred choice for Level 3 hospitals is an overload on these facilities, resulting is very long waiting times and short consultations times. Tensions between patient and hospital staff have become commonplace in China, because of this situation.

This increase in the demand for hospital consultations is fuelled by the current organization of the healthcare system that gives little incentive to consult locally: patients are entitled to go to any hospital in the municipality of residence. If patients go elsewhere, they are penalized by a lower reimbursement from public insurance schemes.[14] As the coverage rate for outpatient consultations is low, or at least judged as insufficient by the healthcare demand, this does not really hurt. However, it creates ambiguity in the recent reforms: they support the development of easily accessible basic healthcare, while offering a very restricted coverage of such care through public insurance schemes, thus giving little incentive to start the patient journey in these structures. Yet, the government seems to now focus on that issue, based on current initiatives that will be described later in the book.[15]

Healthcare Footprint in Urban Areas

In urban areas, from 1949 to 1980, healthcare access was organized at company level. Each state-owned company managed healthcare for its employees and their families and distributed pensions after retirement. The size of these companies was usually gigantic, making possible a pooling of risk. Overall, this was a decentralized organization, in the end comparable to what existed in rural areas.

With economic reforms, many state-owned companies have been privatized. The huge groups have been broken down into smaller entities. As a consequence, medical insurance has been managed at a smaller scale, making it more fragile. The newly formed companies quickly experienced difficulties in financing the system for two main reasons: first, the scale was reduced, so risk was pooled on a smaller number of individuals; then, being profitable became imperative, without direct support from the state. Bankruptcies became commonplace and to avoid a systemic risk of collapse, the government took the burden of social welfare away from the companies. A basic form of public social security was introduced. Even though its coverage was much reduced compared to what was previously offered by state-owned companies, it was still better than the situation in rural areas, where nothing existed.

Companies offering private insurance are today steadily rising, fuelled by the emergence of a wealthy class and self-employment. Direct marketing through phone calls, text messages or emails to sell private health insurance is common place. It is a growing market but one that still encounters difficulties in finding demand for purely health-related products. This point will be developed later in the book.[16]

With the economic reforms and the dismantling of state-owned companies, many hospitals that were previously directly operated by these companies for the benefit of their employees have been turned into local hospitals managed by Health Bureaus. Today, the healthcare system has the following organization structure: local hospitals for basic care make the first layer. They were created after the first reforms from the 1980s. The level of quality they can offer is often considered insufficient, both in terms of equipment and training of physicians. Then, should the severity require it, the patient is directed towards a district hospital, a municipal hospital or a provincial hospital. The highest level is ministry-owned central hospitals. As already mentioned a three-tier classification with three sub-levels has been defined by the State Council. More precisely, the Chinese Hospital Accreditation system was initiated in 1989 by the Ministry of Health. This first version has been refined over time into the current version. The levels are as follows:

- Level 1 refers to hospitals with quite basic equipment. The level of personnel training is also relatively weak.
- Level 2 hospitals offer care of a better quality than Level 1, thanks to better equipment and better trained medical personnel
- Level 3 hospitals are quite similar to big hospital centres that can be found in Europe or the United States. There is also a subcategory that showcases the best level of care that can be offered in China: Level 3AAA.

Within each of these three levels, three sub-categories from A to C are defined, based on criteria set up by each local health bureau. In 2000, the criterion of being state-owned or not was added. Since 2005, qualitative indexes such as scientific management, patient safety or service quality were also introduced. A form of pay for performance (P4P) has been launched in some localities but is still at a pilot stage. This involves government budgetary subsidies for good performance versus fines or risk of disclosure for poor performance, based on accurately defined criteria.[17]

In terms of equipment, China has widely available high-tech devices as well as medicines. For instance, China has more MRI scanners per inhabitant than Thailand, the latter already being very well equipped.[18,19] On the other hand, medical personnel, both quantitatively and in terms of training, are often mentioned as lagging behind.[20] This point will be developed later on.[21]

The Influence of the Hukou on Access to Healthcare in Urban Areas

The categorization of a zone between urban and rural is usually assumed to be quite straightforward. In reality, it can be quite complex in China, as the notion of an urban zone in China is administrative above any other demographic or geographic factor. For any given area, the switch from rural to urban status cannot be accomplished through simple development of habitation and industry. A zone that has rural status has to keep a high percentage of arable land, this percentage being administratively defined. In addition, the quality level of public medical infrastructure in rural zones is limited by the categorization itself. Hospitals in rural areas are designed mainly for primary care and are entitled only to lower levels of equipment and staff qualification.

Each Chinese citizen has a residence permit, which is associated with a specific area. These permits can be split up into two broad types: urban and rural. An individual with a rural permit is constrained in terms of what he or she can do in urban areas, and his or her social and civic rights do not extend to the urban area. An individual with a rural permit moving to an urban area is designated in China as a "migrant", which corresponds to what is elsewhere designated as an "illegal worker".[22] As industrial jobs are most often found in urban areas, workers with rural permits have to circumvent the rules, with the risk of becoming a "non-citizen" and thus losing their social and civic rights. Migration in China (from rural to urban areas)[23] thus involves not only the loss of the home social network, but also the loss of some rights.

This residence permit (*hukou*, a household registration record book) originated well before the communist regime, its objective always being to strictly control the movement of the population. An individual with a rural permit can turn it into an urban one only in a few, very specific cases. Only holders of urban *hukou* are entitled to public goods (e.g. healthcare, education). The consequence of this system has obviously been to strongly limit migration of entire families from rural to urban areas. It has also participated in the financial sustainability of the healthcare system: as it is very decentralized, the offer proposed by each entity is based on the stability of its resources and occurrence of the pathology.

Over the past 40 years, the proportion of the rural population actually working in urban areas has been growing steadily. This could be due to people migrating to settle in cities as well as those commuting regularly between their place of residence and place of work. The *hukou* system has long been an obstacle, slowing this trend. Today, constraints linked to residence permits have been loosened, so there are, for instance, more situations in which a rural permit can be turned into an urban one. In addition, temporary urban permits can be applied for and simply cancelling the *hukou* system is now being discussed.

Until then, to summarize, for those with a rural *hukou*, expenses are only covered if they go back to their place of residence, in a context where the cost of healthcare in urban areas is higher than what can be observed in rural areas.[24] In the case of healthcare need, this incurs costs high enough to give individuals an incentive to return to their place of residence for treatment. Sociologists Bai and He (2002)[25] have used qualitative methods to demonstrate that health status played a big part in the decision to go back to one's home town. In terms of economics, Milcent (2010)[26] shows that migrants are excluded from health services in urban areas due to the lack of a social network as much as the financial hurdle. Empirical results confirm the assumption that migrants with health issues tend to go back to their home towns in rural areas. Social network benefits linked to the residence permit and support from family appear in this study as the main factors driving the decision for migrants to return home.

The residence permit system (*hukou*) is a key driver of accessibility to public services and employment opportunities. Most migrants from rural areas are not entitled to urban citizenship and are left out of the local community. As already mentioned, the central government has recently imposed less stringent rules for obtaining urban permits as well as temporary permits. Depending on the city or province, these temporary permits open up different levels of rights: as far as social welfare is concerned, there is a gulf between fully fledged holders of local resident permits and non-holders. An insurance package offered by employers can sometimes be used by as a top up for healthcare. As a consequence, this migrant population is somewhere in between systems, with a wide variety of actual situations being encountered.

What Lessons Can be Learned from the Evolution of the Chinese Healthcare System?

Until the 1980s, rural inhabitants were fully covered with free—basic—healthcare. It was followed then by a transitional period until the beginning of the 2000s, with an increasingly loose coverage until its total disappearance. This led people with rural *hukou* to change their behaviour and to seek healthcare structures offering the best level of treatment while remaining affordable.

Since the implementation of NCMS in 2003, coverage by public insurance has again been linked to holding a *hukou* from the municipality where the first hospital in the patient journey is located. Rural inhabitants—or, to be more precise, holders of a rural *hukou*—have to start by consulting a healthcare centre located in their home town. If they do not, they face explicit and implicit financial penalties. Yet, because of a weak level of coverage, the habit of turning to structures with higher standards, and lack of trust in the quality of care offered in local hospitals, authorities have struggled to make local hospitals actual points of entry.

Yet, for the rural population with the smallest income, with an agricultural activity or not, the implementation of NCMS has been a key factor in its access to healthcare. Indeed, the cost of healthcare in urban areas is not affordable for rural people, even for those commuting to cities for work, all the more so in that they have to support a bigger share of the cost themselves than their urban counterparts. Going back home is a must to limit the cost and to benefit from NCMS coverage. But as soon as income enables it, most people tend to opt out of full NCMS coverage to benefit from treatment in a more renowned hospital.

It is clear that the period spanning the 1950s to the early 1980s has witnessed a striking improvement in the health status of the Chinese population, whereas the pace of improvement has been slowing since then.[27] Yet, one should not draw conclusions too fast. The first point is that it is possible that in the 1980s the health status metrics of the population had reached a level from which further improvement could only come from an improvement in prevention and primary care, with an improvement in equipment and training of physicians also due. The second point is that it is possible that collected data on health have improved vastly. Previous data may have been affected by a bias leading to more optimistic statistics than in reality.

CURRENT HEALTHCARE INSTITUTIONS AND OWNERSHIP

A deliberate policy to improve the healthcare offer has resulted in a spectacular increase in the number of healthcare structures over the past decade. The number of hospitals has grown from 18,000 in 2003 to more than 25,000 today. Among these, the proportion of private hospitals is steadily increasing, even though public hospital still account for 60% of the total.[28] Yet, the size of public hospitals is usually much larger, be it in number of beds or admissions.

Hospitals cater both for inpatient stays as well as outpatient consultations. The hospital network is complemented by an increasing number of primary healthcare facilities. They include urban healthcare centres (3.6%), rural township healthcare centres (4.1%) and outpatient clinics (20.1%). In total, healthcare centres represent more than 90,000 structures.

This increase masks important geographical inequalities. The vast majority of healthcare structures are mere healthcare posts (72.2%) with little or no equipment and providing low-quality care. The Beijing province has five times more hospital per inhabitants (429 hospitals for 10 million inhabitants) than the province of Guangxi (88 hospitals for 10 million inhabitants). While most provinces tend to have nine level 3 hospitals for 10 million people, Beijing has 41 of these. The same phenomenon is observed with the number of beds.[29] Figure 3.1 highlights the differences between rural and urban areas in terms of medical personnel and capacity.[30]

Village Clinics and Township Hospitals

The first reforms of the healthcare system after the start of the economic reform was to authorize private clinics and favour their development. This private sector then grew, taking advantage of the collapse of the three-tier organization. A large number of private clinics are actually former Tier I centres that have been privatized. Similarly, some Tier II township hospitals have also been shifted into private for-profit hospitals, but to a lesser extent and at a later stage.

From the end of the 1990s, the trend toward full privatization has been slowing down significantly. This can be explained by fiscal constraint and a perception by the public that the quality level of private hospitals is not sufficient.[31,32,33,34,35] Some hospitals returned to public ownership but many opted for public—private joint ownership. In such cases, ownership is shared between public agencies, private individuals and institutional investors. They are much more commonly found in urban rather than rural areas.[36]

Studies measuring the impact of ownership on healthcare prices and quality do not yield consensual results. According to Meng et al. (2000)[37], public and private structures alike tend to over-diagnose and over-prescribe, but both are capable of carrying out prevention activities. The key factor seems to be the financial incentive to perform these prevention activities. When level is considered adequate, type of ownership is not a crucial variable. To understand such results, it is important to bear in mind that even public hospitals enjoy a wide financial autonomy and can therefore generate profits.

In some cases, the "public health" role was detached from the township health centre at the time of privatization. This makes it difficult to compare the impact of ownership in studies.[38] Between 2003 and 2012, the various cycles of reforms have pushed towards a more welfare-state oriented policy. In this particular case, they have mostly aimed at fostering dual status initiatives or repurposing township health centres into public hospitals. Generally speaking, existing studies do not reach a consensus on the effect of ownership on the efficiency of healthcare supply. Data with more granularity than currently available is necessary, such as data at patient level or stay level.[39]

It is important to note that the classification criteria for Chinese hospital accreditation are only loosely applied to village clinics and township hospitals. The scope of their implementation is left to local authorities. A certain number of provinces have neither private hospitals, village clinics nor township hospitals in this scope, introducing disparities and making like with like comparisons difficult, even within China.

Besides ownership, alternatives to fee-for-service (FFS) payment have also been tested in rural areas. For example, in two counties in Xinjiang province, the local NCMS office introduced a fixed payment per month for each village practitioner. In return, the village doctors provided free primary care including free treatment.[40] In a township in Guizhou province, the Township Health Centre (THC) managed all contracted village practitioners. Payments to village doctors were composed of a basic salary, an indicator-based bonus based on the number of home visits and a performance-based bonus bases on on patient satisfaction and cost containment.[41] A similar arrangement could be observed in Wuxue county in

Hubei province and Wushe county in Henan province.[42,43,44] So far, no strong evidence on the effect of quality of care or healthcare spending has been shown.

We have seen that the primary care offering in rural areas had increased significantly over the past decade thanks to a strong push from the government. Yet, this does not necessarily means it is matched to demand. Indeed, newly set-up private health centres struggle to attract patients. Bed occupancy rates are very low, below 40% for Township Health Centres. This situation extends to medical consultation, with a very weak productivity of five visits per physician and 1.5 admissions per general practitioner.[45]

Poor training of physicians and lack of trust in the quality of healthcare from these centres are the main reasons for their low traction. In addition, during the transition period after the disappearance of free healthcare, patients developed other strategies to access healthcare. On the one hand, insurance coverage is not high enough and on the other hand the increased mobility of the population has put alternative solutions within reach.

More details can be found in Chap. 6 on insurance and Chap. 5 on hospital personnel.

Community Health Service Institutions

As early as 1997, the need to set up a primary care network in urban areas emerged as a priority for the government. Pilot experiments to create the first Community Health Centres were carried out in various cities. In 2006, a new step was taken with the promulgation by the State Council of the "Guidance on the Development of Urban Community Health Services". A large number of local hospitals of Level 1 or even Level 2 status have been shifted into Community Health Centres (CHCs). Since the end of 2008, CHCs are present in all Chinese cities and 98% of municipal districts.[46] CHCs are composed of Health Centres (HCs) and Health Stations (HSs). HCs cover zones of 30,000–50,000 inhabitants and are equipped on average with 50 beds for hospital admissions. HSs cover areas of roughly 3000 inhabitants and are not equipped for inpatient admission. CHCs cater for disease prevention, treatment, care, rehabilitation, health education and family planning; they are most commonly state-owned enterprises, but can also be social organizations or individual businesses.[47,48,49,50]

The main objective of CHCs is to determine primary care for the care leading to hospital admission. As this stage, it is important to bear in mind the current patient journey through the system: at present, most primary care consultations are performed in hospitals, there are no medical practices as seen in Western countries. The aim of the Chinese government is thus to change this situation by offering healthcare out of hospitals, not only in urban areas but also in rural areas. The end goal is to reduce congestion in hospitals in the first tier (Level 3 or 3AAA), by separating outpatient consultations from inpatient hospital activity.

Before the 1980s, even if in theory the first layer of the healthcare system was not composed of family doctors, it was often acting as such. Indeed, in rural as well as urban areas, the first step in the patient's care pathway was a small healthcare structure, most commonly composed of only one physician, with sometimes only sparce training. Gratuity of treatment was conditioned by respecting this pathway, be it through the CMS three-tier system in rural areas or through state-owned companies in urban areas.

After the 1980s, the first layer of the healthcare system disappeared with the collapse of the Community Medical System (CMS) in rural areas and the breaking-up of gigantic state enterprises into smaller-scale units. Thus the goal of the CHC reforms is to rebuild a health system that both separates primary care from hospital admission and promotes collaboration between hospitals and CHCs. In the main, CHCs tend to link themselves with Level 3 or Level 3AAA hospitals. According to Xu et al. (2016)[51], there are currently three main forms of collaboration:

- *Loose Collaboration Model*: the collaboration agreement between the CHC and the hospital is not very binding. The hospital has neither financial nor managerial involvement in the activity of the CHC, but supplies medical services or support. It is the most commonly found form of co-operation in China, but it is not specific to China. It is a minimalistic form of vertical concentration that is promoted in countries with a welfare state oriented structure of healthcare, such as France.
- *Medical Consortium Model*: this is a healthcare network built around a Level 3 hospital supported by service centres, including some CHCs. Acting as partners, these centres receive funding. This means binding contracts implying an involvement from the hospital in the management of these centres. This model is quite similar the

Healthcare Management Organizations found in the United States but it is still quite uncommon in China.[52,53]

- *Direct Management Model*: the hospital and related CHCs are managed by local government and do not have any managerial autonomy. The local administration is in charge of their human resources, their medical resources and ultimately their finances. CHCs can then be considered as delocalized units of the hospital.[54] This very centralized model of organization is currently at the pilot stage in China.

The number of CHCs has been rocketing over the past few years, through the sheer number fostered by the policies targeted at developing primary care, but also because some small hospitals have been elevated to CHC status. Liu et al. (2009) and Zhang et al. (2013) have studied the CHC model using the co-operative framework between the Peking University People's Hospital and two CHCs. They find that it tends to generate a decrease in both consultation timing and price of medicines.[55]

CHCs are similar to structures that exist in other countries such as the United Kingdom and Canada, with a small group of physicians and nurses supplying primary health and dental care. Yet, in China, the training of general practitioners (GPs) is fairly recent and is still not very common.[56] The hiring of qualified GPs is one of the main obstacles to the development of these structures. Indeed, as will be shown in detail later in this book (see Chap. 5), there are many different levels of training for physicians in China.

CHCs also differ according to their organization and governance. As newly created entities, they are governed in ways that are often quite innovative compared to existing structures. The objective is to adapt the organization, funding and management to the local socio-economic environment. Basically, three main models have emerged: (1) public establishments employing civil servants; (2) public establishments employing contract workers; (3) private structures. In 2008, 36.5% of CHCs were of type (1), 35.7% of type (2) and 27.8% of type (3).[57]

CHCs of type (1) do not have the same function as public hospitals. Generally speaking, they are directly managed by the local authorities as non-profit healthcare facilities. A new budget procedure called the Separation of Revenue and Expenditure Policy, implemented since 2010,[58] means that collected payments are sent to the local bureau of the Finance Ministry, who in turn allocates funding based on observed costs. As a consequence, the centre is totally disconnected from the profits it may generate, limiting incentives for over-diagnosis and over-prescription. Investment in facilities and medical equipment is not based primarily on profit return considerations. On the other hand, this system means that the local government may have to financially cover the potential losses of the CHCs.

For the CHCs of types (2) and (3), the financing scheme is a fee-for-service payment. Each time an action is performed, the centre is reimbursed at the convened price. Type (2) implies that the structure is part of the public sector but is managed as a private entity, and is often housed in the same building as a public hospital. This means that, to some extent, this type benefits from the financial support of central and local governments to the host hospital. Type (3) are for-profit companies, even though they may receive limited government subsidies and must abide by certain rules. As an example, all CHCs, whatever their status, must comply with precise rules concerning the medical drugs they sell.[59,60]

Today, rebuilding an adequate referral system seems to be key to the better efficiency of the healthcare system. Yet, the current situation is that patients have little or no incentive to go through this referral system. If the number of CHCs increases, their activity will still be well below the expectations of the regulator. Their level of quality is not perceived as meeting the standards expected by most patients, largely due the lower qualification of physicians compared to the average in Level 3 hospitals.[61] In addition, it is a reality that their level of equipment is lower than Level 2 or 3 hospitals.[62] Accounts in the media or on the internet of cases involving improper diagnoses or patient care have contributed to this negative image and severely hamper people's trust in CHCs.

Chinese patients have grown accustomed to using health facilities offering a full array of equipment and medical services, making it possible to have all diagnoses, as well as science and radiology procedures in one place. The end of free healthcare was simultaneous with the improvement of communication channels, be they actual (roads, the transport system) or virtual (information networks, including internet and social networks). These elements drove patients to search for structures offering the safest level of quality: on the one hand they were no longer obliged to follow a predefined pathway with mandatory referral, and on the other hand they had the means to go to the facility that appeared the most capable of treating them. It also drove up the expectation level on the availability of certain advanced treatments and quality of care.

The gradual implementation of universal coverage (Chap. 6) for a basic care basket has amongst its objectives to funnel patients back into a pathway that is more optimal in terms of cost and resource usage. Indeed, afford-ability of the treatment provided is a key success factor for CHCs. In 2009, the government launched a set a reforms, with among others the National Essential Medicine Programme (NEMP). The list of medicines prescribed in primary healthcare facilities has now narrowed down to those on the Essential Medicines List (EML),[63] with a policy of zero mark-up. This has a double objective: to fight over-prescription and make medicines more affordable for patients.[64] Studies show that even if a decrease in over-pre-scription in CHCs and Township Hospitals can be observed, over-prescrip-tion still exists. In addition, marked differences between regions persist.[65,66,67] More details on this can be found in Chap. 7.

Generally speaking, in health centres medical personnel are paid on a fixed salary basis, plus a variable bonus depending on the profit generated by the centre. To be treated in the centre, patients do not need to be pre-registered. They just pay a fixed sum, which covers medical examinations as well as medical drugs. These health centres are a recently created form of healthcare supply for outpatients, but their impact cannot be cleared measured yet. Nevertheless, based on economic theory, as physicians have absolutely no direct incentive to over-diagnose and over-prescribe, we should be witnessing a decrease in the cost of medicines and equipment usage rates. On the flip side, the fact that physicians get a variable bonus based on the profit of the centre, associated with a fixed payment per con-sultation, creates an incentive to increase the number of consultations per patient. This is a mechanism of induced demand: the doctor asks the patient to come back more often than strictly necessary thanks to the asymmetry of information between the two of them. The combined effect of these two contradictory trends, i.e. less over-prescription but an increase in the number of consultations, on global health expenditure is still uncer-tain and will require further study before reaching a consensus.

Current Situational Analysis

The structure of healthcare supply is as follows: 24,709 hospitals, 915,368 primary healthcare facilities and 31,155 specialized public healthcare institutions.[68]

- Hospitals can be general, specialized or performing traditional Chinese medicine, according the NHFPC classification. According to 2011 sta-tistics, general hospitals account for 65.2% of the total, specialized hospitals for 12.9% and traditional Chinese medicine hospitals for the rest. In addition, hospitals are also classified based on their size and the quality of the care they can offer, itself determined by the level of equipment, training and seniority of physicians as well as research activity. The tiering currently defined by NHPFC partially overlaps with the three-tier classification that existed at the beginning of the 1980s.[69]

- Level 3 regroups 1898 hospitals, said to be the "best healthcare establishments in China". This explains why patients are ready to travel long distances to be treated in one of these hospitals. They are university hospitals, have at least 500 beds each and their occupancy rate is above 100%. Depending on sources, this rate varies between 103% (NHFPC, 2014) and 120% (Figure from the National Bureau of Statistics of China, 2015. http://www.stats.gov.cn/english/). The number of patients catered for has reached 121 million a year.
- Level 3 regroups 6807 hospitals. They have between 100 and 500 beds each, with an occupancy rate of 89.7% (NHFPC, 2014). The number of patients is at 104 million a year.
- Level 1 regroups 6853 hospitals, with a capacity ranging from 20 to 99 beds each. Their occupancy rate is 63.5%.
- There are 9951 hospitals that are not categorized; the number of their patients (both in- and outpatients) has reached 21.5 million a year.

• Primary healthcare facilities are composed of health posts/dispensaries in villages, CHCs and THCs.
• Specialized health centres arose from the regrouping of centres for disease control and health supervision institutions.

Overall, this chapter sheds light on the disruption of the healthcare system that followed the economic reforms of the early 1980s, observed both in rural and urban areas. The result is an increase in healthcare access that has been growing continuously. The implementation of a public health insurance scheme, with a progressively increased coverage, curbed this trend but failed to reverse it completely.

Another consequence was the realization by Chinese citizens that the healthcare on offer was very much dependent on the type of health structure. Demand then converged to hospitals with the best quality level, namely Level 3 and 3AAA hospitals. This popularity is observed both for in- and outpatient types of care.

These centres of excellence are thus suffering from a lack of supply. They are no longer able to meet demand, creating extremely tense relationships (that will be studied in Chap. 8), making the re-creation of care pathways the emergency of the moment. Yet, while health expenditure incurred in hospitals is globally well covered by public insurance, this is not the case for care provided by CHCs.[70,71,72] In addition, outpatient consultation fees are almost the same for large tertiary hospitals and community hospitals.[73] This obviously contributes to the patients' preference for Level 3 hospitals, as they can benefit from the best level of equipment and medical staff for a payment equivalent to that of a lower level facility.

Despite China's efforts, a broad shift in patient volumes to CHCs has yet to occur. According to a McKinsey report (2010):[74] "Interviews they conducted suggest that most CHCs have seen only a 10 percent to 15 percent increase in patients following conversion from class I or II hospitals—an insignificant rise given the previous low utilization rates and the 11 percent overall increase in outpatient visits to all health care sites that occurred in 2009 alone."

In parallel, the cost to the community of outpatient consultations in such structures of excellence is much higher than in CHCs. One of the reasons is that these centres regroup state of the art equipment and highly skilled personnel. Using them for basic treatments is a suboptimal use of resources. For the sake of efficiency, patients need to be directed first to primary health centres for medical consultations. This way, an adequate referral would make it possible to funnel them into the structure that is most relevant to their treatment. This system ought to be combined with a fee or any other forms of additional payment carrying out this "adequate referral" mission. The development of CHCs and THCs in urban areas, both strongly regulated in terms of pricing, fits this objective.

One of the routes explored by Chinese authorities is the family doctor, in a form similar to the UK General Practitioner (GP). His or her role is to follow the patient over time, in order to gather historical data and experience on the patient's health, directing the patient towards the relevant medical structure in the event of specialised treatment being needed. Pilot trials have been carried out, but results have appeared too inconclusive to go to a full-scale implementation.

Today, the endorsement of any new health pathway by patients is made difficult by their lack of trust in hospitals that are not top tier. Tools used until now, be they the implementation of public health insurance conditioned by the health pathway or the set-up of CHCs in urban areas and township centres in rural areas with regulated prices for medicines, have produced mixed results.

NOTES

1. Ministry of Health of PRC, China Health Statistics Yearbook 2012, Beijing: Peking Union Medical College Press, 2012.
2. X. Liu and J. Wang, "An Introduction to China's Health Care System," Journal of Public Health Policy, Vol. 12, No. 1, 1991 Spring, pp. 104–116.
3. This system is called in Chinese三級 制.
4. T. Hesketh and X.Z. Wei, "Health in China. From Mao to Market Reform," BMJ, Vol. 314, 1997, pp. 1543.
5. Ibid: W. Yip and W.C. Hsiao, "What Drove the Cycles of Chinese Health System Reforms?" Health Systems & Reform, Vol. 1, No. 1, 2015 Feb 25, pp. 52–61.
6. C. Milcent, "Healthcare Access and Hospital's Violence: Digital as a Response for Inefficiency," China Perspective, Vol. 4, 2016.
7. Ministry of Health, Research Report on China National Health Accounts, Ministry of Health, Beijing, China, 2004.
8. W. Yip and W. Hsiao, "The Chinese Health System at a Crossroads," Health Affairs, Vol. 27, 2008, pp. 460–468.
9. "Baisse de la demande de soins dans les zones rurales en Chine," C. Milcent, under revision for Revue Economique, 2013.
10. K. Eggleston, L. Li, Q. Meng, M. Lindelow, and A. Wagstaff A., "Health Service Delivery in China: A Literature Review," Health Economics, Vol. 17, 2008a, pp. 149–165.
11. J. Akin, W. Dow, and P. Lance, "Changes in Access to Health Care in China, 1989–1997," Health Policy, Vol. 20, 2005.
12. State Council, Implementing Guideline for Classified Administration on Urban Medical Institutions, State Council, 2000a.
13. State Council, State Council General Office Notice to Issue the Instructive Opinions on Urban Medical and Health System Reform, State Council, 2000b.
14. We consider here the situation after the implementation of NCMS in rural areas.
15. See Chap. 6.
16. See Chap. 6.
17. Ministry of Health, Hospital Management Appraisal Guide, MOH, Ministry of Health, Beijing, China (in Chinese), 2000.
18. Data on MRI scanners per million are available in China's health statistical digest.

19. R.C. Hutubessy, P. Hanvoravongchai et al., "Diffusion and Utilization of Magnetic Resonance Imaging in Asia," International Journal of Technology Assessment in Health Care, Vol. 18, No. 3, 2002, pp. 690–704.

20. K. Eggleston, L. Ling, M. Qingyue, M. Lindelow, and A. Wagstaff, "Health Service Delivery in China: A Literature Review," Health Economics, Vol. 17, No. 2, 2008b, pp. 149–165.

21. See Chap. 5.

22. It is however possible to obtain a temporary residence permit for work in urban areas. The way in which such permits are obtained differs from one town to another. The ability to obtain a permanent residence permit is also town-dependent, but severely constrained.

23. In this chapter, the term "migration in China" refers to internal migration between rural and urban areas. This use of language is very frequent in the literature on migration in China.

24. C. Milcent, "Healthcare for Migrants in Urban China: A New Frontier," China Perspectives, Vol. 2010, No. 4, 2010.

25. N. Bai and Yupeng He, "Huiliu haishi waichu—Anhui Sichuan ersheng nongcun waichu laodongli huiliu yanjiu" (Rentrer et émigrer? Etude sur les migrations de retour vers les zones rurales dans les provinces de l'Anhui et du Sichuan), Shehuixue Yanjiu, Vol. 3, 2002, pp. 64–78.

26. C. Milcent, "Healthcare for Migrants in Urban China: A New Frontier," China Perspectives, No. 2010/4, 2010.

27. X.-Y. Gu and S.-L. Tang, "Reform of the Chinese Health Care Financing System," Health Policy, Vol. 32, 1995, pp. 181–191.

28. National Bureau of Statistics of China (2015); Swedish Agency for Growth Policy Analysis (2013): China's healthcare system—Overview and quality improvements; Numbers from the National Bureau of Statistics of China (2015).

29. Source MoH, China National Health Yearbook 2009.

30. China Health Statistics Yearbook, 2012.

31. X. Liu, L. Xu et al., "Reforming China's 50,000 Township Hospitals— Effectiveness, Challenges and Opportunities," Health Policy, Vol. 38, No. 1, 1996, pp. 13–29.

32. W. Li, "Rethinking the Sale of Township Hospitals," Chinese Health Economics, Vol. 4, 2000, pp. 12–14 (in Chinese).

33. J. Xu, "No Choice or Right Choice: Ownership Reform in Township Hospitals," Decision and Consultancy, Vol. 9, 2001, pp. 24–25 (in Chinese).

34. X. Wang and L. Liu, "The Process of Reforming Ownership of Township Hospitals," Health Economics Research, Vol. 3, 2002, pp. 3–5 (in Chinese).

35. Q. Meng, Review of Provider Organization Reforms in China. China Rural Health AAA Background Report, 2005.

36. B. Wang and Y. Zhang, "The Investigation Analysis of 6 Private Hospitals," Chinese Health Economics Magazine, Vol. 21, No. 1, 2002, pp. 52–54 (in Chinese).

37. Q. Meng and X. Liu et al., "Comparing the Services and Quality of Private and Public Clinics in Rural China," Health Policy and Planning, Vol. 15, No. 4, 2000, pp. 349–356.

38. Z. Xu, "Problems after Ownership Reform in Township Hospitals," Jiangsu Health Care Management, Vol. 1, 2003, pp. 35–38 (in Chinese).

39. K. Eggleston, L. Congdong et al., Comparing Public and Private Hospitals in China: Evidence from Guangdong. China Rural Health AAA Background Paper, 2005.

40. S. Hu, "Overview of NCMS models in China," Chinese Journal of Primary Health Care, Vol. 9, 2003, pp. 1–6 (in Chinese).

41. F. Wang, "Improve Rural NCMS in Poor Areas," Guizhou Finance and Economics Journal, Vol. 6, 2003, pp. 62–64 (in Chinese).

42. Z. Wang, S. He, and Zhou, "Why NCMS in Wuxue can be Sustained and Developed," Chinese Rural Health Care Management, Vol. 2, 2003, pp. 25–26 (in Chinese).

43. B. Wang, L. Wang et al., "CMS in Wuxue for 40 Years," Chinese Rural Health Care Management, Vol. 1, 2004, pp. 10–13 (in Chinese).

44. Health Bureau of Wushe County, "Serving the Establishment of Rural Household Contract System," Chinese Rural Health Care Management, Vol. 7, 2002, pp. 28–30 (in Chinese).

45. Ministry of Health, Chinese Health Statistical Digest, Ministry of Health, Beijing, China, 2005.

46. Z. Chen, "Seize the Opportunity, Meet the Challenge, and to Accelerate the Healthy Development of Community Health Services," Journal of Community Healthcare, Vol. 8, No. 5, 2009, pp. 305–309 (in Chinese).

47. Z.X. Lu, Y.B. Li, F. Wang et al., "The Development, Effect and Concerned Issues of Pilot Work of National Community Health Service System Building in Key Contact Cities—Based on the Comprehensive Analysis of the Baseline Survey and Routine Monitoring Data," Chinese Journal of Social Medicine, Vol. 26, No. 6, 2009, pp. 321–325.

48. Division of Maternal and Child Health and Community Health of Chinese Health of Ministry, Department of Social Medicine and Health Management of School of Public Health of Tongji Medical College of Huazhong University of Science and Technology: The Base-line Survey Report of Chinese Community Health Service System Building of 28 Key Contact Cities. Beijing: HOM of P.R. China, 2008.

49. J. Xu, N.N. Wu, S.G. Jin, F. Wang, L.Q. Liu, Y.X. Wang, and Z.X. Lu, "The Analysis of Inpatient Bed Allocation Equity and Utilization in the City Community Health Service Centre of China," Journal of Huazhong

University of Science and Technology [Medical Sciences], Vol. 30, No. 2, 2010c, pp. 141–144. https://doi.org/10.1007/s11596-010-0201-6.

50. J. Xu, W. Wang, Y. Li et al., "Analysis of Factors Influencing the Outpatient Workload at Chinese Health Centres," BMC Health Services Research, Vol. 10, 2010a, pp. 151.

51. J. Xu, R. Pan, R.W. Pong, Y. Miao, and D. Qian, "Different Models of Hospital–Community Health Centre Collaboration in Selected Cities in China: A Cross-Sectional Comparative Study," International Journal of Integrated Care, Vol. 16, No. 1, 2016, p. 8.

52. L. Lu and J. Ma, "Research on Current Situation and Effectiveness of Various Cooperation Modes Between Hospitals and Community Health Service Centers in Wuhan," Chinese Hospital Management, Vol. 31, No. 11, 2011, pp. 20–22 (in Chinese).

53. H.L. Li, X.D. Wang, and Y.Q. Xiao, "Explore on Improving the Ability of Community Health Service Centers Through the Reform of Public Hospitals Direct Management," Journal of Community Medicine, Vol. 11, No. 17, 2013, pp. 22–23 (in Chinese).

54. Y. Xiao and X.M. Ruan, "Practice and Reflection on Regional Medical Consortium in Hubei," Chinese Hospital Management, 2012, Vol. 32, pp. 12–13 (in Chinese).

55. L. Liu, F. Liu, H. Chen, and S. Wang, "Exploration and Practice of Integrated Medical Health Service System," China Digital Medicine, Vol. 4, No. 9, 2009, pp. 11–14 (in Chinese).

56. This will be explained in more detail in Chap. 5 of this book.

57. Centre for Health Statistics and Information Research on Health Services of Primary Health Care Facilities in China. People's Republic of China: Ministry of Health, 2008.

58. With a pilot started in 2006 in Beijing.

59. H. Wang, S. Wong, M. Wong, X. Wei, J. Wang, D. Li, Jin Ling Tang, G. Gao, and S. Griffiths, "Patients' Experiences in Different Models of Community Health Centers in Southern China," Annals Family Medicine, Vol. 11, No. 6, 2013, pp. 517–526.

60. See Chap. 7.

61. G. Dussault and M. Franceschini, "Not Enough There, Too Many Here: Understanding Geographical Imbalances in the Distribution of the Health Workforce," Human Resources for Health, Vol. 4, No. 1, 2006, p. 12.

62. X. Zhang, L.W. Chen, K. Mueller, Q. Yu, J. Liu, and G. Lin, "Tracking the Effectiveness of Health Care Reform in China: A Case Study of Community Health Centers in a District of Beijing," Health Policy, Vol. 100, No. 2–3, 2011, pp. 181–188.

63. L. Yang, C. Liu, J.A. Ferrier, W. Zhou, and X. Zhang, "The Impact of the National Essential Medicines Policy on Prescribing Behaviors in Primary

Care Facilities in Hubei Province of China," Health Policy Plan, Vol. 28, 2013, pp. 750–760.

64. L. Dong, H. Yan, and D. Wang, "Antibiotic Prescribing Patterns in Village Health Clinics across 10 Provinces of Western China," Journal of Antimicrobial Chemotherapy, Vol. 62, 2008, pp. 410–415.

65. Q. Yao, C. Liu, J.A. Ferrier, Z. Liu, and J. Sun, "Urban-Rural Inequality Regarding Drug Prescriptions in Primary Care Facilities—A Pre-post Comparison of the National Essential Medicines Scheme of China," International Journal for Equity in Health, Vol. 14, 2015, p. 58.

66. Y. Song, Y. Bian, M. Petzold, L. Li, and A. Yin, "Effects of the National Essential Medicine System in Reducing Drug Prices: An Empirical Study in Four Chinese Provinces," Journal of Pharmaceutical Policy and Practice, Vol. 7, 2014, p. 12.

67. "Prescribing Patterns in Outpatient Clinics of Township Hospitals in China: A Comparative Study Before and After the 2009 Health System Reform," International Journal of Environmental Research and Public Health, 13, No. 7, 2016.

68. Source: National Bureau of Statistics of China, 2015.

69. The number of hospitals shown here is as described in November 2014 by NHFPC.

70. Z.X. Lu, J.H. Chen, K. Wang et al., Social Health Insurance Science, Beijing: People's Medical Publishing House, 2, 2007.

71. J. Xu, F. Wang, and Z.X. Lu, "The Survey Analysis of the Health Insurance Compensation Impact on the Income of City Community Health Center in 28 Chinese Cities," Chinese Health Economics, Vol. 4, 2010b.

72. Z.X. Lu, J. Xu, W.X. Wang, N.N. Wu, and W. Qin, "Analysis of Medical Insurance Reimbursement Rates of Community Health Stations Sponsored by Various Entities," The Chinese Journal of Hospital Administration, Vol. 26, No. 3, 2010, pp. 205–208.

73. Qi Li and Peng Xie, "Outpatient Workload in China," Vol. 381, No. 8, 2013.

74. http://www.mckinsey.com/~/media/mckinsey/dotcom/client_service/healthcare%20systems%20and%20services/health%20international/hi10_china_healthcare_reform.ashx. Accessed September 2017.

Bibliography

Akin, J., W. Dow, and P. Lance, "Changes in Access to Health Care in China, 1989–1997," Health Policy, Vol. 20, 2005.

Bai, N., and Yupeng He, "Huiliu haishi waichu—Anhui Sichuan ersheng nongcun waichu laodongli huiliu yanjiu," (Rentrer et émigrer? Etude sur les migrations de retour vers les zones rurales dans les provinces de l'Anhui et du Sichuan), Shehuixue Yanjiu, Vol. 3, 2002, pp. 64–78.

"Baisse de la demande de soins dans les zones rurales en Chine," C. Milcent, Under Revision for Revue Economique, 2013.

Chen, Z., "Seize the Opportunity, Meet the Challenge, and to Accelerate the Healthy Development of Community Health Services," Journal of Community Healthcare, Vol. 8, No. 5, 2009, pp. 305–309 (in Chinese).

Division of Maternal and Child Health and Community Health of Chinese Health of Ministry, Department of Social Medicine and Health Management of School of Public Health of Tongji Medical College of Huazhong University of Science and Technology: The Base-line Survey Report of Chinese Community Health Service System Building of 28 Key Contact Cities. Beijing: HOM of P.R. China, 2008.

Dong, L., H. Yan, and D. Wang, "Antibiotic Prescribing Patterns in Village Health Clinics Across 10 Provinces of Western China," Journal of Antimicrobial Chemotherapy, Vol. 62, 2008, pp. 410–415.

Dussault, G., and M. Franceschini, "Not Enough There, Too Many Here: Understanding Geographical Imbalances in the Distribution of the Health Workforce," Human Resources for Health, Vol. 4, No. 1, 2006, p. 12.

Eggleston, K., L. Congdong et al., Comparing Public and Private Hospitals in China: Evidence from Guangdong, China Rural Health AAA Background Paper, 2005.

Eggleston, K., L. Li, Q. Meng, M. Lindelow, and A. Wagstaff, "Health Service Delivery in China: A Literature Review," Health Economics, Vol. 17, 2008a, pp. 149–165.

Eggleston, K., L. Ling, M. Qingyue, M. Lindelow, and A. Wagstaff, "Health Service Delivery in China: A Literature Review," Health Economics, Vol. 17, No. 2, 2008b, pp. 149–165.

Gu, X.-Y., and S.-L. Tang, "Reform of the Chinese Health Care Financing System," Health Policy, Vol. 32, 1995, pp. 181–191.

Health Bureau of Wushe County, "Serving the Establishment of Rural Household Contract System," Chinese Rural Health Care Management, Vol. 7, 2002, pp. 28–30 (in Chinese).

Hesketh, T., and X.Z. Wei, "Health in China. From Mao to Market Reform," British Medical Journal, Vol. 314, 1997, pp. 1543.

Hu, S., "Overview of NCMS Models in China," Chinese Journal of Primary Health Care, Vol. 9, 2003, pp. 1–6 (in Chinese).

Hutubessy, R.C., P. Hanvoravongchai et al., "Diffusion and Utilization of Magnetic Resonance Imaging in Asia," International Journal of Technology Assessment in Health Care, Vol. 18, No. 3, 2002, pp. 690–704.

Li, W., "Rethinking the Sale of Township Hospitals," Chinese Health Economics, Vol. 4, 2000, pp. 12–14 (in Chinese).

Li, H.L., X.D. Wang, and Y.Q. Xiao, "Explore on Improving the Ability of Community Health Service Centers through the Reform of Public Hospitals Direct Management," Journal of Community Medicine, Vol. 11, No. 17, 2013, pp. 22–23 (in Chinese).

Li, Qi, and Peng Xie, "Outpatient Workload in China," The Lancet, Vol. 381, No. 8, 2013.

Liu, L., F. Liu, H. Chen, and S. Wang, "Exploration and Practice of Integrated Medical Health Service System," China Digital Medicine, Vol. 4, No. 9, 2009, pp. 11–14 (in Chinese).

Liu, X., and J. Wang, "An Introduction to China's Health Care System," Journal of Public Health Policy, Vol. 12, No. 1, 1991 Spring, pp. 104–116.

Liu, X., L. Xu et al., "Reforming China's 50,000 Township Hospitals— Effectiveness, Challenges and Opportunities," Health Policy, Vol. 38, No. 1, 1996, pp. 13–29.

Lu, Z.X., J.H. Chen, K. Wang et al., Social Health Insurance Science, Beijing: People's Medical Publishing House, 2, 2007.

Lu, Z.X., Y.B. Li, F. Wang et al., "The Development, Effect and Concerned Issues of Pilot Work of National Community Health Service System Building in Key Contact Cities—Based on the Comprehensive Analysis of the Baseline Survey and Routine Monitoring Data," Chinese Journal of Social Media. Vol. 26, No. 6, 2009, pp. 321–325.

Lu, L., and J. Ma, "Research on Current Situation and Effectiveness of Various Cooperation Modes Between Hospitals and Community Health Service Centers in Wuhan," Chinese Hospital Management, Vol. 31, No. 11, 2011, pp. 20–22 (in Chinese).

Lu, Z.X., J. Xu, W.X. Wang, N.N. Wu, and W. Qin, "Analysis of Medical Insurance Reimbursement Rates of Community Health Stations Sponsored by Various Entities," The Chinese Journal of Hospital Administration, Vol. 26, No. 3, 2010, pp. 205–208.

Meng, Q., Review of Provider Organization Reforms in China, China Rural Health AAA Background Report, 2005.

Meng, Q., and X. Liu et al., "Comparing the Services and Quality of Private and Public Clinics in Rural China," Health Policy and Planning, Vol. 15, No. 4, 2000, pp. 349–356.

Milcent, C., "Healthcare for Migrants in Urban China: A New Frontier," China Perspectives, No. 2010/4, 2010.

Milcent, C., "Healthcare Access and Hospital's Violence: Digital as a Response for Inefficiency," China Perspective, Vol. 4, 2016.

Ministry of Health, Chinese Health Statistical Digest, Ministry of Health, Beijing, China, 2005.

Ministry of Health, Hospital Management Appraisal Guide, MOH, Ministry of Health, Beijing, China, (in Chinese), 2000.

Prescribing Patterns in Outpatient Clinics of Township Hospitals in China, "A Comparative Study Before and After the 2009 Health System Reform," International Journal of Environmental Research and Public Health, Vol. 13, No. 7, 2016.

Song, Y., Y. Bian, M. Petzold, L. Li, and A. Yin, "Effects of the National Essential Medicine System in Reducing Drug Prices: An Empirical Study in Four Chinese Provinces," Journal Pharmaceutical Policy Practice, Vol. 7, 2014, p. 12.

Wang, F., "Improve Rural NCMS in Poor Areas," Guizhou Finance and Economics Journal, Vol. 6, 2003, pp. 62–64 (in Chinese).

Wang, Z., S. He, and D. Zhou, "Why NCMS in Wuxue can be Sustained and Developed," Chinese Rural Health Care Management, Vol. 2, 2003, pp. 25–26 (in Chinese).

Wang, X., and L. Liu, "The Process of Reforming Ownership of Township Hospitals," Health Economics Research, Vol. 3, 2002, pp. 3–5 (in Chinese).

Wang, B., L. Wang et al., "CMS in Wuxue for 40 Years," Chinese Rural Health Care Management, Vol. 1, 2004, pp. 10–13 (in Chinese).

Wang, H., S. Wong, M. Wong, X. Wei, J. Wang, D. Li, Jin Ling Tang, G. Gao, and S. Griffiths, "Patients' Experiences in Different Models of Community Health Centers in Southern China," Annals Family Medicine, Vol. 11, No. 6, 2013, pp. 517–526

Wang, B., and Y. Zhang, "The Investigation Analysis of 6 Private Hospitals," Chinese Health Economics Magazine, Vol. 21, No. 1, 2002, pp. 52–54 (in Chinese).

Xiao, Y., and X.M. Ruan, "Practice and Reflection on Regional Medical Consortium in Hubei," Chinese Hospital Management, 2012, Vol. 32, pp. 12–13 (in Chinese).

Xu, J., "No Choice or Right Choice: Ownership Reform in Township Hospitals," Decision and Consultancy, Vol. 9, 2001, pp. 24–25, (in Chinese).

Xu, Z., "Problems after Ownership Reform in Township Hospitals," Jiangsu Health Care Management, Vol. 1, 2003, pp. 35–38 (in Chinese).

Xu, J., R. Pan, R.W. Pong, Y. Miao, and D. Qian, "Different Models of Hospital–Community Health Centre Collaboration in Selected Cities in China: A Cross-Sectional Comparative Study," International Journal of Integrated Care, Vol. 16, No. 1, 2016, p. 8.

Xu, J., W. Wang, Y. Li et al., "Analysis of Factors Influencing the Outpatient Workload at Chinese Health Centres," BMC Health Services Research, Vol. 10, 2010a, pp. 151.

Xu, J., F. Wang, Z.X. Lu, "The Survey Analysis of the Health Insurance Compensation Impact on the Income of City Community Health Center in 28 Chinese Cities," Chinese Health Econics, Vol. 4, 2010b.

Xu, J., N.N. Wu, S.G. Jin, F. Wang, L.Q. Liu, Y.X. Wang, and Z.X. Lu, "The Analysis of Inpatient Bed Allocation Equity and Utilization in the City Community Health Service Centre of China," Journal of Huazhong University of Science and Technology [Medical Science], Vol. 30, No. 2, 2010c, pp. 141–144. https://doi.org/10.1007/s11596-010-0201-6

Yang, L., C. Liu, J.A. Ferrier, W. Zhou, and X. Zhang, "The Impact of the National Essential Medicines Policy on Prescribing Behaviors in Primary Care Facilities in Hubei Province of China," Health Policy Plan, Vol. 28, 2013, pp. 750–760.

Yao, Q., C. Liu, J.A. Ferrier, Z. Liu, and J. Sun, "Urban-rural Inequality Regarding Drug Prescriptions in Primary Care Facilities—A Pre-post Comparison of the National Essential Medicines Scheme of China," International Journal of Equity Health, Vol. 14, 2015, p. 58.

Yip, W., and W. Hsiao, "The Chinese Health System at a Crossroads," Health Affairs, Vol. 27, 2008, pp. 460–468.

Yip, W., and W.C. Hsiao, "What Drove the Cycles of Chinese Health System Reforms?" Health Systems & Reform, Vol. 1, No. 1, 2015 Feb 25, pp. 52–61.

Zhang, X., L.W. Chen, K. Mueller, Q. Yu, J. Liu, and G Lin, "Tracking the Effectiveness of Health Care Reform in China: A Case Study of Community Health Centers in a District of Beijing," Health Policy, Vol. 100, No. 2–3, 2011, pp. 181–188.

Zhang, L., R.Y. Yang, and D.F. Qian, "Evaluation on Collaborative Services Under Medical Group Model by Patients in Community Health Service Centers," Chinese General Practice, Vol. 16, No. 10, 2013, pp. 3298–3300.

CHAPTER 4

Hospital Institutional Context and Funding

Abstract This chapter focuses on hospital ownership and supervision. Public hospitals are mostly, but not always, under the supervision of the Health Ministry. There are a certain number of other governing bodies that are directly involved in the management of hospitals. A cross-ministry group was set up in 2006 to facilitate the implementation of hospital reforms. Apart from the organizational structure, the funding of hospitals and its evolution is studied. Between 1979 and 1991, the government introduced a co-payment system in healthcare establishments. In 1992, the Ministry of Health officially granted greater autonomy to public hospitals. They were authorized to deliver paid services and to make profits, but were made responsible for their losses and debts. By 2003, central government funding had fallen to 8% of the hospital budget. As a result, public hospitals in China behave very similarly to for-profit firms, while being governed as any traditional public structure. The next step is the current experiment of a Diagnostics Related Group-based payment in China. Along with the financial autonomy of public hospitals, different reforms have been directed at developing private hospitals, even though many obstacles still remain.

Keywords Healthcare institution • Funding and ownership • Healthcare quality • Healthcare expenditure • Evolution

© The Author(s) 2018
C. Milcent, *Healthcare Reform in China*,
https://doi.org/10.1007/978-3-319-69736-9_4

In this chapter, we separate the hospital by ownership (public/private) for discussion. Because of the historical healthcare system context, the public sector is more mature than the private one. As a consequence, some pilot reforms are introduced only in the public sector. As example is the implementation of a Diagnostics Related Group- (DRG)-based payment presented at the end of the first section of this Chapter. Actually, this does not mean that the private sector will be immune to these new forms of funding. In the United States, for instance, when the DRG-based payment was introduced, it was designed for Medicare patient (patients aged over 65) without focusing on a specific hospital ownership by also targeting private hospitals.

PUBLIC HEALTH ESTABLISHMENTS

Institutional Context

Ownership
After the implementation of the "three-tier public provision system", most hospitals were under the direct supervision of the Health Ministry, with support from local Health Offices. Nevertheless, some remained dependent on state-owned companies or the army. Other governing bodies were involved in maternity and family planning centres, at county and township level. Whatever the governing body, the healthcare supply was provided by the public sector.

Today, health centres in both rural and urban areas are split between public and private structures. In rural zones, community clinics are mostly private whereas urban county hospitals remain mostly public.

Comparing Figs. 4.1 and 4.2 illustrates that the healthcare supply shift from the public sector to the private sector is an ongoing process.

Governing Bodies
Public hospitals are mainly but not solely under the supervision of the Health Ministry. There is still a certain number of governing bodies, ministries or state-owned companies that are directly involved in the management of hospitals. For instance, the People's Liberation Army (PLA) and some large state-owned industries, such as the railways, have their own hospitals and medical schools. Most hospitals and medical schools affiliated with the PLA are considered to be of a high quality and provide services to political leaders.[1]

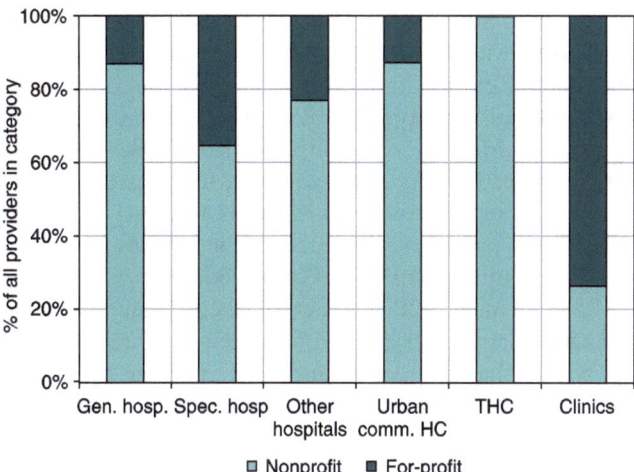

Fig. 4.1 Ownership and healthcare services in 2006. Note: Data are from the 2006 MOH Health Statistical Digest (online) (Ministry of Health, 2006) and refer to 2005. Estimates exclude a small number of providers (<1%) that have not yet been classified. The "non-profit" category mainly consists of organizations owned by the government and companies (available data do not permit a disaggregation of the non-profit category by ownership)

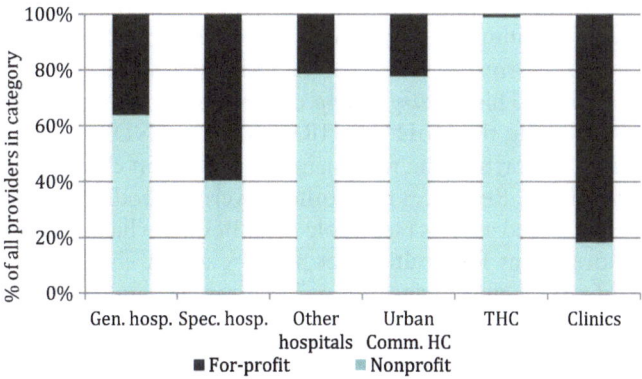

Fig. 4.2 Ownership and healthcare services in 2012. Note: Data are from the 2012 MOH Health Statistical Digest (online) (Ministry of Health, 2012) and refer to 2011. Estimates exclude a small number of providers (<1%) that have not yet been classified. The "non-profit" category mainly consists of organizations owned by government and companies (available data do not permit a disaggregation of the non-profit category by ownership)

This fragmented structure is a hurdle to the implementation of any hospital reform, with four main ministries involved: the National Development and Reform Commission (NDRC), the Ministry of Human Resources and Social Security (MoHRSS), the Ministry of Finance (MoF) and obviously the Ministry of Health (MoH). These ministries do not have the same objectives. As a consequence, healthcare suppliers do not respond to the same incentives, which leads to a lack of co-ordination between healthcare providers. The effect of the reforms implemented may be affected by this multiplicity of governing bodies.

The SARS epidemics in 2003 has crystallized the importance of public health and care. Many experts and officials have pointed out the flaws in the health system that led to the quick spread of the SARS virus.[2] As a consequence, a think tank was created to give strategic direction to future reforms: the Development Research Centre (DRC) reports to the Chinese State Council. One of its reports heavily influenced the 2009 reform package.[3]

To solve the complexity of implementing Chinese health system reforms, a cross-ministry group was set up in 2006 to facilitate the implementation of hospital reform. This Leading Group for Coordination Healthcare System Reform is dependent on the NDRC and Health Ministry and its first chairman was the future Prime Minister Li Keqiang.

In 2008, this group in the state council was restructured with the mission to co-ordinate all stakeholders of healthcare reform, from provincial governments to ministries involved and administrations in charge of implementing reforms.[4] It made various and important policy initiatives at the central level. This *leading group* consists of representatives from 20 ministries including the MoH, MoHRSS, MoF and NDRC. As a support, one agency from each of the four main ministries is in charge of a specific part of the reform. Resources from other governing bodies are also tapped for more specialized aspects (see Table 4.1). Besides which, every province set up a local team for health reform. They are in charge of a specific checklist of tasks from the state council that can be completed by the provincial authority.

As a consequence, all reforms implemented since 2009 are not co-ordinated by the Ministry of Health but by a special unit reporting directing to the State Council (or more precisely to the Health Reform Office of the State Council). Yet, this unit does not have the ability to actually implement the decisions taken. It needs to go the ministries to execute decisions. In reality, these reforms involve a large numbers of governing

Table 4.1   Agencies in charge of healthcare reform

Governing body	Role
Ministry of Health (MoH)	Healthcare service per se, public hospital reform, rural co-operative schemes, list of authorized medicines and medical devices, long-term planning
National Development and Reform Commission (NDRC)	Payment rules and regulation, national list of reimbursed medicines, training
Ministry of Human Resources and Social Security (MoHRSS)	State-financed health insurance
Ministry of Finance (MoF)	Investment in healthcare
State Food and Drug Administration of China (SFDA)	Safety of care products and care-related products
State Intellectual Property Office (SIPO)	Patent regulation and application in the domain of healthcare
China Insurance Regulatory Council (CIRC)	Organization and regulation of private insurance market

Source: US-China Business Council

bodies. The National Development and Reform Commission (NDRC) and the Ministry of Finance (MoF) in particular have a key role.

The different ministries involved can sometimes have conflicting priorities. For instance, if we take the example of health insurance, MoHRSS is in charge of insurance in urban areas, whereas the Ministry of Civil Affairs (MoCA) manages a programme for the underprivileged that includes insurance covering basic care. In parallel, the China Insurance Regulatory Commission (CIRC) has a mission to encourage the development of a private health insurance market.

Another example is any reform touching hospital human resources. The Office of Central Institutional Organization, the Ministry of Education as well as MoHRSS, because it manages the career of civil servants, are necessarily involved.

Daily governance is also complex. For instance, for investment decisions for public hospitals, two ministries share responsibility: the MOH and the National Development and Reform Commission (NDRC). As a result, public hospitals may receive conflicting policies and regulations.

In addition, for the execution of policies, many other bodies are involved: authorities at provincial level, district level and city level, bureaus of Labour and Social Security, Health and Finance. This huge number of stakeholders shows the complexity of hospital reform in China. If the central government defines the general direction and objectives, this actual implementation takes place under steering at a more granular level—provincial and below. This, combined with a large financial autonomy, makes it possible to factor in local specificities in the actual execution of reforms but can also generate important territorial inequalities. A costly reform implemented in an area hit by economic downturn will not produce the same effect as when implemented in a soaring region.

To mitigate this risk, each authority in charge of implementation at the local level is given measurable targets, for instance, the number of people covered by public health insurance at a certain date. These targets are cascaded into the individual objectives of local political leaders, having a direct impact on their career advancement and promotion into the party's apparatus. Nonetheless, many health reform objectives are not easily quantifiable, for instance better governance, leaving widespread nuances in interpretation.

Evolution of Funding

At the beginning of the 1980s, the central government was paying for 60% of hospital expenditure. Over the 1979–1991 period, the government introduced a co-payment system in healthcare establishments. The aim was to provide greater flexibility in terms of profit, and thus to incite establishments to improve the quality of the services they offered and professionalize their medical staff (Du, 2009).[5] In 1992, the Ministry of Health officially granted greater autonomy to public hospitals, through an official document published in September 1992 by the State Council, "Instructions on Health Reform".[6] By this, public hospitals were authorized to deliver paid services and to make profits, but were made responsible for their losses and debts. They have to self-finance their investment in equipment and infrastructure as well as a salary bonus policy. They are also entitled to enter into joint ventures with private companies, including setting up for-profit departments within the public hospital itself. As a result of this 1992 reform, bigger hospital structures developed, as well as improved quality, thanks to the acquisition of high-tech equipment.

Since then, public hospitals in China have the particularity that they behave as companies, aiming to maximize profit through investment and price setting, while being governed as any traditional public structure. They are the sole recipient of public funding,[7] be it from the central or local governments. Staff management is under the supervision of central governing bodies, mainly the MoRHSS, from both a resource allocation perspective as well as individual career management. While they keep this strong bond with central authorities, they have financial autonomy. They are able to determine their price policy, which can turn out to be a problem in cases where they are in a monopoly situation in certain geographical areas, and hence without the market regulation of pricing.

By 2003 central government funding had fallen to 8% of hospital expenditure. The fall in state financing was offset by charging for medicines and diagnosis procedures. In China, as in many other Asian countries, patients do not consult doctors in their doctor's office—outside any healthcare facilities—but in the hospital outpatient department. Prescriptions are given at the end of the consultation by default (patients are not asked if they want to purchase them). The total cost is the sum of the price of the consultation and that of the prescribed medicine. Patients do not have an explicit choice in not accepting the doctor's prescription. In this context, prescription prices can be varied in order to compensate for the fall in the hospital's central funding. This practice has been severely questioned during the recent healthcare reforms in China. Prescriptions currently account for about half of healthcare expenditure. The over-prescription of medicine and the over-use of high-tech equipment for diagnostic purposes have often been identified as the cause of the rapid increase in healthcare expenditure (Eggleston et al., 2008a[8]; Wang, 2005)[9]. The current healthcare system has been judged to be both too costly and more sophisticated than is medically necessary (World Bank, 2004[10]; Blumenthal and Hsiao, 2005[11]). It is very likely that these factors affect the demand for and use of healthcare.

Following the 1992-reform, some public facilities set up healthcare centres with a fee-for-service payment. As expected, these for-profit firms reoriented their activity to the most profitable healthcare areas. These for-profit health centres did not have to provide any public-service mission. The healthcare prevention programme was then neglected: epidemic control, health education, maternal and child health all suffered.

The 2003 SARS epidemic put the public health role of public hospitals to the forefront again. The negative side-effects of financial autonomy appeared sharply in that context. This led to a clear split between medical operations and hospital management functions. Additionally, it was demanded that for-profit activities be clearly split from the rest in hospital books of account.[12]

Nonetheless, in 2008, health expenditure for pharmaceutical products still accounted for 43% of total health expenditure.[13] This compares with a 17% average share in Organisation for Economic Co-operation and Development (OECD) countries.[14] Per capita medicine expenditure reach RMB 574. Nearly 40 million surgeries were performed in China in 2015. This figure is nearly one-sixth of the world's total surgical operations. The biggest share of procedures is in the obstetrical and gynecological areas, followed by digestive and gastrointestinal system procedures.[15] According to Yip and Hsiao (2015), "from 1978 to 2011, personal health spending per capita increased by a multiple of 164 from 11 RMB to 1801 RMB (or from roughly 6 to 280 USD) while the Consumer Price Index increased by 5.65 times during this period. A huge portion of this expenditure was for high-tech tests and unnecessary drugs."[16,17]

Improving Healthcare Quality and Reducing Hospital Expenditure Funding

In the 1980s, the main objective of the regulator was to make it possible for hospitals to acquire technology and to improve their level of quality. In parallel, the aim was also to reduce the burden of hospital expenditure funding. The series of reforms implied three main changes:

- Financial autonomy of public hospitals
- Managerial autonomy for a part of public hospital staff
- Financial incentives for physicians to profit.

Financial autonomy of public hospitals: This has been achieved at the expense of accessibility for many. The share of health expenditure in total income has rocketed during the past 35 years. In 1990, per capital health expenditure in urban areas was still contained at a very low level of RMB 26, whereas it reached more than RMB 1,000 in 2013.

Another effect of the financial autonomy of public hospital has been a certain loss of authorities over medical practices.

Managerial autonomy: In parallel, hospitals have autonomy in person-nel management for their for-profit activity. For that part of the activity, personnel are not under the same governance and control by authorities. This co-existence is bound to create tensions, as salary differences appear between the official public salary scale and unregulated salaries of the for-profit activities. Additional benefits can be granted to physicians and other medical personnel, based on a very non-transparent basis, leading to many frustrations. Pursuit of profit can become the top priority while it was totally disregarded in previous situations. The objective function of medical personnel includes an increasing component of profit maximization.

Financial incentives for physicians: In public hospitals, physicians are civil servants (*bianzhi*)[18]. This status implies certain benefits that will be described later and ensures a fixed income, independent from their volume of activity. Yet, this fixed income is often described as being fairly low in view of both their responsibilities and other revenue sources. An additional income source has been authorized dependent on the for-profit activity of the hospital. One can then easily see that physicians have an incentive to develop the for-profit activities, for instance increasing the number of consultations, delivering over-diagnoses or over-prescribing. In such cases, it is a win–win situation for both medical personnel and hospital management.

In addition, this healthcare system nurtures the pre-existing practices of bribes and other types of corruption. They tend to become widespread, creating an increasingly tense atmosphere between patients and hospital personnel.

Funding of Public Hospitals Today

The Chinese healthcare system has long been accused of failing to efficiently deliver healthcare services at an affordable cost. In 2009, a set of reforms were implemented, giving the state a bigger role in the production and distribution of health services.

Nonetheless, public hospitals receive only limited funding from the regulator. Figure 4.3 shows the different sources of funding. It is quite striking that direct public funding from the government only represents a minimal share of the total (8%). In reality, the involvement is more pronounced with indirect funding through public health insurance set up in both rural and urban areas. Companies also participate in the financing of healthcare, accounting for almost one-third of the total.

Patients' share accounts for 50% of hospital revenue, but patients usually do not bear the total costs, as part is covered by public or private health insurance. The covered part has been increasing steadily over the past few years. In the end, patients' out-of-pocket payments rose from 20% in 1980 to 59% in 2000, but then decreased to a current rate of around 35%).[19,20]

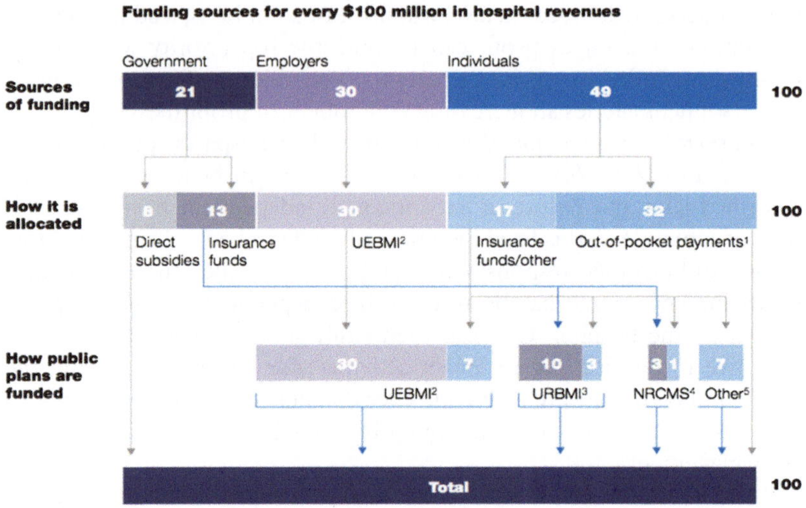

Funding sources for every $100 million in hospital revenues

Fig. 4.3   Funding sources of public hospitals in China. Out-of-pocket payment: sum paid by patients and not reimbursed by any kind of insurance. It includes $6 million from the uninsured and $26 million in co-payments from the insured. [2]UEBMI: Urban Employee Basic Medical Insurance. [3]URBMI: Urban Resident Basic Medical Insurance. [4]NRCMS: New Rural Cooperative Medical System. [5]"Other" includes private health insurance (both supplementary and stand-alone); employer contribution to group private health insurance, which is around $1 million. Total funding is around $7 million. Source: Hospital interviews; government statistics 2010, "Healthcare in China," A Kieger Report on the Chinese Healthcare Market 2015. www.mckinsey.com/...service/healthcare%20systems%20and%20 services/health%20international/hil0_china_healthcare_reform.ashx

A landscape analysis of the health insurance market in China is presented in Chap. 7.

Early Forms of Prospective Payment in China

Some experiments, presented here, aimed at switching from a fee-for-service payment to any form of prospective payment. The goal is to modify incentives for healthcare providers: from driving up service prices to introducing and encouraging competition with a price ceiling system. In urban areas, the insurance schemes existing before the economic reform were based on a principle of regulated pricing. When the Basic Medical

Insurance (BMI) scheme was introduced, a mechanism to contain expenditure from the demand side was implemented (the Medical Savings Accounts—MSA). On the supply side, there was no change in the provider payment introduced by central government. However, at local government level, examples of the implementation of some form of prospective payment can found from the early BMI pilot.

In 1997, the Social Insurance Bureau of Hainan province implemented a prospective payment, concerning six key hospitals. This payment was quite similar to a global budget system. Studies led by Yip and Eggleston (2001 and 2004)[21,22] show that average expenditure by admission fell below that of other hospitals on a fee-for-service basis. Besides, spending growth on expensive drugs and high-tech services was reduced dramatically.[23] The defined limits of these studies concerns the fact that the data were not available to control for the potential reduction of quality of care, risk selection and cost shifting to the uninsured. Implementation of similar forms of prospective payment systems were nonetheless implemented in many areas throughout China, as in Qingdao, Shandong province, for instance.[24]

Some other cities introduced payment per capita as an alternative prospective payment form. In 2001, Jiujiang city switched to capitation: a fixed amount per capita (contrary to per inpatient or per inpatient day as presented so far) on a defined geographic area. Medical expenditure per insured inpatient fell dramatically and the share of drug expenditure in total spending fell drastically.[25] However, lack of information about the impact on the healthcare level of quality prevents any conclusion being drawn.

First Implementation of the DRG Payment in China

The Diagnosis Related Group (DRG) payment is a reimbursement scheme that was first implemented in the United States at the beginning of the 1980s. This type of payment is a form of prospective payment system and consists of a lump sum based on the pathology and procedures to be carried out on the patient. A categorization of pathologies, diagnoses and actions is made *ex-ante*. All patients are affected in one these categories, collectively called the Diagnosis Related Group (DRG).

Each DRG defines a pathology, associated diagnoses and all procedures already implemented or yet to be implemented. This way, each patient falls into a DRG and each DRG corresponds to a predefined lump sum, based on the expenses the hospital has to incur to carry out treatment for this type of patient. The advantage of this lump sum is that it is not correlated with the treatment actually performed while covering the theoretical expenses necessary to cure the patient. This gives an incentive to limit cost, explaining why this type of payment is widespread, not only in China but in a vast majority of OECD countries.

The efficiency of such a system relies heavily on the quality of the information system that goes with it. It is quite complex, as, for each patient, information regarding diagnoses, procedures and comorbidities is to be collected and compiled. China aims at putting in place a comprehensive information system with medical history and patient admission details. This project is still in the early stages though.

Zhenjiang, a BMI pilot city, started to experiment with a DRG payment system for 82 diseases.[26] The reimbursement rate for each disease was set according to average expenditure incurred over the previous three years in treating each disease, minus any "unreasonable" expenditure.[27] In 2003, the average spending for diseases using the DRG payment was 25% lower than the province average in hospitals of the same level. Once again, because of the poor quality of data at the micro-level, studies on the impact of the DRG payment system on the quality of care and risk of selection impact have unfortunately not been published yet.

After that, DRG-based payment systems spread across China, for instance, in cities such as Guangzhou, Dalian, Liushou and Mudanjiang. In Guangdong province, as early as 2002, a total of 13 out of 18 municipalities were already using such systems. However, this DRG-based payment is still restricted to specific diseases. Besides, these cities also use different prospective payment systems alongside a fixed charge per inpatient. Studies on this aspect provided less strong evidence for DRG-based payments or other forms of prospective payment on a reduction of healthcare spending.[28,29,30]

Following the BMI offices' example, some local offices of NCMS (public health insurance for inhabitants in rural areas)[31] adopted a prospective payment system to reimburse the health providers. For instance, two counties in Shaanxi province adopted a fixed-price reimbursement system for some selected THCs and selected county hospitals according to specific criteria.[32]

Some providers moved from a FFS service to a prospective payment system but not in conjunction with a public insurance scheme. In

Heilongjiang province, by the end of 2000, 16 hospitals started to use a DRG-based payment system. One goal was to attract private investment and more business by developing a reputation for transparency in pricing.[33,34] So far, there is no scientific study paper on the effect on quality of care or strong evidence on healthcare expenditure.

To date, there are two main viable DRG systems, the Beijing-DRG (2011) and the C-DRG system set up by the NHFPC (2017). Because of inconclusive results, in 2017, these different forms of prospective payment are still being studied and this is an on-going field of research.

PRIVATE HEALTH ESTABLISHMENTS

Is the Private Hospital Sector Really Booming?

We use here "private" in a wider sense, to cover all hospital structures apart from the public ones (*minying*), be it through joint ventures, co-operatives or private structures with capital from mainly Hong-Kong, Macao, Taiwan but also all over the world.

Until 1980, it was legally impossible to set up a private hospital. Different reforms since then have been directed at developing them, along with the financial autonomy of public hospitals. As of 2005, 15.9% of hospitals were registered as private structures, most of them being specialized establishments. Nonetheless, the average size of private hospitals is much smaller than public hospitals. In 2008, the average number of inpatient beds for a private hospital was 42, which is in sharp contrast to the average number of 228 beds for a public hospital.[35]

Recently, when classifying hospitals by their ownership, 58% of the hospitals in China are public, including state-owned and indirectly state-owned ones; the remaining 42% are private. In terms of level, according to the official hospital classification, the percentage of publicly owned hospitals by admissions is 96% for Level 3 and 91% for Level 2 hospitals. As a result, 90% of Chinese patients choose to visit public hospitals. Private hospitals in China only account for around 10% of the service volume and for 14% of beds while being operated at a lower level (Fig. 4.4).[36] The picture is quite the opposite in the United States, where public hospitals make up 15% of total hospitals and only 27% of patient visits.[37]

Nonetheless, the private hospital sector has been steadily increasing over the past few years. In 2013, the share of beds in private hospitals reached 15.6%, 1.6% up from the previous year. The number of public

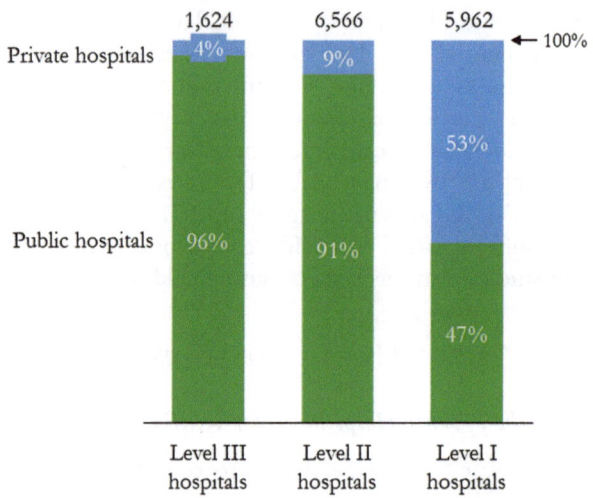

Fig. 4.4   Hospital ownership by hospital level. Source: NHFPC (2014), figures from 2012

hospitals grew from roughly **5400** in **2008** to **10,877** in **2014**.[38] From 2012 to 2013, the number of patients treated in a private hospital grew by 1.1%. We can then observe a constant increasing trend but no sharp change (Fig. 4.5).

In rural zones though, the situation is totally different. A large part of primary care is carried out in dispensaries that are now almost exclusively private and paid for on a fee-for-service mode. Yet, it is quite difficult to precisely measure the actual progression of the activity of private health-care establishments. Until very recently, the information on the public or private status of a hospital was not made available in official statistics.

In conclusion, the number of private healthcare facilities is increasing but, in terms of number of visits, there is no private hospital boom.

How to Explain the Difficulty of Growing the Private Hospital Sector?

The Ministry of Health has stated on various occasion that it wants to develop the private health sector. The objective set by the State Council is for it to command 20% of the market by 2020. Why such support? As previously explained, public hospitals are largely in a monopoly situation

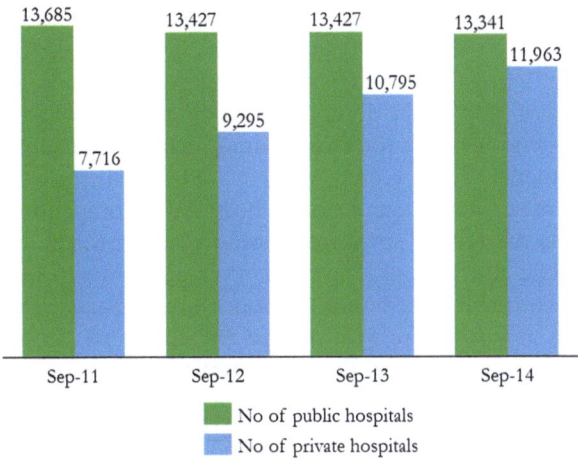

Fig. 4.5 Number of public and private hospitals in China. Source: NHFPC (2014)

in their geographical area. The decrease in public funding has led to a deregulation of healthcare pricing. The partially stated goal here is to increase competition between public and private hospitals to help regulate pricing. This is very similar to the mechanism in place in the United States for a large part of the population. Using competition between public and private sectors to better regulate hospital care is also increasingly popular in a number of European countries (e.g. Germany, the United Kingdom, the Netherlands and France).

In China, the 12th Five Year Plan (2012–2016) and the 13th Five Year Plan (2016–2020) emphasize the development of private hospitals. Until then, setting up a private healthcare structure had been legally possible for two decades, but almost impossible in practice, in particular due to the difficulties of hiring medically qualified personnel.[39] Private hospitals have been addressing, as a priority, three markets segments: high-end healthcare for expats and the affluent local population, healthcare targeted to very specific pathologies and finally healthcare in direct competition with that offered by public hospitals.

The first segment enjoys sold growth. Initially directed at expat consumers, it turns out to be increasingly used by high-end consumers. "Half of our outpatients are expats working or living in China, such as diplomats and executives of foreign-invested companies. And the other half is high-income Chinese residents. We sell by word of mouth," said Zhu Ying, President of the Beijing Bayley & Jackson Medical Centre in downtown Beijing, a private hospital with headquarters in Hong Kong.[40] This is an example of what can be observed in very big cities in China. However, so far, this phenomenon is too new to draw an conclusion apart from this initial assessment.

In the third segment, that of private hospitals in competition with public structures, the former sometimes have to face distorted competition, through public subventions. However, they also have to overcome the difficulties of attracting the best practitioners and resistance from the public towards a new structure with neither a track record nor endorsement from the community. This difficulty in attracting patients seems hard to understand in the context of dissatisfaction over the service provided by public hospitals, but it actually sheds light on the priority criteria of patients/customers. The quality and reliability offered by public hospital, through their high level of equipment and skilled and trained personnel, prevails over the annoyance of congestion and the price of care.

As mentioned previously, recruitment of highly skilled professionals is one of the main obstacles to the development of private hospitals. The status of physicians in public hospitals, the benefits it brings and the additional wages received in various forms are often roadblocks to a migration to a private structure.[41] A 2010 McKinsey report entitled "China Healthcare Reform" gives the example of Beijing municipality. It addresses Community Healthcare Centres[42] (CHCs) but the configuration is identical for private hospitals: "A few cities have tried to force more patients to go to CHCs, but these efforts have generally been unsuccessful. In January 2010, for example, one local government implemented a policy of requiring patients with certain chronic diseases to be treated at a CHC before they could receive care at a class III hospital. However, the local department of health withdrew this policy one month later, saying that the quality of the CHCs needed to be improved before the policy could be implemented."[43]

The status and financial obstacles to hiring well-known professionals in private hospitals creates a vicious circle. As they do not manage to hire renowned physicians, private hospitals are obliged to hire young doctors with little experience. For both patients and professionals, this type of structure tends to become a second choice, when public hospitals are not an option. The story of An Hua and Li Peng provides a good example. They are reputed physicians in a Level 1 hospital in Beijing. They confided that working in a private structure could resolve their current, difficult, working conditions. Where they work, they have to deal with an extended number of working hours, an excessive number of patients and a patient–hospital staff antagonistic climate. However, according to them, the size of private facilities is too small to attract a sufficient number of patients; the healthcare equipment is too limited; and the professional environment does not provide a sufficiently stimulating setting in which to work and grow.[44] This difficulty in recruitment is a recurring theme mentioned by professionals as well as academics. Dr. Wang Zhen, from the Chinese Academy of Social Sciences (CASS) gives the example of the creation of a private hospital in Shenzhen in 2012. It was a showcase collaboration between Hong Kong University (HKU) and the Shenzhen municipality. In 2015, this state of the art facility has not managed to fill all the physician positions. Out of 300 full-time positions, 100 are yet to be filled, to a point where it is seriously considering shift the establishment to a public status to solve the recruitment issue.[45]

In parallel, another obstacle to the development of private hospitals is the restrictive conditions on the reimbursement of healthcare expenses by public insurance. This does not include the reimbursement of healthcare in private facilities. However, a main part of the population can only afford to get healthcare access using public insurance. As a consequence, the restrictive rule of public insurance excludes a large part of the population from access to private facilities. Recently, in some cases and in some areas, expenses in private facilities have been partially reimbursed by public health insurance.[46] It would be interesting to assess the effect of such a change on the individual's preference in the choice of healthcare providers.

So far, if some reforms have tended to develop the private health sector, there are still some keys determinants that limit this central state support.

A True Story of the Challenges Behind Opening a Clinic

Yu Ying, a former physician in a famous Beijing hospital, the Peking Union Medical College Hospital, is a key figure and spokesperson for public hospital doctors. Her Weibo blog (Chinese equivalent of Twitter) has more than 3 million followers. On it, she has been describing her hesitation about leaving the public sector, her difficulties after crossing the bridge, but also the fulfillment it created for her.[47] Yu Ying, who had chosen "Emergency Room superwoman" for her pseudoname, is one of the few professionals to have left a Level 3 hospital to create a private medical centre. When she decided to leave her public hospital, her objective was to open her clinic in Beijing city, within the Fifth Ring Road. However, as she explained, this was not as easy as expected. A series of administrative constraints and barriers prevented her from opening a centre there. All her efforts failed. Having resigned from her previous hospital and given up her civil servant status, returning to the public sector was no longer an option. She decided to take her chance in Chengdu, Sichuan province, where she tried again to open a private clinic providing the most basic medical services. She failed again. During this time, she used her Weibo blog to explain part of her difficulties and the obstacles encountered along the way. When I interviewed her, the term "bribery" was never mentioned. As she said, she was able to explain her disappointment without going too far into detail about the local administrative process. In March 2014, she used her Weibo account to explicitly address the authorities about her situation asking, "Which deputy of the National People's Congress can tell me why it is so difficult for a doctor, who has worked in the country's top-grade hospital for 12 years and has held a doctorate degree after eight years of professional medical education, to open a regular clinic through formal channels?"[48] The timing was perfect. It was between the plenary session of the National People's Congress and the Chinese People's Political Consultative Conference, allowing a strong echo to her protest. The outcome was finally positive, even though she had to drop the idea of setting up her own facility. She is now the CEO of a private general clinic in Beijing city run by the Amcare group,[49] a public–private partnership joint venture, two and a half years after having resigned from a top public hospital. Despite her 3 million fans, she has to struggle to both promote the quality of a market-oriented institution and recruit staff members from big public hospitals.

Her experience illustrates the difficulty faced by medical professionals in opening their own private health centres compared to the situation in most OECD countries.

Regulatory and Para-regulatory Context for Private Health Structures

New Series of Policies
Since 2009, a new series of policies have been released. The goal of these policies is to lower the barrier to entry for private health establishments.

This should create a more adequate business environment and improve the share of private health structures in the healthcare market. In 2010, a notification on "further encouraging and leading social capital to participate in healthcare institutions" was published.[50] This document promotes and encourages social capital to run private hospitals. It covers more practical, detailed information on beneficial policies for running a private health structure. In order to facilitate the development of the private hospital sector, it also allows a lowering of the entry barriers for private medical institutes with foreign capital. As a pilot experiment, some local governments have lifter some constraints on public hospitals: for instance, experimenting with the privatization of public hospitals.

The Model—Chains of Private Specialized Hospitals
Currently, the private healthcare market has developed a model based on chains of private specialized hospitals. More specifically, the medical services provided by the private sector are mostly for dental treatment, ophthalmology and plastic surgery, as well as diagnosis labs and centres. These sectors are medical sectors where customized services may generate higher margins. Maternity is also considered as a potentially profitable sector. For instance, by May 2013, AmCare had assisted in more than 10,000 births and its total revenue soared 50% to 300 million yuan ($49 million). In 2014, US-based Warburg Pincus LLC invested $100 million in Beijing-based AmCare Women's and Children's Hospital to support its expansion. Today AmCare accounts for about half of the high-end healthcare market for women and children in Beijing, which is now dominated by private hospitals.[51]

According to the Roland Berger report illustrated in Fig 4.6, "investors with various backgrounds are entering China's private hospital market. Foreign hospital chain investors, such as Chindex have built up high-end chain hospitals in smaller size in China. Local financial investors, real estate companies and pharmaceutical companies are mostly targeting at mid-end market and specialty hospitals. Pharmaceutical companies such as Shanghai Fosun Pharmaceutical Group aim at broadening their value chain and boost selling of their own drugs by establishing hospitals or participating in public hospital privatization".[52]

A cluster of private medical companies and hospitals owned by people from the city of Putian, commonly known as the "Putian clan" (*Putian ji*), also constitutes great power in the healthcare industry as over 80% of private medical companies in China are affiliated with the Putian clan.[53]

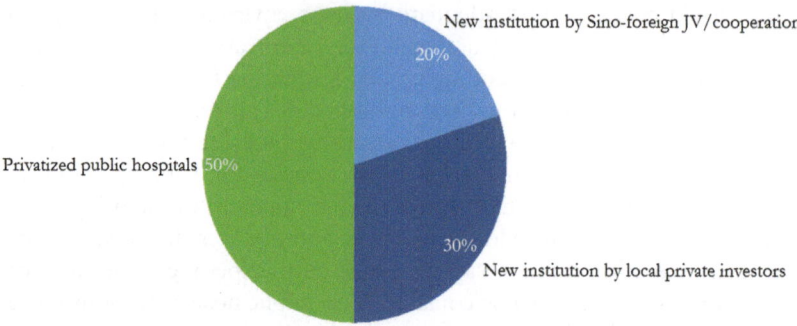

Fig. 4.6   Investors with various backgrounds in 2012. Source: Roland Berger (2014)

The members of the Putian clan have organized themselves into a chamber of commerce named "Putian (Chinese) Health Industry Association" (*Putian (Zhongguo) Jiankang chanye zong shanghui*) since 2014.

Public Funding and Private Healthcare Providers
Another part of the reform aimed at developing private hospitals is their inclusion into public health insurance schemes. Until recently, a patient admitted into a private hospital was not eligible for reimbursement from public insurance. This constraint is progressively eased, in one province after the other. Rules tend to vary depending on the area, but there is an increasing number of cases for which care provided in private healthcare centres can be covered by public insurance schemes.

In addition, in some provinces or municipalities, private hospitals can be directly subsidized. Again, it is important to note the decentralized structure of the Chinese healthcare system. General direction and target is given by the central government but provinces have wide autonomy in actual implementation. In August 2015, the National Health and Family Planning Commission jointly announced with the Ministry of Commerce that fully foreign-owned private hospitals were allowed in seven provinces (Beijing, Tianjin, Shanghai, Jiangsu, Guangdong, Hainan and Fujian).[54,55]

Challenges for Private Health Establishments

In future, key factors private health structures need to develop are: (1) patient recognition that private health establishments can be as trustworthy as a public ones; (2) obtaining sufficiently skilled and reputable doctors and medical staff including nurses; and (3) full inclusion in healthcare insurance schemes.

This point (1) is a prerequisite condition. The development of the private sector is based on a high level of healthcare quality. The over-arching goal of profit maximization must not contaminate the level of quality provided. In 2016, press articles drew attention to private healthcare companies that severely undermined doctors' medical professionalism. As witnesses, doctors previously employed by Putian clan hospitals, stated that to achieve profit targets set by their superiors they performed unnecessary medical treatments. They added that these practices are not uncommon in these hospitals as doctors are directly employed by the hospitals they serve.[56] A necessary challenge will be to make a profit without undermining the level of quality provided.

Even at a slower pace than anticipated, things are starting to change and the private sector is now showing significant growth. According to the NHFPC, from September 2013 to September 2014, the number of private hospitals has increased by 1168, while the cohort of public hospitals was reduced by 86. From 2008 through 2014, patient visits to private hospitals have increased by 12.5% from third trimester 2013 to third trimester 2014, overstepping the growth of visits to public hospitals, which have grown at 7.9% on a quarter-to-quarter basis.[57]

In fact, since the economic reforms of the 1980s, there have been two schools of thought regarding the direction the health system in China should take.[58] One is a pro-market group that advocates market liberalism to improve the quality of healthcare and efficiency. The other is a pro-government group that advocates the need for a large government role in the production and distribution of health services. The latter prioritize issues of equity or fairness and aim at reducing social inequities. Depending on the period, each school of thought has had the upper hand in the direction given to reform. The last round of reform since 2013 is very much market-oriented, the market being expected to play a decisive role in the allocation of resources. The Third Plenum of the 18th Central Committee of the Communist Party, in November 2013, emphasized a higher priority for economic growth. Therefore, the conditions required for the development of the private sector in the healthcare market are fully in place with favourable policies.

In a near future, with this preferential environment and the ongoing governmental commitment, a rapid growth of the private sector is to be expected. This evolution should have, at least, two consequences. One could be to put pressure on public hospitals and push them to keep going at improving their level of quality, not only in terms of medical services but also in the overall service quality (including accommodation, catering, etc.) and operational efficiency. The other consequence could be to limit the demand for public hospital access (for in- and outpatients) and reduce congestion in the Level 3 and 3AAA public hospitals.

These forecasts on the effect of a more prominent presence of private healthcare providers in the healthcare market are based on a major assumption: that the income or wealth of a society is equitably distributed. The hypothesis is very strong and very restrictive. With increasing income inequality, the part of the population who cannot afford to access to healthcare will increase. An adequate and efficient alternative may be universal healthcare access for all. While this may be too costly for society it may avoid the failure of the market in providing equal access to healthcare. The Healthy China 2020 project includes universal healthcare access by the year 2020 for basic healthcare supplies. Besides the success of this programme, the central question will be "What is included in the 'basic healthcare supplies' basket?"

NOTES

1. Sheila Hillier and Jie Shen, "Health Care Systems in Transition: People's Republic of China. Part I: An Overview of China's Health Care System," Journal of Public Health Medicine, Vol. 18, No. 3, 1996, pp. 258–265.
2. S. Wang, "China's Health System: From Crisis to Opportunity," Yale-China Health Journal, Vol. 3, 2004, pp. 5–49.
3. Y. Ge and S. Gong, Chinese Health Care Reform: Problems, Reasons and Solutions, Beijing: China Development Publishing House, 2007.
4. K. Eggleston, L. Ling, M. Qingyue, M. Lindelow, and A. Wagstaff, "Health Service Delivery in China: A Literature Review," Health Economics, Vol. 17, No. 2, 2008b, pp. 149–165.
5. J. Du, "Economic Reforms and Health Insurance in China," Social Science and Medicine, Vol. 69, 2009.
6. State Council of PRC, Opinions on Further Reforming of Health Care Systems, 1992. http://www.reformdata.org/content/19920923/25367.html. Accessed September 2017.
7. There are a few exceptions to that rule.
8. K. Eggleston, L. Li, Q. Meng, M. Lindelow, and A. Wagstaff, "Health Service Delivery in China: A Literature Review," Health Economics, Vol. 17, 2008a, pp. 149–165.

9. H. Wang, "Impacts of Medicine Price on New Cooperative Medical Scheme," China Price, Vol. 11, 2005, pp. 23–24 (in Chinese).
10. World Bank, Taking Stock of China's Rural Health Challenge, Washington, DC: The World Bank, 2004.
11. D. Blumenthal and W. Hsiao, "Privatization and its Discontents: The Evolving Chinese Health Care System," New England Journal of Medicine, Vol. 353, 2005, pp. 1165–1170.
12. W. Yip and W.C. Hsiao, "What Drove the Cycles of Chinese Health System Reforms?" Health Systems & Reform, Vol. 1, No. 1, 2015 Feb 25, pp. 52–61.
13. Chinese MoH: Report of China National Health Accounts, Beijing: China Health Economics Institute, 2009.
14. W. Yip, William C. Hsiao, Wen Chhen, Shanlian Hu, Jin Ma, and Alan Maynard, "Early Appraisal of China's Huge and Complex Health-Care Reforms," The Lancet, Vol. 379, No. 9818, 2012, pp. 833–842.
15. http://www.kaloramainformation.com/article/2014-04/Nearly-40-million-Surgeries-Performed-China-Last-Year. Accessed September 2017.
16. G.X. He, S. van den Hof, M.J. van der Werf, H. Guo, Y.L. Hu, J.H. Fan, W.M. Zhang, C.P. Tostado, and M.W. Borgdorff, "Inappropriate Tuberculosis Treatment Regimens in Chinese Tuberculosis Hospitals," Clinical Infectious Diseases: Oxford Journals, Vol. 52, 2011.
17. National Bureau of Statistics of PRC. China Statistical Year-book, Beijing, China Statistics Press, 2012.
18. We will see later that *bianzhi* status is very specific.
19. Shanlian Hu, Shenglan Tang, Yuanli Liu, Yuxin Zhao, Maria-Luisa Escobar, and David de Ferranti, "Reform of How Health Care is Paid for in China: Challenges and Opportunities," The Lancet, Vol. 372, No. 9652, 2008, pp. 1846–1853.
20. S. Kuruvilla, J. Schweitzer, D. Bishai, S. Chowdhury, D. Caramani, L. Frost, R. Cortez, B. Daelmans, A. de Francisco, T. Adam, R. Cohen, Y.N. Alfonso, J. Franz-Vasdeki, S. Saadat, B.A. Pratt, B. Eugster, S. Bandali, P. Venkatachalam, R. Hinton, J. Murray, S. Arscott-Mills, H. Axelson, B. Maliqi, I. Sarker, R. Lakshminarayanan, T. Jacobs, S. Jack, E. Mason, A. Ghaffar, N. Mays, C. Presern, and F. Bustreo, "Success Factors for Women's and Children's Health Study Groups," Bulletin of World Health Organization, Vol. 92, No. 7, 2014, pp. 533–544. http://www.who.int/pmnch/successfactors/en/. Source of data is the China Health Statistics Yearbook.
21. W. Yip and K. Eggleston, "Provider Payment Reform in China: The Case of Hospital Reimbursement in Hainan Province," Health Economics, Vol. 10, No. 4, pp. 325–339.
22. W. Yip and K. Eggleston, "Addressing Government and Market Failures with Payment Incentives: Hospital Reimbursement Reform in Hainan, China," Social Science and Medicine, Vol. 58, 2004, pp. 267–277.

23. The authors used a difference-in-difference econometric method using data from June 1995, before the introduction of the prospective payment, to June 1997, after the implementation of the prospective payment for six of the hospitals.

24. Qingdao Municipal Department of Labor and Social Security. 2003. Payment Arrangements for Contract Hospitals. Policy Document No. 52, Qingdao Municipal Department of Labor and Social Security (in Chinese).

25. Jiujiang Health Insurance Office, The '413' Urban Health Insurance Arrangement. Project Report, Jiujiang Health Insurance Office, Jiujiang, Jiangxi Province (in Chinese), 2004.

26. Q. Meng, "The Impact of Provider Payment Reforms on Cost Containment," Chinese Health Economics Research, Vol. 9, 2002, pp. 18–20 (in Chinese).

27. A. Wu, Y. Li et al., "DRG-based Payment Reform for Urban Health Insurance Scheme," Chinese Journal of Health Economics, Vol. 9, 2004, pp. 38–39 (in Chinese).

28. Q.Y. Meng, C. Rehnberg et al., "The Impact of Urban Health Insurance Reform on Hospital Charges: A Case Study from Two Cities in China," Health Policy, Vol. 68, No. 2, 2004, pp. 197–209.

29. G. Liu, R. Cai et al., "Reform of Medical Insurance System in Chinese Cities: Discussion on Equity of Cost Allocation," Journal of Economics (Quarterly), Vol. 2, No. 2, 2003, pp. 435–452 (in Chinese).

30. A. Wu, Y. Li et al., "DRG-based Payment Reform for Urban Health Insurance Scheme," Chinese Journal of Health Economics, Vol. 9, 2004, pp. 38–39 (in Chinese).

31. Actually, as said before, the eligibility of the NCMS depends on the rural *hukou* and sometimes the place of residence.

32. World Bank Mission Team, "Notes for BTOR: Shaanxi Field Visit," 2004.

33. Y. Bai, "About DRG Payment Reforms," Modern Medicine, Vol. 8, 2004, p. 25 (in Chinese).

34. Q. Meng, "Review of Provider Organization Reforms in China," China Rural Health AAA Background Report, 2005.

35. C. Tang, Y. Zhang, L. Chen, and Y. Lin, "The Growth of Private Hospitals and their Health Workforce in China: A Comparison with Public Hospitals," Health Policy and Planning, Vol. 29, No. 1, 2014 Jan, pp. 30–41.

36. NHFPC, 2014.

37. X. Ji and S. Tong, UBS Research. China Healthcare: Where to Position for Growth, 2014.

38. Ministry of Health website: https://www.moh.gov.cn/publicfiles/business/mohwsbwstjxxzx/s7967/201112/53508.htm

39. See Chap. 5.

40. Yu Nan, "Investment Injection," Beijing Review, September 24, 2015. http://www.bjreview.com/Nation/201509/t20150921_800038844. html. Accessed September 2017.
41. See paragraph on *bianzhi* status.
42. CHC is a healthcare facility providing care for outpatients.
43. http://www.mckinsey.com/~/media/mckinsey/dotcom/client_service/ healthcare%20systems%20and%20services/health%20international/hi10_ china_healthcare_reform.ashx. Accessed September 2017.
44. Interviews in Beijing, June 2015. Translated from Chinese.
45. Interviews in Beijing, Dr Wang Zhen, Chinese Academy of Social Sciences, September 2015. Translated from Chinese.
46. When expenses incurred in private facilities are reimbursed by public health insurance, the reimbursement rates are lower than those for public facilities.
47. The BMJ Blogs, 23/06/2015. http://blogs.bmj.com/bmj/2013/09/11/ liu-xu-et-al-chinese-doctors-leaving-public-hospitals-brain-drain-or-emanci-pation/. Accessed September 2017.
48. Kate Wu, "Yu Ying: China's 'Face of ER' Who Runs New Beijing Hospital," China Youth Daily, January 27, 2016. http://www.womenofchina.cn/ womenofchina/html1/people/others/1601/1728-1.htm
49. Amcare Corporation operated seven medical facilities for women and children in China in 2015.
50. The PRC government's No.58 document (03.12.2010): Notification on further encouraging and leading social capital to participate in healthcare institutions.
51. http://www.bjreview.com/Nation/201509/t20150921_800038844. html. Accessed September 2017.
52. Roland Berger, Entering China's private hospital segment, 2014.
53. See, for example, Zhang Yue and Wang Leping, "Putian Ji: youyi zhong cheng wangguo—Zhongguo de minying yiyuan bacheng du shi tamen de" (Putian Clan: Wandering Doctors Become a Kingdom—Eighty Percent of Private Hospitals in China Belongs to Them), Southern Weekly.
54. Restrictions Loosened on Overseas Ownership of Hospitals, China Daily, August 2015. http://www.chinadaily.com.cn/business/2014-08/28/ content_18500131.htm. Accessed September 2017.
55. This rate was about 70%.
56. Chai Huiqun, "Tamen shi zai biliangweichang pu ji yisheng zi jie yiyuan xi jin shu" ("They are Forcing Us to be Immoral: Putian-clan Doctors Revealed How Hospitals make Money), Southern Weekly, 12 May 2016.
57. China Healthcare: 2015 Outlook.
58. H. Zhang, "The Argument about the New Health Reform Lines: Government and Market," The Reform and Open-up, Vol. 4, 2013, p. 009.

BIBLIOGRAPHY

Bai, Y., "About DRG Payment Reforms," Modern Medicine, Vol. 8, 2004, p. 25 (in Chinese).

Blumenthal, D., and W. Hsiao, "Privatization and its Discontents: the Evolving Chinese Health Care System," New England Journal of Medicine, Vol. 353, 2005, pp. 1165–1170.

Du, J., "Economic Reforms and Health Insurance in China," Social Science and Medicine, Vol. 69, 2009.

Eggleston, K., L. Li, Q. Meng, M. Lindelow, and A. Wagstaff, "Health Service Delivery in China: A Literature Review," Health Economics, Vol. 17, 2008a, pp. 149–165.

Eggleston, K., L. Ling, M. Qingyue, M. Lindelow, and A. Wagstaff, "Health Service Delivery in China: A Literature Review," Health Economics, Vol. 17, No. 2, 2008b, pp. 149–165.

Ge, Y., and S. Gong, Chinese Health Care Reform: Problems, Reasons and Solutions, Beijing: China Development Publishing House, 2007.

He, G.X., S. van den Hof, M.J. van der Werf, H. Guo, Y.L. Hu, J.H. Fan, W.M. Zhang, C.P. Tostado, and M.W. Borgdorff, "Inappropriate Tuberculosis Treatment Regimens in Chinese Tuberculosis Hospitals," Clinical Infectious Diseases: Oxford Journals, Vol. 52, 2011.

Hillier, Sheila, and Jie Shen, "Health Care Systems in Transition: People's Republic of China. Part I: An Overview of China's Health Care System," Journal of Public Health Medicine, Vol. 18, No. 3, 1996, pp. 258–265.

Hu, Shanlian, Shenglan Tang, Yuanli Liu, Yuxin Zhao, Maria-Luisa Escobar, and David de Ferranti, "Reform of How Health Care is Paid For in China: Challenges and Opportunities," The Lancet, Vol. 372, No. 9652, 2008, pp. 1846–1853.

Huiqun, Chai, "Tamen shi zai biliangweichang pu ji yisheng zi jie yiyuan xi jin shu" ("They are Forcing Us to be Immoral: Putian-clan Doctors Revealed How Hospitals Make Money), Southern Weekly, 12 May 2016.

Ji, X., and S. Tong, UBS Research. China Healthcare: Where to Position for Growth, 2014.

Jiujiang Health Insurance Office, The '413' Urban Health Insurance Arrangement. Project Report, Jiujiang Health Insurance Office, Jiujiang, Jiangxi Province (in Chinese), 2004.

Kuruvilla, S., J. Schweitzer, D. Bishai, S. Chowdhury, D. Caramani, L. Frost, R. Cortez, B. Daelmans, A. de Francisco, T. Adam, R. Cohen, Y.N. Alfonso, J. Franz-Vasdeki, S. Saadat, B.A. Pratt, B. Eugster, S. Bandali, P. Venkatachalam, R. Hinton, J. Murray, S. Arscott-Mills, H. Axelson, B. Maliqi, I. Sarker, R. Lakshminarayanan, T. Jacobs, S. Jack, E. Mason, A. Ghaffar, N. Mays, C. Presern, and F. Bustreo, "Success Factors for Women's and Children's Health Study Groups," Bulletin of World Health Organisation, Vol. 92, No. 7, 2014, pp. 533–544.

Liu, G., R. Cai et al., "Reform of Medical Insurance System in Chinese Cities: Discussion on Equity of Cost Allocation," Journal of Economics (Quarterly), Vol. 2, No. 2, 2003, pp. 435–452 (in Chinese).

Meng, Q., "The Impact of Provider Payment Reforms on Cost Containment," Chinese Health Economics Research, Vol. 9, 2002, pp. 18–20 (in Chinese).

Meng, Q., "Review of Provider Organization Reforms in China," China Rural Health AAA Background Report, 2005.

Meng, Q.Y., C. Rehnberg et al., "The Impact of Urban Health Insurance Reform on Hospital Charges: A Case Study from Two Cities in China," Health Policy, Vol. 68, No. 2, 2004, pp. 197–209.

Nan, Yu, "Investment Injection," Beijing Review, September 24, 2015. http://www.bjreview.com/Nation/201509/t20150921_800038844.html. Accessed September 2017.

Qingdao Municipal Department of Labor and Social Security. 2003. Payment Arrangements for Contract Hospitals. Policy Document No. 52, Qingdao Municipal Department of Labor and Social Security (in Chinese).

Tang, C., Y. Zhang, L. Chen, and Y. Lin, "The Growth of Private Hospitals and their Health Workforce in China: A Comparison with Public Hospitals," Health Policy and Planning, Vol. 29, No. 1, 2014 Jan, pp. 30–41.

Wang, S., "China's Health System: From Crisis to Opportunity," Yale-China Health Journal, Vol. 3, 2004, pp. 5–49.

Wang, H., "Impacts of Medicine Price on New Cooperative Medical Scheme," China Price, Vol. 11, 2005, pp. 23–24 (in Chinese).

World Bank, Taking Stock of China's Rural Health Challenge. Washington, DC: The World Bank, 2004.

Wu, Kate, "Yu Ying: China's 'Face of ER' Who Runs New Beijing Hospital," China Youth Daily, January 27, 2016. http://www.womenofchina.cn/womenofchina/html1/people/others/1601/1728-1.htm

Wu, A., Y. Li et al., "DRG-based Payment Reform for Urban Health Insurance Scheme," Chinese Journal of Health Economics, Vol. 9, 2004, pp. 38–39 (in Chinese).

Yip, W., and K. Eggleston, "Addressing Government and Market Failures with Payment Incentives: Hospital Reimbursement Reform in Hainan, China," Social Science and Medicine, Vol. 58, 2004, pp. 267–277.

Yip, W., and K. Eggleston, "Provider Payment Reform in China: The Case of Hospital Reimbursement in Hainan Province," Health Economics, Vol. 10, No. 4, 2001, pp. 325–339.

Yip, W., and W.C. Hsiao, What Drove the Cycles of Chinese Health System Reforms? Health Systems & Reform, Vol. 1, No. 1, 2015 Feb 25, pp. 52–61.

Yip, W., William C Hsiao, Wen Chhen, Shanlian Hu, Jin Ma, and Alan Maynard, "Early Appraisal of China's Huge and Complex Health-Care Reforms," The Lancet, Vol. 379, No. 9818, 2012, pp. 833–842.

Zhang, H., "The Argument About the New Health Reform Lines: Government and Market," The Reform and Open-up, Vol. 4, 2013, p. 009.

CHAPTER 5

Medical Staff

Abstract China has around 2.79 million licensed physicians, among which 90% have received some kind of training in Western medicine in addition to Chinese traditional medicine. China has far more doctors than nurses. This is inherited from Chinese history, with the barefoot doctor system. In terms of education level, as many as 70% of healthcare suppliers did not have a bachelor degree in 2013. One of the current goals of Chinese authorities is to reinforce the training level and to ensure sufficient access to skilled healthcare personnel. Besides, there are important disparities in healthcare access between rural and urban areas. These disparities concern not only the number of medical employees per bed but also the average level of qualification available. In this chapter, we also explore the administrative status of public medical staff (*bianzhi* status) and their working conditions (salary, financial incentives and informal bonuses amounting to bribery). The development of the family doctor, through specific training and career paths, is usually seen as a key reform, which is now at the pilot programme stage.

Keywords Supply • Medical staff • Doctors and nurses • Medical education and training • *Bianzhi* status

© The Author(s) 2018
C. Milcent, *Healthcare Reform in China*,
https://doi.org/10.1007/978-3-319-69736-9_5

OVERVIEW OF SUPPLY

China has roughly 2.79 million licensed physicians, among which 90% have received some kind of training in Western medicine in addition to Chinese traditional medicine. In terms of education level, in 2013, only around 28.5% of healthcare suppliers had a bachelor degree or above, but this was an increase (of 26.7%) on the previous year. One of the current goals of Chinese authorities is to reinforce this trend and to ensure sufficient access to skilled healthcare personnel. In this chapter, we will see how the central state introduced reforms to cope with this goal and the challenges faced.

Still, compared to the developed countries, the shortage of healthcare professionals in China is vast. Qin et al. (2013)[1] compared five high-income countries, namely, Japan, Australia, Germany, the United Kingdom and the United States in 2008. The number of nurses per 1000 people was around 10, in each of these five countries, while this ratio was only about 1.3 in China. In terms of physicians, the ratio ranged from 2 to 4 in the above-mentioned countries, to be compared with about 1.7 in China. The difference, although it does not seem much, hides a crucial factor. The term "doctor" in China is given to a wide spectrum of medical qualification, from very short training to qualified doctors with more than 10 years of education and training.

As an overview of the historical context, before 1980, the main purpose of the medical education system was to provide sufficient health professionals to rural villages in order to provide medical assistance in rural areas, which covered 80% of the inhabitants. After 1980, China prioritized the steady development of its medical universities to provide sufficient qualified doctors to the health system overall.[2]

There are important disparities in healthcare access between the rural and urban areas. According to Fig. 5.1, since the early 1980s the number of doctors and university-certified physicians in cities exceeded that in the counties. The number of medical doctors and physicians has stagnated or even declined in the counties since 1988.

According to the *China Statistical Yearbook* (2015), the number of hospital beds was 5.33 million. This figure was about 2.45 million in 2005. The number of physicians per 1000 population was 2.06 according to the Chinese Ministry of Health (2013). In 2004, the urban to rural ratio for hospital beds per 10,000 inhabitants was 2.2 and 2 for healthcare personnel employed, meaning that there are twice as many medical

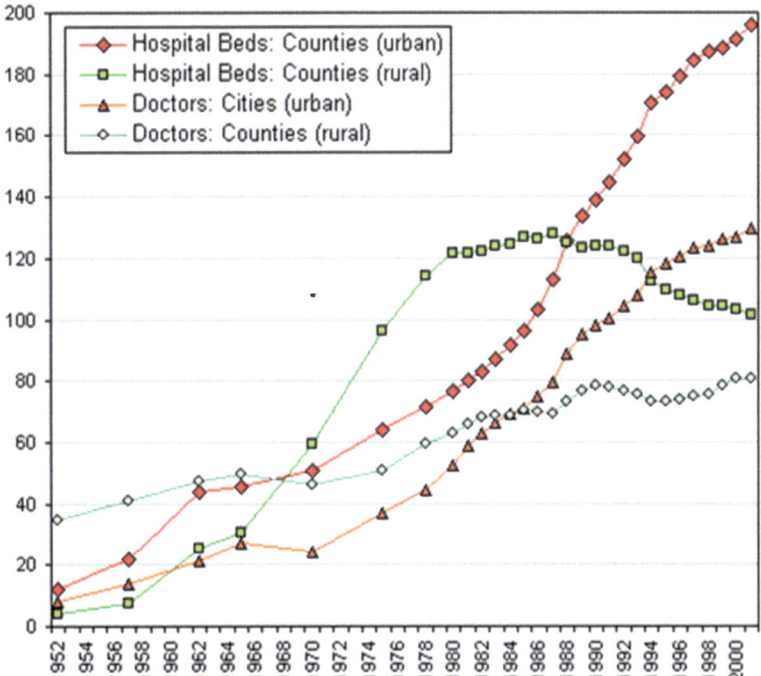

Fig. 5.1   Number of hospital beds and doctors in cities and counties 1952–2002 (in 10,000). Source: China Statistical Yearbook, 2003, Table 21–36, p. 806. Note 1: Before 1978 statistical data are questionable—particularly during the period of the Great Leap Forward and the Cultural Revolution. Note 2: Doctors include traditional healers, university-trained doctors and physicians with a university certification.   http://www.china-profile.com/data/fig_health_1.htm.   Accessed September 2017

professionals in urban areas versus rural ones. Today, the disparities in geographical accessibility to hospitalization between urban and rural areas, between different income levels of different regions, and between eastern, western and central China, have narrowed down considerably, but gaps still exist.[3]

Of course, these figures are an obvious consequence of the hospital organization system, where a large size and high-tech hospitals are located in urban areas. However, we will see in this chapter that it goes beyond this in terms of implications. The quality of medical staff training is also considerably lower in rural areas and even worse in underdeveloped poor areas.[4] A study by Wang et al. (2005)[5] found that 70% of village doctors did not have any formal medical education. This study was based on data coming from 46 poor counties. The quality of health care services that patients receive by these low trained doctors is by definition lower than what would be provided by highly trained doctors.

The patients' level of wealth and education emphasizes the urban/rural difference. Indeed, patients who are unaware of quality differences do not consider the options for a better quality of healthcare but with the inconvenience of a possibly longer journey to access it.[6]

Doctors and Nurses

China has far more doctors than nurses. This feature is very specific to the Chinese context, and is a historical feature inherited from the Chinese barefoot doctor system.

In 2005, the national ratio of doctors to nurses was only 1.4 to 1. Breaking it down between urban and rural areas, this ratio was 1.3 to 1 in urban areas and almost 2 to 1 in rural zones.[7,8] Since then, the number of nurses has been increasing rapidly. By 2013, the number of licensed doctors reached 2.06 per 1000 inhabitants and the number of licensed nurses reached 2.05 per 1000 inhabitants, getting close to a 1 to 1 ratio.[9]

Looking back to 1960, we observe overall a dramatic increase in the number of healthcare workers (Fig. 5.2). This increase accelerated from the early 2000s. However, there are still not enough healthcare workers to cater for China's immense population. The recent series of reforms from 2009 onwards support the objective to promote the recruitment and training of a health workforce. China now has 1.65 million nurses but with a population of 1.3 billion and an increasingly ageing population, the country needs 5 million more nurses to catch up with the global standards.[10]

In a paper from 2010, Yun, Jun and Anli, three members of a nursing faculty group in Shanghai, described the actual context of the nursing shortage in China:

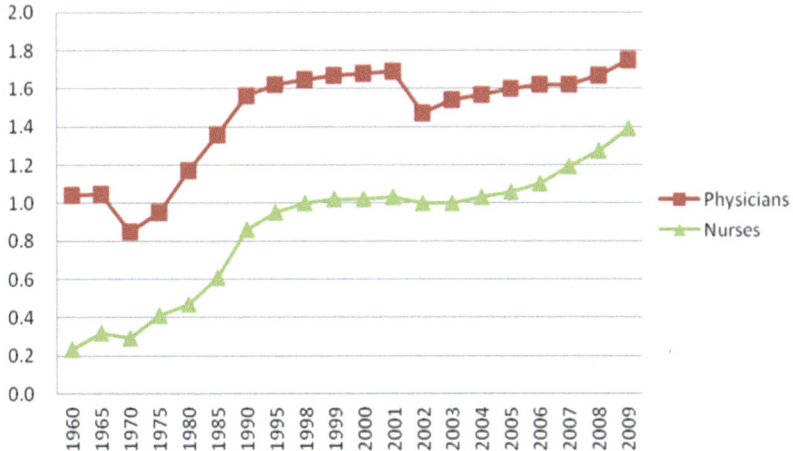

Fig. 5.2   Number of Nurses and Physicians per 1000 in China, 1960–2009. Source: 2010 China Yearbook of Health Statistics. Qin, X. and Li, L. and Hsieh, C-R (2013) "Too Few Doctors or Too wages? Labor supply of healthcare professionals in China" China Economic Review, 24(1)

"With a population of 1.3 billion people, China has 1.65 million nurses. To meet the global standards, it needs 5 million more nurses. 90% of China's nurses are prepared in what are called "associate degree programs" but these actually are the equivalent of high school level programs. Students usually are individuals who are not eligible for college. Many of these nurses have knowledge and skills equivalent to those of nurses' aides or technicians in the United States. About 7% hold what is called a diploma in nursing. Only 2–3% have college degrees, most of these at the Bachelor of Science level. Graduate education is in its infancy. In a country with twice as many physicians than nurses, and with a relatively low level of knowledge and skill among its nurses, it is usually a physician who stands at the patient's bedside when the patient is very ill."

This picture is probably over pessimistic. However, it reflects the urge to have a higher standard of nursing and gives a global idea of the shortage and training challenges China has to face regarding its nurses.

BECOMING A DOCTOR

From 1949 to the 1980s in Rural Areas

At the inauguration of the People's Republic of China in 1949, the country had only 40,000 doctors to care for a population of nearly 540 million. Most physicians were concentrated in cities, despite a low urbanization rate.

One of the first priorities of the new power was to put more emphasis on health work in rural areas.[11] The "barefoot doctor" system was introduced in the mid-1960s. These "barefoot doctors" were recruited from farmers with a secondary education level. They were trained by urban physicians for 3–6 months and then were considered qualified to meet the basic health needs of the rural inhabitants. With the Co-operative Medical System (CMS), the barefoot doctors represented Tier I of the three-tier system. Given their limited training, they provided preventive and basic health services to rural inhabitants accounting for 80% of the whole population. They referred their patients to higher-level units (Tier II or above) if necessary. Usually, they still remained in farming activity.[12,13,14]

Applying both Western and local remedies, barefoot doctors remarkably improved the population's health at a very low cost.[15,16] In spite of a lack of training and equipment, the increase in life expectancy that can be observed from 1949 to 1980 is the fastest ever witnessed.[17] Life expectancy at birth rose from around 40 years in 1949 to 60.5 years in 1980.

With the economic reforms, the barefoot system was abolished. The existing barefoot doctors were offered the option of taking a national exam. Those passing the exam became *village doctors*. Those who failed could still carry on their activity, but without the doctor title. Later, they were called *village health aides*. In 1985, the Ministry of Health (MoH) officially phased out support for barefoot doctors.[18] That same year, the title "barefoot doctor" was officially abandoned. About 0.64 million doctors who passed the qualifying examination obtained a certificate as village doctors.[19]

The behaviour of the rural doctor changed in two main ways. First, village doctors started charging patients for the healthcare provided.[20] Rapidly, they adopted a fee-for-service payment system as was already commonly applied in cities. Because the CMS scheme collapsed (see Chap. 2), medical costs were borne directly by rural Chinese inhabitants. Secondly, village doctors began to shift their focus to the treatment of chronic conditions rather than preventive care.[21] Subsidies were implemented by central and local authorities for their work on preventive health, anti-epidemic work, maternal and child health and other administrative affairs. But they were not enough to overcome the shift away from preventive medicine as they only represented 5–10% of the village doctors' income.[22,23,24] More than that, health workers were forced to seek alternative sources of income for their survival. Eventually, a fee-for-service system became the dominant way to pay village doctors.[25]

Current Situation in Rural Areas

Taking effect in 1999, the Law on Physicians defined the training requirements for medical practice licences. This law was adopted at the 3rd Meeting of the Standing Committee of the Ninth National People's Congress on 26 June 1998. "The Doctors" referred to in this Law include licensed doctors and licensed assistant doctors.[26] It applies to medical workers who have, in accordance with the law, obtained the licences of qualified doctors or qualified assistant doctors, who are registered and employed in medical treatment institutions, disease-prevention institutions or healthcare institutions.

In Article 8, this law sets up an examination system to determine the qualifications of doctors including licensed doctors and licensed assistant doctors. Standardized qualifications and skills are needed to pass the diploma for both categories, but the actual organization of examinations is left to the public health administrative departments of the people's governments at or above the provincial level.

According to Article 9, to be a licensed doctor means at least:

- Having graduated from the faculty of medicine of a university and, under the guidance of a licensed doctor, worked on probation for at least one year in a medical treatment, disease-prevention or healthcare institution; or
- After obtaining the licence for an assistant doctor, having reached the level of a graduate from the faculty of medicine of a university and worked for at least two years in a medical treatment, disease-prevention or healthcare institution; or
- Having reached the level of a graduate from the specialty of medicine of a polytechnic school and worked for at least five years in a medical treatment, disease-prevention or healthcare institution.

In Article 13 of the same law, the state authorities determine a system of registration for licensed doctors. A certified doctor has to apply for registration to the administrative department for public health of the local people's government at or above county level.

This law thus implies a more homogeneous definition of what is meant by "to be a doctor". It highlights the fact that licences and accreditations are important tools for policy makers to improve provider performance. Besides, it clearly shows the lack of qualification of medical staff and the doctors before this period. It also emphasizes the fact that the qualification required by this law "to be a doctor" remains lower than that required in Western countries.

For the *village doctors*, the authority also prioritized their training and qualification, and some practice regulations were established. The minimum requirement for medical practice in village clinics was to pass the local examination held by the county health bureau and to obtain Village Doctor Certification, while some village doctors could also pass the National Licensed (Assistant) Doctors Examination and become a licensed (assistant) doctor. By 2010, only a minority (around 14.2%) of the village doctors had passed the national examination.[27]

More accurately, a series of policies began in the 1990s to improve the quality of village doctors. In 1991, the MOH released the "1991–2000 National Education Plan of Village Doctors", which required 80% of village doctors to reach the requirements of Systematization and Normalization. In 2002, the "2001–2015 Health Workforce Development Outlines" were published with specific goals: village doctors should obtain an educational degree of secondary school or above, and 85% of village doctors should pass the exam and get their assistant doctor licence by the end of 2015. The "Village Doctors Practitioners Regulation" was published by the State Council in 2003; it particularly regulated the certification, practice, training and legal obligations of village doctors, establishing the first set of national regulations for them. After the regulations were implemented, the number of village doctors swiftly decreased to 0.8 million in 2003.

However, the implementation of the New Co-operative Medical System (NCMS) and other factors led to a sharp increase in healthcare demand from rural residents. The number of healthcare workers in rural areas was subsequently increased, including 1 million village doctors at the end of 2011.[28,29] Recently, there have been several new policies implemented regarding village doctors, mainly targeted at improving quality, strengthening management and prioritizing public health services. Since the health reform of 2009, the MOH has required village doctors to provide both medical and public health services to rural residents.[30] In fact, there was still no consistent or sufficient public funding to really implement a change in the type of healthcare provided in village clinics, although village doctors could receive some remuneration.[31]

Medical Education Programme

Doctors in Medicine

The training of physicians in China has quite a complex organization, for both geographical and historical reasons. In theory, a physician from a rural area cannot work in an urban area. Nevertheless, seniority can be taken into consideration to make such transfers possible. As a physician from a Level 3 hospital in Beijing puts it: "Here, all doctors have more or less a medical diploma. They all are senior."[32] In most cases, doctors educated to university level work in Level 3 hospitals where they are increasingly able to benefit from continuing education.

For Level 2 healthcare institutions, doctors are on average underqualified. While doctors at Level 2 hospitals are increasingly qualified with higher education degrees, many of them still leave with training that is roughly equivalent to taking a specialist subject at sixth-form (a specialist subject after vocational high school). However, this situation is constantly evolving (Table 5.1).

Table 5.1 Distribution of doctors and nurses by level of education, 2005

	Urban		Rural		Total	
	Doctors (%)	Nurses (%)	Doctors (%)	Nurses (%)	Doctors (%)	Nurses (%)
College or above	42.8	3.0	12.9	0.7	32.8	2.5
Secondary school	52.8	90.4	79.0	89.2	61.6	90.0
High school or less	4.4	6.6	8.1	10.1	5.6	7.5

In China, college level refers to a bachelor's education or higher, while secondary school level includes secondary schools, secondary technical schools and junior colleges.

Source: Ministry of Health, 2006 China Human Resources for Health Report, Beijing: Peking Union Medical Press, 2007 (in Chinese). Anand, S., Fan V., Zhang J., Zhang L., Ke Y., Dong Z., and Chen L., "China's Human Resources for Health: Quantity, Quality, and Distribution," The Lancet, Vol. 372, No. 9651, 2008, pp. 1774–1781

The MoH launched a regulation for the Standardized Residency Training Programme in the late twentieth century that became effective from 2003.[33] However, the training quality varies from centre to centre.[34]

As described by Anand et al. (2008),[35] the medical education programme is extended with training ranging from one to 11 years. Three ranks need to be considered:

- Primary education (1–3 years) for training of village doctors as described above;
- Secondary education (2–3 years) for training of hospitals at Level 1 and Level 2;
- Tertiary education (3–11 years) for doctors who will work in secondary and tertiary hospitals. For this rank, there exists a subdivision based on the official degree received:
  - a three-year bachelor's degree
  - a five-year bachelor's degree
  - a seven or more years' master's or doctoral degree.

Today, the medical programme involving high-school level and three years' vocational training is being phased out. There is a political switch to a unique medical programme with a university-level, three-year programme leading to a certificate.

The medical academic degree system in China is organized around a three-level degree system awarding bachelor, master and doctorate degrees. Medical universities provide a five-year undergraduate medical curriculum for candidates who have completed high-school education and passed the National Admission Examination.

In order to obtain a licence to practise medicine, graduates must pass the National Medical Licensing Examination (NMLE) also known as the doctor licensing examination (DLE) and have hospital experience.[36]

Similarly, medical graduates with lower degrees are eligible to become licensed assistant doctors but they must: (1) undergo an internship in a hospital, where the length of the internship depends on the degree obtained; and (ii) pass the assistant doctor licensing examination (ADLE). A legal gateway exists for a licensed assistant doctor to become a licensed doctor. ADLE candidates can take the DLE after a period of time practising that depends on their original degree.

Standards of education are also very variable from one geographical zone to another. This can be observed as well in clinics, township health centres and community health centres, and from Level 1 to the high-tech Level 3 hospitals. The medical curriculum also varies from one Chinese university to another. Only the top 12 leading medical schools in China have been authorized by the Ministry of Education to develop a dedicated eight-year programme with a limited number of students.[37]

In addition, the training of physicians focuses on specialties. There is no general practitioner training as such. In Western countries, medical training usually starts with a very general training, with students choosing to specialize only in the last years of their curriculum. In China, specialization starts from the second year. As hospitals are also organized by specialties, with little contact across departments, physicians tend to have a very fragmented assessment of their patients' health.

As a result, there is no dedicated physician's training for outpatients (i.e. there are no general practitioners). Different types of specialists provide consultations for outpatient. The patient has to choose which specialist will be the most relevant for his or her pathology, but there are too few mechanisms to steer a patient to the right specialist. This aspect of the healthcare system contributes to its inefficiency.

Nurses

As far as training for nurses is concerned, there are two tiers:

- A two-year secondary education programme corresponding to training in Level 1 and Level 2 hospitals. Then, graduate students have to pass the nursing certification examination;
- A five-year secondary education programme corresponding to a training in Level 3 hospitals. Medical graduates are then exempt from the nursing certification examination.

This low standard, for qualifying as a doctor or a nurse, and the important variability in what is called a doctor, may explain the widespread mistrust of doctors and medical staff regarding their skills and the strong preference by patients to be treated in a Level 3 hospital. This situation may explain what is evidenced later in this book, with an over-burden on tertiary hospitals and the resulting long queues in these hospitals.

WORK STATUS

"Civil Servant" Status

After obtaining the Doctor Licensing Examination (DLE), every young practitioner gets a job in a health institution or a health centre. He then becomes a salaried worker of this structure, being captive of it to some extent. Indeed, to be a doctor implies registering with one medical institution and only one. Getting a position in a public medical institution is associated with *bianzhi* status, comparable to civil servant status in OECD countries, with some specific advantages:

1. *Social security benefits*: Under the protection of *bianzhi*, medical professionals benefit from a stable salary, bonus and all kinds of social security benefits from the hospital for their whole life.
2. *Double career*: To be *bianzhi* implies a double career as a doctor in a public medical institution and as party cadre. These two careers are symbiotic.
3. *Lifetime employment*: *Bianzhi* is also a kind of lifetime employment warranty for the medical professionals according to the government's promise. Professionals cannot be fired by a hospital, even though they can resign.
4. *Juridical protection*: Medical liability insurance is under-developed. In such a context, the *bianzhi* status appears to be a form of legal protection. We will see later in this book (Chap. 8) that the relationship between doctors and patients has become a very tense one. This context may fuel the patient–doctor relationship into one of violence.
5. *Publication*: Professionals can also take advantage of lots of academic and research opportunities, which are provided by the giant public hospital network. Today, the performance of medical doctors is mainly evaluated through the number of their published papers.

Once a professional has left *bianzhi*, he or she has no chance of going back. This aspect may be part of why doctors are reluctant to quit the public sector in order to be recruited into the private sector.

Village Doctor Status

Medical workers in Township Health Centres (THCs) can be recruited by the government. They have *bianzhi* status and a certificate of permanent urban residence (*Chengzhen Hukou*) so they can enjoy urban welfare. The situation for rural village doctors is quite different from the medical workers in THCs. They have a certificate of permanent rural residence (*Nongcun Hukou*) and because they are still farmers they are not registered in the official system under the identity of a civil servant. In China, the Household Registration System (*hukou*) prohibited the free migration of farmers from accessing the urban welfare system.[38] To become state employees, residential status (*hukou*) needs to be changed from rural to non-rural.[39] As a result, village doctors cannot have *bianzhi* status and the advantages associated with this status. They then worried about their welfare, especially regarding endowment insurance. Strictly speaking, village doctors are not a formal professional title. Historically, after the start of economic reforms, they have been self-employed, temporary, medical and agricultural workers. As already described, many started copying urban doctors' strategies, by introducing fee-for-service payment and over-prescribing drugs and injections, thus inflating drug mark-ups.[40] These changes can be seen as a response to inadequate remuneration and poor supervision.[41,42] Recently, some of them have been put under the supervision of THCs. Their incomes are restricted and their working time is regulated.

In some areas, village doctors work and are managed just in the same way as a THC outreach worker. Administratively they cannot obtain the same advantages as a regular employee in THCs associated with *bianzhi* status. The lack of legitimacy granted to village doctors by health professionals with a degree is another barrier to defining their work roles and wage rates as workers in THCs.[43]

All of the above took the shape of a vicious circle and explains the staff shortage in primary health facilities in rural China.

Impact of "Bianzhi" Status on Mobility

We will see that the greatest impact of the lack of "freedom of practice" is on:

- The lack of enrolment in private activity:
- Kickbacks and *hongbao*;
- The age of personnel in private hospitals;
- The level of quality in private hospitals.

In China today, due to *bianzhi* status, medical staff working in a public hospital cannot work in parallel in another structure in the same municipality or elsewhere. Their professional registration number is linked to a specific medical structure. In this context, individual doctors are tied to their healthcare institution. Working in a private healthcare institution means renouncing *bianzhi* status and, in most situations, a permanent loss of this status.

For some academic researchers, lacking "freedom of practice" for medical staff is part of the problem of what is pointed out as being doctors' "immoral" behaviour. Behind this term, practices such as treating patients with indifference, practising defensive medicine, and receiving kickbacks and *hongbao* (bribery in the form of red envelopes containing cash) are pinpointed.[44]

The current system in which doctors' salaries are regulated and fixed at a low level, and the obligation to practise in a registered hospital and only in that particular hospital, results in medical staff displaying such "immoral" behaviour. There is no example of such a strict organization in developed countries. In the United States, medical doctors obviously enjoy both socio-economic and technical professional autonomy because of minimal government involvement. In United Kingdom, the state directly manages the National Health Service, in which medical professionals are civil servants. However, doctors from the NHS are still allowed to open private clinics and hospitals, and they are allowed to practise in both public and private medical service organizations simultaneously. In France, where physicians are highly regulated by strong state intervention, medical doctors can still work in private practices in parallel to their jobs in public structures.

Some academic think tanks reckon that in-depth reformation of *bianzhi* status would make it possible to improve the motivation and engagement of medical staff. The deputy director of the Institute of Economics and head of research in public policies of the Chinese Academy of Social Sciences (CASS), Hengpeng Zhu, explains that this status undermines the efficiency of hospitals and that it should be reformed or that its application should be limited.[45] Currently, *bianzhi* status is offered not only to physicians but also to a large portion of the medical staff, including nurses. Over 85% of medical professionals, both doctors and nurses, have signed such a contract with public hospitals in China.[46]

Reforms have been implemented to make the system less rigid. Among the different options tested, physicians can practise in another structure to that where they are registered. This can be seen as a transitional layer to the free practice model. On 1 March 2011 the municipal Health Bureau in Beijing implemented "The Tentative Measures of Practitioners' Practising in Several Points" (*Beijingshi Yishi Duodian Zhiye Guanli Banfa (Shixing)*). These measures allow medical doctors to apply to practise in different medical institutions. So far, to be eligible, doctors have to:

- Be physician-in-charge or higher-ranking doctors;
- Have all their practice locations within Beijing;
- Finish their duties at the current institution.[47]

According to Yan (2014),[48] there were a total of 1355 practising doctors who registered a several-point practice in Beijing in November 2013. The number of practising doctors was about 44,000 in this province-level municipality. These multi-sites doctors only accounted for approximately 3% of the total and this figure remains quite small. A plausible explanation is based on the disincentives exercised by hospital authorities: (i) using the "finish their duties" criterion to justify denial; and (ii) putting pressure on the amount of financial compensation and promotion and career development.

According to academics from CASS and Fudan University, even if this is theoretically possible at the experimental stage of the reforms, public hospital management and administrators talk physicians out of it. Among the disincentives used, physicians mention a reduction of their bonuses and the impact on their career development.[49]

As a result, skilled doctors prefer to stay with high-quality public hospitals instead of running independent clinics or working for private hospitals due to the uncertain welfare and pension benefits, limited research resources and extremely complicated application procedures. This last point was widely described in Chap. 3, with the example of Yu Ying, a former doctor employed in a very big Level 3 public hospital in Beijing.

Another impact is the age of personnel in private hospitals.[50] Overall, the mandatory retirement age in China is 60 for men and 55 for women. Strictly speaking, medical workers, physicians, as well as other categories, have to retire at that age and leave public healthcare institutions. For them, working in a private hospital becomes an opportunity, as they do not have to give up any advantages. According to Tang et al. (2014), 22.03% of physicians who practise in private hospitals are over 60. Other authors also obtained similar results.[51,52] This demonstrates that private hospitals have hired many older doctors who cannot or do not want to work in public structures anymore. This fact may have an impact on the innovative medical technics used in private hospitals. Indeed, according to evidence collected from developed countries, it seems that decreasing performance was associated with increasing years in practice for all outcomes assessed.[53,54]

In parallel, the standards of performance and quality expected by patients have been increasing along with the standard of living. People demand skilled doctors and medical staff as well as high-tech and innovative equipment. The concentration of the highest-skilled professionals in a small set of hospitals and the lack of mobility contributes to patient congestion in the highest-level public hospitals.

WORKING CONDITIONS

To introduce this section, I will recount the experience of a Chinese doctor, Yu Ying (See Chap. 3), who formerly worked at a Level 3 hospital, the Peking Union Medical College Hospital. She is a key public figure and emblematic of the current situation faced by doctors in the healthcare system. She has created a Weibo account (Chinese equivalent of Twitter) that has now more than 2 million followers.[55] Her resignation, widely commented on, was explained on the web.[56] She mentioned:

- The excessive workload and unreasonably long hours with 150 patients per day at some times;
- Patients travelling more than 1500 km to get a consultation in this Level 3 hospital;
- The mediation role of doctors to avoid conflicts between patients and medical staff;
- A promotion system based only on publication and thus totally disconnected from medical activity.

Salary, Bribery and Financial Interest

According to the National Bureau of Statistics, the average salary of a physician amounts to RMB 35,478 per annum, which is not much more than the average salary of an employee in an urban area (RMB 32,244). This salary is defined at the national level, taking into account different factors, such as seniority and level of responsibilities.[57]

According to Qin et al. (2013),[58] the shortage of healthcare professionals in China can be explained by the low salaries in medical careers,

Table 5.2   Comparison of public and private hospitals nationwide, 2013

	Public	%	Private	%	Total
Number	13,396	54.22	11,313	45.78	24,709
Beds	3,865,385	84.42	713,216	15.58	4,578,601
Hospital personnel (10,000)	460.6	85.76	76.4	14.22	537.1
Health personnel (10,000)	383.9	86.76	58.6	13.24	442.5
Outpatients (100,000,000)	24.6	**89.78**	2.9	**10.58**	27.4
Inpatients (10,000)	12,315	87.92	1692	12.08	14,007

Source: National Health and Family Planning Commission 2014. The total number of outpatients does not equal the number of public hospitals added to the number of private hospitals. The same problem also occurs for the number of inpatients. The statistical report shows the same problem. Yao, Z., "The Changing Relationship between the Chinese Urban Medical Profession and the State since the Republican Period: The Perspective of the Sociology of Professions", The Journal of Chinese Sociology, Vol. 3, No. 2, 2016

compared to other occupational categories. The government has reduced financial support for public healthcare institutions but at the same time has largely retained a monopoly on the supply of healthcare. As a consequence, the majority of medical practitioners are dependent on public institutions. In China, public hospitals provide more than 90% of out- and inpatient healthcare services (Table 5.2). The majority of healthcare professionals, including physicians and nurses, are employees of public hospitals and receive payments on a salary basis, regulated by the government.[59] In this context, the healthcare sector is not sensitive to market forces when fixing wages. Consequently, the mean earnings in the regulated health sector are ranked among the lowest in the Chinese economy, comparable to what is observed in the regulated educational sector.[60,61]

For Bloom et al. (2001),[62] the consistently low wage levels in the healthcare sector forces many healthcare professionals, especially physicians, to seek compensation from other sources of revenue. Yet, as we saw above, *bianzhi* status prevents doctors from working in another institution to achieve that goal.

In fact, many salary supplements and bonuses top up the basic salary. A well-known phrase in Chinese is "Neike kao huikou, waike kao shoushu", which translates as "Physicians rely on commissions, surgeons rely on operations". According to a November 2013 study, salary supplements represent on average 45% of the basic salary in Level 3 hospitals,[63] but these additional amounts are obviously very heterogeneous. An article published in March 2014 by *China Medical News* reckons that the total salary of a physician working in a Level 3 hospital in Beijing would reaching RMB 180,000 per month, up from the RMB 46,000 basic salary, when all extra income is taken into account (the bonus from the hospital based on the number of patients treated, commission on drug and test prescriptions, plus all kind of bribery and moonlighting activities).[64,65] He and Qian (2013)[66] also suggest that medical doctors are incentivized to prescribe profitable tests and over-prescribe because of the correlation between hospital revenue and their bonuses, which account officially for 50–60% of their payroll income, and can be much more according to physicians from Level 3AAA hospitals in Beijing.[67] They are fully aware of this correlation, even if the incentive is neither direct nor official.

Another perverse effect of this system is in patient prioritization. In a context of very long waiting lists, "red envelopes" enable some patients to jump the queue. This is a widespread practice and explains the tense relationship between medical staff and their patients who feel obliged to give bribes in order to obtain a decent waiting time. Some 70% of doctors claim to have experienced violent disputes with their patients.

Zhu Hengpeng from the Chinese Academy of Social Sciences argued that the phenomenon of doctors relying on selling medicines and medical check-ups to increase their income partly results from the fact that the prices for their medical services were set by the government and they do not adequately compensate doctors.[68] Low income as a predicator of perverse economic incentives for physicians is also shown by He (2014).[69]

Working Time and Workload

On the Supply Side
The number of Community Health Centres (CHCs) increased massively in just a few years. However, patient demand to consult in the Level 3 hospitals providing the highest care quality level kept going.

The number of hospitals with more than 800 wards rose from 488 in 2008 to 976 in 2011. According to Roemer's law, any beds provided will always be filled. In the Chinese context, a recent study shows that Roemer's law is deemed to be satisfied for public high-tech hospitals.[70] This increase occurred in the context of too few physicians and qualified doctors to meet the healthcare demand.

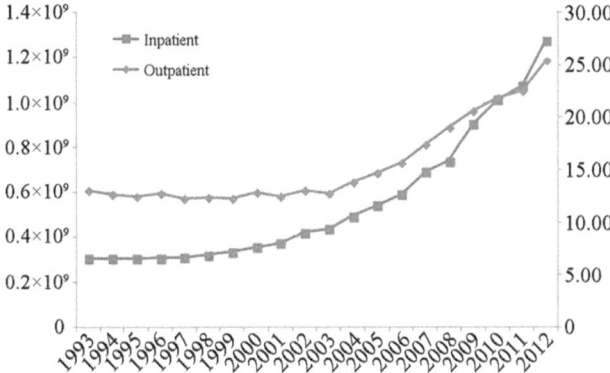

Fig. 5.3 In-hospital admissions and outpatient visits in hospitals, 1993–2012. Source: Chinese Health Statistics Yearbook 2012. Wang et al., "Comparison of Chinese Inpatients with Different Types of Medical Insurance Before and After the 2009 Healthcare Reform," BMC Health Services Research, Vol. 14, 2014, p. 443

On the Demand Side

As a result, the number of out- as well as inpatients increased over the same period. From 2007 to 2011, the inpatient admission number increased by 56% and the outpatient visit number increased by 33% (Fig 5.3). It has been estimated that 30% of admissions are not medically justified. The cost is approximated by calculation to be 37 times more expensive for inpatient admissions than outpatient consultations. In addition, the inhospital length of stay in China is, on average, twice as much compared to an OECD country. Although these are averages, discounting geographical heterogeneity these figures enable us to understand the worrisome evolution of healthcare costs.

Overload

For a physician in a Level 3 hospital, the average number of consultations per day is 70 and can be much higher in a renowned hospital, reaching 100 outpatient consultations and hitting a peak of 200 on certain days.[71] For Anzhen hospital, the number of outpatient consultations was 2.41 million in 2014. This hospital is one of the top 10 hospitals. For the Beijing Children Hospital, Nie Xiaolu, a medical doctor, reckoned the number of outpatient consultations reached 3.37 million in 2014, stating:[72] "Now, it is common to witness more than 1000 out-patients and their relatives waiting to be seen since the early morning."

This situation leads to incredibly long waiting times for patients, an increased workload for physicians and reduced consultation times, to less than 5 minute per patient, creating friction between medical staff and patients.

In all the hospitals I had the opportunity to visit, physicians often mention a two-minute consultation time per patient.

A study carried out in Shaanxi province determined that doctors were spending less than one and a half minute with each patient. This results in turning patients and their family totally unreasonable. The *New Yorker* magazine quotes an American physician visiting the Beijing United Family Hospital, a Level 3 hospital (with AAA status, implying a superior quality standard) and catering for many expatriate families in Beijing:[73] "Joe Passanante, a doctor from Chicago who did a stint at Beijing United Family Hospital, told [the reporter] that he was once performing CPR on a woman when the parents of a girl with a fever walked into the room. 'Here I am pushing on a dead person's chest, trying to revive her, and they're asking me to see their daughter,' he recalled". In this article, the journalist also cited a physician on his work overload of work: "A leading radiologist in Shanghai told [the reporter] he'd heard that the record number of patients seen in a day is three hundred and fourteen. 'That was at the Shanghai Children's Hospital,' he said. '"One doctor, 8 a.m. to 6 p.m., ten hours, two minutes per patient.'

However, whatever the audience—academic researchers, professional providers or consumers—there is a consensus that to queue and/or be on a waiting list for a consultation in a Level 3 hospital is preferable to consulting a doctor in a closer healthcare centre without waiting times. From the list of benefits, the two main ones are:

- The level of quality provided in the Level 3 hospitals even just for a consultation;
- The all-in-one healthcare supply: a consultation, blood test, radiology, and so on. (In the healthcare centres the care supply is fragmented.)

According to China's *Health Statistics Yearbook 2012*, the number of patients visiting Chinese hospitals increased from 4 billion in 2005 to 6.2 billion in 2011, whereas inpatient admissions soared from 71 million in 2005 to more than double—152 million—in 2011. Meanwhile, between 2008 and 2011, the number of doctors only increased by 170,000.[74]

Publication

Since the late 1980s, the larger hospitals in China have used publications in the Science Citation Index (SCI) as the main indicator for medical career evaluation, promotion and recognition. Most medical doctors are under pressure to publish as many articles as possible every year. This system is one chosen to evaluate doctors in public hospitals and leads to doctors spending part of their time writing articles. On the one hand, this means less time to treat patients; on the other hand, writing articles is a way to encourage them to remain connected to the medical and scientific improvements.

In the context of a shortage of medical doctors, an evaluating system based on publication affects the quality of treatment and the doctor-patient relationship. Another aspect concerns the reliability of the system and how trustworthy the articles are. The system pushes medical doctors to cheat, falsifying data. Firms of ghostwriters appeared on the market and are growing rapidly.[75] This point was widely discussed by bloggers such as Yu Ying.

Low Social Status

In Western countries, medicine is a profession that implies prestige and a high salary. Conversely, in China, this profession has a low social status. McKinsey in 2012 found that "physicians [in China] report that their job satisfaction is quite low, averaging 4.3 out of 10, and only 20 percent of physicians are 'satisfied' with their job". McKinsey also found that the top three reasons why Chinese physicians are not happy were: (1) "professional risks"; (") a "suboptimal level of compensation"; and (3) "low social status".

A non-negligible proportion of medical school graduates choose to pursue other professions, such as in the pharmaceutical industries. The 12th Five Year Plan asserts a goal of training 150,000 new primary care physicians and this objective appears realistic. Indeed, recently, there are approximately 600,000 doctors a year graduating. The problem is that, of those, an estimated 500,000 will never practise medicine.[76] Li Ling, a professor at the National Development Research Institute of Beijing University, who is also China's medical reform expert, presents the same figures: "China trains about 600,000 medical students each year, but only about 100,000 of them actually become doctors."[77]

According to a survey of 61 major medical schools conducted by the Economic Observer, overall the national admission scores for medical students have decreased in recent years. In a *Financial Times* article (2013), a student who wanted to study engineering had been reoriented to medicine because of too low grades in his southern China university. Except for the prestigious medical schools, recruiting good students has become a major challenge.[78] That reinforces the gap in quality between the Level 3 hospitals that drain the brightest medical graduates and the other health institutions.

Occupation Changes

Family Doctors: A Possible Future

Healthcare access is regulated in the sense that patients cannot consult a physician outside their municipality of residence if they want to be fully reimbursed by the public insurance scheme. Nevertheless, they are at liberty to choose the physician they want within their municipality. The concept of a referring doctor, as it exists in the United Kingdom or in France, is at experimental stage.

The 2009 reform introduced specific training for family doctors, as explained above. However, most physicians, including community physicians, do not have any special family medical training. The Chinese medical education system aims to train medical specialists.[79] Therefore, the ability of health centres to provide adequate family medicine is also key to improve the quality of care and to promote the primary health centees. Over the past decade, healthcare system policy has focused on the introduction of General Practitioners training.

In July 2011, the State Council published a document announcing the implementation of a system of referring doctors covering the entire country by 2020. This document targets the formation of **400,000** General Practitioners or family doctors. It involves not only attracting young medical graduates into a career as family doctors but also training the doctors in service who are working in village or community clinics. The objective is to foster the skills of medical staff working in village or community clinics. In fact, this reform is not wholeheartedly supported by either medical staff or patients.

On the Demand Side

This reform deals with the need for confidence building in the whole healthcare system. For a large part of the population, the expected healthcare quality can only be obtained in a Level 3 hospital. The new hospital classification based on equipment level and medical staff skill level, introduced with the reform, emphasized this belief.

So far, the level of quality provided by the healthcare centres and clinics is still quite poor. A lack of training for medical staff and insufficient financial resources does not contribute to the restoration of public confidence. However, the implementation of reform needs the support of the demand side.

On the Supply Side
The reform implies the support of the medical community. The government has to guarantee a sustainable referral doctor system, and the young graduate doctors have to trust it. Referral doctor training did not exist a few years ago. This career choice requires visibility about career opportunities and progression. Working in public hospitals has advantages and benefits clearly established over time.

The difficulties in recruiting referral doctors have been increased by a deterioration in the image of the doctor in Chinese society. They are no longer considered the elite in society. According to a 2011 survey, conducted by the Chinese Medical Doctors Association, 78% saw a career as a medical doctor as being a bad choice for their children. At Xiamen University, Doctor Wang reckons that among the first year medical school students (the 2006 cohort), more than half have reoriented their careers to work with pharmaceutical and biotechnology companies.[80]

Pilot Trials
One of the pilot trials has been carried out in Haidian district, Beijing, from November 2015. According to the first results, the local doctors were willing to participate in the pilot. They received a referral doctor's training and had to provide healthcare to a defined number of patients. Their wages were not connected to the care performed on patients. On the demand side, people were more reluctant. The lack of freedom to choose their doctor was one of the obstacles.

Internet
These new developments in the healthcare system are intensively viewed and considered by internet companies. With the widespread use of online medical consultations, the referral doctors could be a link to a more global system where the healthcare system would be networked organized. Wang

Lei, CEO of Alibaba Health Information Technology (Ali Health), has considered the implementation of a healthcare medical service network with online access. The gatekeeper would be the referral doctor, supported by telemedical services. It would be an online-to-offline (O2O) service.[81]

NOTES

1. X. Qin, L. Li, and C.-R. Hsieh, "Too Few Doctors or Too Low Wages? Labor Supply of Healthcare Professionals in China," China Economic Review, Vol. 24, No. 1, 2013.

2. D. Xu, B. Sun, X. Wan, and Y. Ke, "Reformation of Medical Education in China," Lancet, Vol. 375, No. 9725, 2010a May 1, pp. 1502–1504.

3. H. Zhang and P. Yuen, "Medical Savings Account Balance and Outpatient Utilization: Evidence from Guangzhou, China," Social Science and Medicine, Vol. 151, 2016.

4. Q. Meng, "Developing and Implementing Equity-promoting Health Care Policies in China," A case study commissioned by the Health Systems Knowledge Network, 2007.

5. F. Wang and W. Luo, "Assessing Spatial and Non-spatial Factors for Healthcare Access: Towards an Integrated Approach to Defining Health Professional Shortage Areas," Health & Place, Vol. 11, No. 2, 2005, pp. 131–146.

6. J. Vedom and H. Cao, "Health Care Access and Regional Disparities in China," Risques de santé en sociétés, 2011/1, 2011.

7. S. Anand, V. Fan, J. Zhang, L. Zhang, Y. Ke, Z. Dong, and L. Chen, "China's Human Resources for Health: Quantity, Quality, and Distribution," The Lancet, Vol. 372, No. 9651, 2008, pp. 1774–1781.

8. J. Moe, S. Chen, and A. Taylor, "Initial Findings in a Landscaping Study of Healthcare Delivery Innovation in China, IPIHD Research Report 14-01, 2014.

9. http://en.nhfpc.gov.cn/2014-06/25/content_19004549.htm. Accessed August 2016.

10. H. Yun, S. Jie, and J. Anli, "Nursing Shortage in China: State, Causes, and Strategy," Nursing Outlook, Vol. 58, No. 3, 2010, pp. 122–128.

11. World Bank, Main Report. China Health Policy Notes; No. 2, 2010.

12. D.Q. Zhang and P.U. Unschuld, "China's Barefoot Doctor: Past, Present, and Future," Lancet, Vol. 372, 2008, pp. 1865–1867.

13. Y. Liu, "The Essential of Primary Health Care and A Review of its Development in China," Chin Health Econ, Vol. 26, 2007, pp. 11–15.

14. V. Lin, Y. Guo, D. Legge, and Q. Wu, Health Policy in and for China, 1st ed., Beijing: Peking University Medical Press (PUMP), 2010.

15. D. Blumenthal and W. Hsiao, "Privatization and its Dis-contents—The Evolving Chinese Health Care System," The New England Journal of Medicine, Vol. 353, 2005, pp. 1165–1170.
16. X.Z. Kong (ed.), "Chapter 9," In: China's Three Dimensional of Agro Issues Prospects Report [in Chinese], Beijing: China Modern Economic Publishing House, 2009.
17. N.G. Miller, K. Eggleston, and Q. Zhang, "Understanding China's Mortality Decline Under Mao: A Provincial Analysis, 1950–1980," Stanford University Working Paper, Presented at the International Economics Association World Congress in Beijing, July, 2011.
18. D. Zhang, and P. Unschuld, "China's Barefoot Doctor: Past, Present, and Future," Lancet, Vol. 372, 2008, pp. 1865–1867. https://doi.org/10.1016/S0140-6736(08)61355-0.
19. G. Youlong, A. Wilkes, and G. Bloom, "Health Human Resource Development in Rural China," Health Policy Plan, Vol. 12, No. 4, 1997.
20. J. McConnell, "Barefoot No More," Lancet, Vol. 341, 1993, p. 1275.
21. H. Wang, L. Zhang, W. Yip, and W. Hsiao, "An Experiment in Payment Reform for Doctors in Rural China Reduced Some Unnecessary Care but Did Not Lower Total Costs," Health Affairs (Millwood), Vol. 30, 2011, pp. 2427–2236.
22. H.D. Shanlian Hu, C. Qian, X. Liu, and X. Liu, "A Study on Rural Doctor's Health Service and Payment (in Chinese)," Chinese Primary Health Care, Vol. 8, 1994, pp. 7–9.
23. Youlong Gong, Fei Yan, and Lingfang Feng, "Village Doctors' Distribution, Training and Remuneration (in Chinese)," Chinese Rural Health Service Administration, Vol. 17, 1997, pp. 15–16.
24. S.C. Airong Wang, Xueshan Feng, Lieping Chen, Tao Hong, and Jingwen Huang, "Analysis of Rural Doctors' Pay Level, Pay Structure, Origin and Influencing Factors (in Chinese)," Academic Research, Vol. 14, 2000, pp. 9–10.
25. W. De Geyndt, X. Zhao, and S. Liu, From Barefoot Doctor to Village Doctor in Rural China, Washington, DC: World Bank, 1992.
26. http://www.npc.gov.cn/englishnpc/Law/2007-12/11/content_1383574.htm. Accessed September 2017.
27. D. Hipgrave, S. Guo, Y. Mu, Y. Guo, F. Yan, R. Scherpbier, and H. Brixi, "Chinese-style Decentralization and Health System Reform," PLoS Medicine, Vol. 9, No. 11, 2012. http://www.ncbi.nlm.nih.gov/pmc/articles/PMC3491007/. Accessed September 2017.
28. Huiwen Xu, Weijun Zhang, Xiulan Zhang, Zhiyong Qu, Xiaohua Wang, Zhihong Sa, Yafang Li, Shuliang Zhao, Xuan Qi, and Donghua Tian, "Longitudinal Study of Rural Health Workforce in Five Counties in China: Research Design And Baseline Description," Human Resource Health, Vol. 11, 2013, p. 17.

29. Ministry of Health, 2012 China Health Statistics Yearbook (in Chinese), Beijing: Beijing Union Medical University Press, 2012.
30. The Central People's Government of the People's Republic of China, The Guideline for Improving the Village Doctors by State Council (in Chinese). http://www.gov.cn/zwgk/2011-07/14/content_1906244.htm. Accessed September 2017.
31. H. Xu, W. Zhang, X. Zhang, Z. Qu, X. Wang, Z. Sa, Y. Li, S. Zhao, X. Qi, and D. Tian, "Longitudinal Study of Rural Health Workforce in Five Counties in China: Research Design and Baseline Description," Human Resources Health, Vol. 11, 2013, p. 17. http://www.ncbi.nlm.nih.gov/pmc/articles/PMC3656804/. Accessed September 2017.
32. Interview in Beijing, October 2015 (translated from Chinese).
33. X.Y. Wang, A.C. Rodriguez, and M.R. Shu, "Challenges to Implementation of Medical Residency Programs in China: A Five-year Study of Attrition from West China Hospital," Academic Medicine, Vol. 85, 2010, pp. 1203–1208.
34. Z. Yang, "Quantity or Quality? Implications for Postgraduate … Quantity or Quality? Implications for Postgraduate Medical Training System in China," QJM: An International Journal of Medicine, Vol. 170, No. 2, 2013, pp. 169–170.
35. S. Anand, V. Fan, J. Zhang, L. Zhang, Y. Ke, Z. Dong, and L. Chen, "China's Human Resources for Health: Quantity, Quality, and Distribution," The Lancet, Vol. 372, No. 9651, 2008, pp. 1774–1781.
36. L. Wu, Y. Wang, X. Peng, M. Song, X. Guo, H. Nelson, and W. Wang, "Development of a Medical Academic Degree System in China," Medical Education Online, Vol. 19, 2014. https://doi.org/10.3402/meo.v19.23141. Accessed September 2017.
37. L.X. Wang, "A Comparison of Metropolitan and Rural Medical Schools in China. Which Schools Provide Rural Physicians?" Australian Journal of Rural Health, Vol. 10, 2002, pp. 94–98.
38. J. Wang, J. Su, H. Zuo, M. Jia, and Z. Zeng, "What Interventions Do Rural Doctors Think Will Increase Recruitment in Rural Areas: A Survey of 2778 Health Workers in Beijing," Human Resource Health, Vol. 11, 2013, p. 40.
39. Y. Zhong. Local Government and Politics in China: Challenges from Below. Armonk: M. E. Sharpe, 2004.
40. L. Dong, H. Yan, and D. Wang, "Drug Prescribing Indicators in Village Health Clinics Across 10 Provinces of Western China," Family Practice, Vol. 28, 2011, pp. 63–67.
41. C. Weiyuan, "China's Village Doctors take Great Strides," Bulletin of the World Health Organization, Vol. 86, 2008, pp. 914–915.

42. L.N. Henderson and J. Tulloch, "Incentives for Retaining and Motivating Health Workers in Pacific and Asian Countries," Human Resource Health, Vol. 6, 2008, p. 18.
43. Z. Huixuan, W. Zhang, S. Zhang, F. Wang, Y. Zhong, L. Gu, Z. Qu, X. Liang, Z. Sa, X. Wang, and D. Tian, "Health Providers' Perspectives on Delivering Public Health Services Under the Contract Service Policy in Rural China: Evidence from Xinjian County," BMC Health Services Research, Vol. 15, 2015, p. 75.
44. Z. Yao, "The Changing Relationship Between the Chinese Urban Medical Profession and the State since the Republican Period: The Perspective of the Sociology of Professions," The Journal of Chinese Sociology, Vol. 3, No. 2, 2016.
45. Interviews in Beijing, November 2015 (Translated from Chinese).
46. https://healthintelasia.com/lack-talent-chinas-private-hospital-operators/.
47. Wei Liu, "Liberating Doctors," Southern Weekly, 2013, January 31.
48. Gong Yan, "Doctors' Several-point Practice has Breakthrough in Beijing," Health News, 2014, January 21.
49. Interviews à Pékin et Shanghai, November 2015 (traduit du chinois).
50. C. Tang, Y. Zhang, L. Chen, and Y. Lin, "The Growth of Private Hospitals and their Health Workforce in China: A Comparison with Public Hospitals," Health Policy and Planning, Vol. 29, No. 1, 2014 Jan, pp. 30–41.
51. H. Xu and J. Huang, "Discussion about Challenge and Strategy for Private Hospital (Shi lun ming ying yi yuan de kun jing he dui ce)," Journal of Chinese Community Doctors, Vol. 8, 2006, p. 124.
52. D. Xue, "The Health Workforce Development of Private Hospital (Ming ying yi yuan ren cai dui wu jian she xian zhuang)," China Health Human Resources, Vol. 5, 2008, pp. 21–22.
53. N.K. Choudhry, R.H. Fletcher, and S.B. Soumerai, "Systematic Review: The Relationship Between Clinical Experience and Quality of Health Care," Annals of Internal Medicine, Vol. 142, 2005, pp. 260–273.
54. J.F. Waljee, L.J. Greenfield, J.B. Dimick, and J.D. Birkmeyer, "Surgeon Age and Operative Mortality in the United States," Annals of Surgery, Vol. 244, 2006, pp. 353–362.
55. The BMJ Blogs, 23/06/2015. http://blogs.bmj.com/bmj/2013/09/11/liu-xu-et-al-chinese-doctors-leaving-public-hospitals-brain-drain-or-emancipation/. Accessed September 2017.
56. Interviews in Beijing, November 2015 (Translated from Chinese).
57. Li-mei Ran et al., "An analysis of China's Physician Salary Payment System," Journal of Huazhong University Sciences Technology [Medicine Science], Vol. 33, No. 2, 2013, pp. 309–314.

58. ibid., X. Qin, L. Li, and C.-R. Hsieh, "Too Few Doctors or Too Wages? Labor Supply of Healthcare Professionals in China," China Economic Review, Vol. 24, No. 1, 2013.

59. ibid., X. Qin, L. Li, and C.-R. Hsieh, "Too Few Doctors or Too Wages? Labor Supply of Healthcare Professionals in China," China Economic Review, Vol. 24, No. 1, 2013.

60. Source: 2005 China Yearbook of Labor Statistics.

61. http://www.scmp.com/news/china/article/1502551/doctors-paid-less-barbers-may-see-salaries-rise-china-mulls-increasing. Accessed September 2017.

62. G. Bloom, L. Han, and X. Li, "How Health Workers Earn a Living in China," Human Resources for Health Development Journal, Vol. 5, No. 1, 2001, pp. 25–38.

63. The Global Hospital Management Survey—China (GHMS-China), Harvard Business School, November 2013. http://www.hbs.edu/faculty/conferences/2014-world-management-survey/Documents/GlobalHospital_Management_Survey_Horak.pdf. Accessed September 2017.

64. http://www.chinesemedicalnews.com/2014/03/how-much-does-average-chinese-doctor.html. Accessed September 2017.

65. http://www.chinesemedicalnews.com/2014/03/dr-zhong-nanshan-whats-wrong-with.html. Accessed September 2017.

66. J.A. He and J. Qian, "Hospitals' Responses to Administrative Cost-containment Policy in Urban China: The Case of Fujian Province," China Quarterly, Vol. 216, 2013, 946–969.

67. Interview in Beijing. November 2016.

68. http://china.caixin.com/2016-08-25/100981795.html. Accessed September 2017.

69. A. He, "The Doctor-Patient Relationship, Defensive Medicine and Over-prescription in Chinese Public Hospitals: Evidence from a Cross-sectional Survey in Shenzhen City," Social Science & Medicine, Vol. 123, 2014, pp. 64–71.

70. P.L. Delamater, J.P. Messina, S.C. Grady, V. WinklerPrins, and A.M. Shortridge, "Do More Hospital Beds Lead to Higher Hospitalization Rates? A Spatial Examination of Roemer's Law," PLoS One, Vol. 8, No. 2, 2013.

71. Interviews in Beijing and Shanghai of Level III Hospital Physicians, February, November 2015 and December 2015 (translated from Chinese).

72. No More Long Queues in China's Smart Hospitals, August 2015, China Daily. http://www.chinadaily.com.cn/china/2015-08/05/content_21511189.htm. Accessed September 2017.

73. Ch. Beam, "Under the Knife _Why Chinese Patients are Turning Against their Doctors," NewYorker Magazine, August 2014. http://www.newyorker.com/magazine/2014/08/25/under-the-knife. Accessed September 2017.

74. http://www.worldcrunch.com/culture-society/why-becoming-a-doctor-in-china-is-no-longer-a-dream-job/china-doctor-medical-student-school/c3s9693/. Accessed September 2017.
75. B. Ye and J. Liu, "Inadequate Evaluation of Medical Doctors in China," The Lancet, Vol. 381, 2013.
76. https://healthintelasia.com/where-chinas-best-doctors-go-will-patients-follow/. Accessed September 2017.
77. http://www.worldcrunch.com/culture-society/why-becoming-a-doctor-in-china-is-no-longer-a-dream-job/china-doctor-medical-student-school/c3s9693/. Accessed September 2017.
78. http://www.ft.com/cms/s/0/35a081ae-2653-11e3-8ef6-00144feab7de.html. Accessed September 2017.
79. J. Xu, X. Wang, H. Li, J. Zhang, M. Pavlova, and H. Liu, "Analysis of Factors Influencing the Outpatient Workload at Chinese Health Centres," BMC Health Services Research, Vol. 10, 2010b, p. 151.
80. http://www.ft.com/cms/s/0/35a081ae-2653-11e3-8ef6-00144feab7de.html#axzz3tzD25070. Accessed September 2017.
81. Blen Perez, "Ali Health to Expand Despite Loss," South China Morning Post, 25 November 2015.

Bibliography

Airong Wang, S.C., Xueshan Feng, Lieping Chen, Tao Hong, and Jingwen Huang, "Analysis of Rural Doctors' Pay Level, Pay Structure, Origin and Influencing Factors (in Chinese)," Academy of Research, Vol. 14, 2000, pp. 9–10.

Anand, S., V. Fan, J. Zhang, L. Zhang, Y. Ke, Z. Dong, and L. Chen, "China's Human Resources for Health: Quantity, Quality, and Distribution," The Lancet, Vol. 372, No. 9651, 2008, pp. 1774–1781.

Beam, Ch., "Under the Knife_Why Chinese Patients are Turning Against their Doctors," NewYorker Magazine, August 2014. http://www.newyorker.com/magazine/2014/08/25/under-the-knife. Accessed September 2017.

Bloom, G., L. Han, and X. Li, "How Health Workers Earn a Living in China," Human Resources for Health Development Journal, Vol. 5, No. 1, 2001, pp. 25–38.

Blumenthal, D., and W. Hsiao, "Privatization and its Discontents—The Evolving Chinese Health Care System," New England Journal of Medicine, Vol. 353, 2005, pp. 1165–1170.

Choudhry, N.K., R.H. Fletcher, and S.B. Soumerai, "Systematic Review: The Relationship Between Clinical Experience and Quality of Health Care," Annals of Internal Medicine, Vol. 142, 2005, pp. 260–273.

De Geyndt, W., X. Zhao, and S. Liu, From Barefoot Doctor to Village Doctor in Rural China, Washington, DC: World Bank, 1992.

Delamater, P.L., J.P. Messina, S.C. Grady, V. WinklerPrins, and A.M. Shortridge, "Do More Hospital Beds Lead to Higher Hospitalization Rates? A Spatial Examination of Roemer's Law," PLoS One, Vol. 8, No. 2, 2013.

Dong, L., H. Yan, and D. Wang, "Drug Prescribing Indicators in Village Health Clinics Across 10 Provinces of Western China," Family Practice, Vol. 28, 2011, pp. 63–67.

Gong, Youlong, Fei Yan, and Lingfang Feng, "Village Doctors' Distribution, Training and Remuneration (in Chinese)," Chinese Rural Health Service Administration, Vol. 17, 1997, pp. 15–16.

He, A., "The Doctor-Patient Relationship, Defensive Medicine and Over-prescription in Chinese Public Hospitals: Evidence from a Cross-sectional Survey in Shenzhen City," Social Science & Medicine, Vol. 123, 2014, pp. 64–71.

He, J.A., and J. Qian, "Hospitals' Responses to Administrative Cost-containment Policy in Urban China: The Case of Fujian Province," China Quarterly, Vol. 216, 2013, 946–969.

Henderson, L.N., and J. Tulloch, "Incentives for Retaining and Motivating Health Workers in Pacific and Asian Countries," Human Resources of Health, Vol. 6, 2008, p. 18.

Hipgrave, D., S. Guo, Y. Mu, Y. Guo, F. Yan, R. Scherpbier, and H. Brixi, "Chinese-style Decentralization and Health System Reform," PLoS Medicine, Vol. 9, No. 11, 2012.

Huixuan, Z., W. Zhang, S. Zhang, F. Wang, Y. Zhong, L. Gu, Z. Qu, X. Liang, Z. Sa, X. Wang, and D. Tian, "Health Providers' Perspectives on Delivering Public Health Services Under the Contract Service Policy in Rural China: Evidence from Xinjian County," BMC Health Services Research, Vol. 15, 2015, p. 75.

Kong, X.Z. (ed.), "Chapter 9," In China's Three Dimensional of Agro Issues Prospects Report [in Chinese]. Beijing: China Modern Economic Publishing House, 2009.

Lin, V., Y. Guo, D. Legge, and Q. Wu. Health Policy in and for China, 1st ed. Beijing: Peking University Medical Press (PUMP), 2010.

Liu, Y., "The Essential of Primary Health Care and A Review of its Development in China," Chinese Health Economics, Vol. 26, 2007, pp. 11–15.

Liu, Wei, "Liberating Doctors," Southern Weekly, 2013, January 31.

McConnell, J., "Barefoot No More," Lancet, Vol. 341, 1993, p. 1275.

Meng, Q., Developing and Implementing Equity-promoting Health Care Policies in China. A Case Study Commissioned by the Health Systems Knowledge Network, 2007.

Miller, N.G., K. Eggleston, and Q. Zhang, "Understanding China's Mortality Decline under Mao: A Provincial Analysis, 1950–1980," Stanford University Working Paper, Presented at the International Economics Association World Congress in Beijing, July, 2011.

Ministry of Health, 2012 China Health Statistics Yearbook (in Chinese). Beijing: Beijing Union Medical University Press, 2012.

Moe, J., S. Chen, and A. Taylor, "Initial Findings in a Landscaping Study of Healthcare Delivery Innovation in China," IPIHD Research Report 14-01, 2014.

Perez, Blen, "Ali Health to Expand Despite Loss," South China Morning Post, 25 November 2015.

Qin, X., L. Li, and C.-R. Hsieh, "Too Few Doctors or Too Low Wages? Labor Supply of Healthcare Professionals in China," China Economic Review, Vol. 24, No. 1, 2013.

Ran, Li-mei et al., "An Analysis of China's Physician Salary Payment System," Journal of Huazhong Univ Sciences Technology [Medicine Science], Vol. 33, No. 2, 2013, pp. 309–314.

Shanlian Hu, H.D., C. Qian, X. Liu, and X. Liu, "A Study on Rural Doctor's Health Service and Payment (in Chinese)," Chinese Primary Health Care, Vol. 8, 1994, pp. 7–9.

Tang, C., Y. Zhang, L. Chen, and Y. Lin, "The Growth of Private Hospitals and their Health Workforce in China: A Comparison with Public Hospitals," Health Policy and Planning, Vol. 29, No. 1, 2014 January, pp. 30–41.

Vedom, J., and H. Cao, "Health Care Access and Regional Disparities in China," Risques de santé en sociétés, 2011/1, 2011.

Waljee, J.F., L.J. Greenfield, J.B. Dimick, and J.D. Birkmeyer, "Surgeon Age and Operative Mortality in the United States," Annals of Surgery, Vol. 244, 2006, pp. 353–362.

Wang, L.X., "A Comparison of Metropolitan and Rural Medical Schools in China. Which Schools Provide Rural Physicians?" Australian Journal of Rural Health, Vol. 10, 2002, pp. 94–98.

Wang, F., and W. Luo, "Assessing Spatial and Non-spatial Factors for Healthcare Access: Towards an Integrated Approach to Defining Health Professional Shortage Areas," Health & Place, Vol. 11, No. 2, 2005, pp. 131–146.

Wang, X.Y., A.C. Rodriguez, and M.R. Shu, "Challenges to Implementation of Medical Residency Programs in China: A Five-year Study of Attrition from West China Hospital," Academy Medicine, Vol. 85, 2010, pp. 1203–1208

Wang, J., J. Su, H. Zuo, M. Jia, and Z. Zeng, "What Interventions do Rural Doctors Think Will Increase Recruitment in Rural Areas: A Survey of 2778 Health Workers in Beijing," Human Resources of Health, Vol. 11, 2013, p. 40.

Wang, H., L. Zhang, W. Yip, and W. Hsiao, "An Experiment in Payment Reform for Doctors in Rural China Reduced Some Unnecessary Care But did not Lower Total Costs," Health Aff (Millwood), Vol. 30, 2011, pp. 2427–2236.

Wang, S. et al., "Comparison of Chinese Inpatients with Different Types of Medical Insurance Before and After the 2009 Healthcare Reform," BMC Health Services Research, Vol. 14, 2014, p. 443.

Weiyuan, C., "China's Village Doctors Take Great Strides," Bulletin World Health Organization, Vol. 86, 2008, pp. 914–915.

Wu, L., Y. Wang, X. Peng, M. Song, X. Guo, H. Nelson, and W. Wang, "Development of a Medical Academic Degree System in China," Medical Education Online, Vol. 19, 2014. https://doi.org/10.3402/meo.v19.23141. Accessed September 2017.

Xu, H., and J. Huang, "Discussion About Challenge and Strategy for Private Hospital (Shi lun ming ying yi yuan de kun jing he dui ce)," Journal of Chinese Community Doctors, Vol. 8, 2006, p. 124.

Xu, D., B. Sun, X. Wan, and Y. Ke, "Reformation of Medical Education in China," Lancet, Vol. 375, No. 9725, 2010a May 1, pp. 1502–1504.

Xu, J., X. Wang, H. Li, J. Zhang, M. Pavlova, and H. Liu, "Analysis of Factors Influencing the Outpatient Workload at Chinese Health Centres," BMC Health Services Research, Vol. 10, 2010b, p. 151.

Xu, H., W. Zhang, X. Zhang, Z. Qu, X. Wang, Z. Sa, Y. Li, S. Zhao, X. Qi, and D. Tian, "Longitudinal Study of Rural Health Workforce in Five Counties in China: Research Design and Baseline Description," Human Resources Health, Vol. 11, 2013, p. 17. http://www.ncbi.nlm.nih.gov/pmc/articles/PMC3656804/. Accessed September 2017.

Xue, D., "The Health Workforce Development of Private Hospital (Ming ying yi yuan ren cai dui wu jian she xian zhuang)," China Health Human Resources, Vol. 5, 2008, pp. 21–22.

Yan, Gong, "Doctors' Several-Point Practice has Breakthrough in Beijing," Health News, 2014, January 21.

Yang, Z., "Quantity or Quality? Implications for Postgraduate … Quantity or Quality? Implications for Postgraduate Medical Training System in China," QJM: An International Journal of Medicine, Vol. 170, No. 2, 2013, pp. 169–170.

Yao, Z., "The Changing Relationship Between the Chinese Urban Medical Profession and the State Since the Republican Period: The Perspective of the Sociology of Professions," The Journal of Chinese Sociology, Vol. 3, No. 2, 2016.

Ye, B., and J. Liu, "Inadequate Evaluation of Medical Doctors in China," The Lancet, Vol. 381, 2013.

Youlong, G., A. Wilkes, and G. Bloom, "Health Human Resource Development in Rural China," Health Policy Plan, Vol. 12, No. 4, 1997.

Yun, H., S. Jie, and J. Anli, "Nursing Shortage in China: State, Causes, and Strategy," Nursing Outlook, Vol. 58, No. 3, 2010, pp. 122–128.

Zhang, D.Q., and P.U. Unschuld, "China's Barefoot Doctor: Past, Present, and Future," Lancet, Vol. 372, 2008, pp. 1865–1867.

Zhang, H., and P. Yuen, "Medical Savings Account Balance and Outpatient Utilization: Evidence from Guangzhou, China," Social Science and Medicine, Vol. 151, 2016.

Zhong, Y., Local Government and Politics in China: Challenges from Below, Armonk: M. E. Sharpe, 2004.

CHAPTER 6

Health Insurance in China

Abstract Health insurance in China is the topic of this chapter. Up until the economic reforms of the 1980s, communities (a village or a group of villages) were managing the social welfare of their inhabitants. The system was extremely decentralized. With the collapse of the community medical system, existing public establishments were either replaced by private ones, or put into competition with them. As a result, the healthcare access system was no longer free of charge and became unaffordable to many. During the period of absence of a centralized public insurance system, this lack of access to treatment became a major problem; at first for the most vulnerable part of the population, and gradually for a greater and greater proportion of rural dwellers. As the question of healthcare costs causing widespread poverty became a pressing issue, different public health insurance programmes were implemented. Today, geographical inequity is still observed for these programmes. There is variability not only in terms of funding eligibility, types of illness or services to be covered, but also in terms of levels of benefits and payments methods. Concerning the private health insurance market, it was next to nothing in the early 2000s. Today, the rise of private health insurance schemes is supported by the Chinese government and is finding an audience among the emerging upper middle class.

Keywords Insurance • Public Insurance programmes • Geographical inequity • Private health insurance

© The Author(s) 2018   125
C. Milcent, *Healthcare Reform in China*,
https://doi.org/10.1007/978-3-319-69736-9_6

In Urban Areas

The Labour Insurance System

In urban areas, from 1949 to 1980, access to treatment was largely organized by and within state-owned enterprises. Each enterprise managed access to treatment on behalf of its employees and their children, as well as setting up a pension in preparation for retirement. These enterprises were gargantuan in size, and their sheer scale made it possible to pool risks of illness. Just as in rural areas, the system was extremely decentralized.

In 1951, the Labour Insurance System (LIS) was set up for employees of state-owned enterprises (SOEs), the collectively-owned enterprises and their dependants. The Medical Insurance System for Urban Employees was part of the labour insurance package of these firms. It covered in- and outpatient care, free of charge for the employee and at 50% of the costs for their dependants. This insurance was financed by the firms.

As far as healthcare facilities were concerned, each patient was cared for by the establishment that was affiliated to his or her enterprise. Then, according to the severity of the patient condition and the establishment's ability to treat, the patient would be sent either to a district hospital, a municipal hospital or a provincial hospital. At the highest level was the central hospital.

With the economic reforms, this social protection system has been eroding, and eventually disappeared altogether in some places. The root causes of this evolution are quite different from those found in rural areas. In cities, many state enterprises have been turned into private or semi-private firms. Simultaneously, they were divided up into smaller-scale units or just dismantled. The collective aspect of social welfare, managed independently by each enterprise, was thus seriously weakened: enterprises that were now smaller in scale soon found they were struggling to fund their own social welfare. Two main reasons accounted for this: first, since the units were smaller, insurance was supported by a smaller number of individuals; in addition, these units were then supposed to turn a profit without any support from the state. However, a portion of their profits was used to provide social welfare for their employees. Bankruptcies piled up and threatened to destabilize the whole system, as employees lost their jobs and health insurance packages. User fees were implemented as public funding declined and out-of-pocket payments progressively increased.[1]

The Government Insurance System

For workers in government organizations and public institutions, there was a specific insurance system before the economic reform that is still used partially today. In 1952, the Government Insurance System (GIS) was established for government staff and retired government staff, as well as university students. It has been progressively dissolved into the new schemes being set up but the process is very long and GIS is still partially in use in some areas.

The Urban Employees Basic Medical Insurance System from 1998

Threatened with impending economic collapse, the government was forced to take action, and decided to relieve enterprises of the financial burden that came with social security. At the same time, the government introduced a public form of social protection. This was much less extensive than its previous incarnation, but had the advantage of at least existing, in contrast to the situation in rural areas. As a result, urban residents were subjected to a decline in quality within their social welfare system, while the overall structure was preserved.

From a series of pilot programmes, the State Council released the 1998 Decisions in establishing the Urban Employees Basic Medical Insurance System (UEBMI). People eligible for this new urban insurance are those eligible for LIS and GIS[2] as well as employees of private sector companies and small public firms.

One major change of this new system is to pool the health insurance at city or county level and not at firm level as before. The funding for this scheme is based on social pooling plus individual accounts, to which employers contribute 6% and employees 2% of their wages. This funding is split into two accounts:

- Individual accounts are funded by individual contributions plus 30% of the contributions made by enterprises;
- Social accounts are funded by the rest of the firms' contribution.

Medical expenditure is covered according to a minimum that depends on the discretion of the local government. Healthcare costs below the minimum can be covered either by the individual accounts or by the individual. Local governments had discretion to determine the exact rates for the minimum and the maximum, as well as the percentages for reimbursement. Besides, depending on the area, if no money was left in an individual's account then he or she became eligible for the social pooling account. In 2004, one in-patient episode was estimated to amount to two-thirds of the average annual household expenditure in urban areas.[3] At the same time, employees were encouraged to enrol in private medical insurance schemes.

Urban Residents' Basic Medical Insurance Programme from 2010

In 2008, the Urban Residents' Basic Medical Insurance Programme (URBMI) was covering 64% of the active urban population. However, only 31% of the urban population was eligible for this health insurance system.

For residents who are not urban employees, URBMI was implemented nationwide in 2010, with pilot cities from 2007. This public health insurance is designed for household subscription on a voluntary basis. This system is funded by contributions from households and government subsidies (from central government and local governments). Since then, those eligible include college students, workers with an informal occupation who are not eligible for the UEBMI and migrant workers who are also not eligible for the UEBMI[4]. In short, the URBMI is for those living in urban areas who are ineligible for the UEBMI. Today, these programmes cover around 95% of the urban population, including some migrant workers, in other words those who are both eligible and choose to participate.

A very important point is that there is *no portability of rights*. In other words, rights acquired are available only in geographically defined areas.

IN RURAL AREAS

The Community Medical System

Up until the 1980s, the communities (a village or a group of villages) were managing the social welfare of their local inhabitants. The system was extremely decentralized. The profit generated from the farmlands was managed by a local authority that was spending on public goods including social welfare, health and retirement. This system was set up in a context of strict control of the population's movements, particularly between cities and rural areas.

As explained in Chap. 3, The individual residents permit restraint the population in the possibility to settle down from one place to another.[5] This control also ensures the sustainability of the decentralized social welfare system.

As highlighted by Hesketh and Xingzhu,[6] and also by Yip and Hsiao,[7] between the 1950s and the start of the 1980s the structure of China's healthcare system allowed the country to make clear improvements to the health of its population. A number of indicators attest to this. Treatment was mostly guaranteed free of charge. However, the level of care available was relatively low, using equipment of mediocre quality.

The Chinese healthcare system was divided into three levels of treatment access.[8] The first level was equivalent to free clinics in villages called Tier I; the second comprised health centres for the township, called Tier II; the third was represented by the county hospital, called Tier III.[9] This was the structure that made up the public healthcare system for each community.[10] In addition, there was an obligation to pass through Tier I organizations in order to reach Tier II and Tier III.

From 1991 onwards, the Chinese government promoted the creation of private organizations. The services provided by these private establishments were, overall, of higher quality than those offered by public healthcare establishments.

In parallel, the progressive privatization of land allowed workers to generate profit from its exploitation. However, communities were deprived of a portion of the profit from farms which had helped to finance social protection. This harmed the capability and quality of public institutions' services, leading to a considerable degree of protest. The poor quality of healthcare was no longer counterbalanced by the perception of free care, as taxes were levied to pay for healthcare.

At the same time, demand for healthcare was changing. The emergence of more middle-class farmers led to demand for better-quality healthcare. An analogous rise in healthcare demand came from rural inhabitants with industrial jobs in urban areas, who had greater than average incomes. At the government's instigation, some of those living in rural areas turned to private healthcare offered by private health centres. In the end, the social protection system was financed only by those whose income was too low to afford the healthcare available in private clinics, but high enough to pay social insurance contributions. This subset of the population, being small, meant that the social protection system ended up either being drastically reduced in size or entirely wiped out.

The Disappearance of Any Health Insurance

The community medical system found its funding cut dramatically, and sometimes this funding even disappeared completely. Existing public establishments were either replaced by private ones, or put into competition with them. As a result, Tier I public establishments began to collapse due to a lack of funding, leaving rural areas without public healthcare treatment. This meant that in rural areas, where people had to only travel a relatively short distance to reach the nearest health centre, they now had to travel further in order to reach a public establishment, as noted by Akin et al.[11] The overall effect of this was that local populations discovered that the sources of treatment made available to them had become private, and more expensive.

At the same time, Tier II and Tier III public healthcare providers acquired an increasing level of autonomy, including the management of their profits. This allowed them to develop their equipment and acquire new medical technology. This was coupled with a rapid withdrawal of funding from the state and the provinces.[12]

Since they had little or no public subsidy to rely on, public establishments were no longer subject to a duty of public service. Moreover, with public health establishments now behaving like commercial enterprises, economic theory dictated that suppliers should seek to maximize their profits.[13] They were helped by the fact that they had an effective monopoly over their local geographic area, allowing them to set their own prices.

As the price of healthcare (consultations, treatment and medication) was rocketing, average income also increased steadily, but with huge inequalities. The differences in the quality of treatment on offer between the cities and countryside became more pronounced. In addition, there was no longer an obligation to pass through Level I organizations in order to reach Levels II and III. *De facto*, the rural population found itself offered a choice of establishments at which to seek medical consultation.

As a result, the rural population developed a preference for establishments in urban areas, especially those that offered an excellent level of quality. This was also facilitated by greater mobility among a certain sector of that population: there was a rapid decrease in the proportion of rural residents within the total population, and a growing number of them began commuting and working further from home. These changes were concomitant to an amazing improvement of the transportation network[14].

In 1998, only 9.5% of the Chinese population was covered by a public health system[15] and this figure dropped to 7% one year later. The private health insurance market was next to nil at that time.[16]

For financial reasons, the lack of access to treatment became a major problem, first for the most vulnerable among China's population, and then for a greater and greater proportion of rural dwellers.[17]

The New Co-operative Medical Scheme

Along with the economic reforms of the 1980s came the dissolution of the rural Co-operative Medical System, and illness emerged as a leading cause of poverty in rural China. The high cost of healthcare has deterred many families from obtaining necessary healthcare. In response, the Chinese government started pilot programmes of the New Co-operative Medical System (NCMS) in 2003. NCMS programmes have several key features: (1) the programme is targeted at rural residents;[18] (2) participation is voluntary but must be at the household level; (3) participants are required to pay flat-rate premiums, but their contributions are heavily subsidized by governments; (4) the programmes mainly reimburse large expenses so as to ease the economic burden resulting from catastrophic disease and alleviate illness-caused poverty; (5) the programmes are operated at the county level rather than the township or village level. The primary goal of the NCMS is to reduce impoverishment resulting from illness and improve the affordability of healthcare (Central Committee of CPC, 2002). Local governments have been granted autonomy to design, implement and supervise the programmes.

While local governments have some discretion over the level of financing of the programme, the standard in 2003 was for each participating household to pay at least RMB 10 (about $1.2) for each household member every year, with the local government providing more than RMB 10 for each person per year. The central government would also match this with RMB 10 per year for each beneficiary living in the central and western provinces. As of 2006, while individual contributions generally remained at the existing level, subsidies from local and central government increased (Wagstaff and Yu 2007). NCMS insurance mainly provides financial risk protection to patients with catastrophic health problems. Many services—particularly outpatient care—are not covered, deductibles are high, ceilings are low, and co-insurance rates are high.

There are more than 2800 rural counties in China. The NCMS pilot programme began in 310 rural counties in 2003. It expanded to 617 counties in 2005, 1451 counties in 2006 (i.e., 50.7% of the total number of counties) and started to spread across the country in 2007. By the end of June 2007, the programme had expanded to cover 84.9% of all rural counties and 82.8% of all rural residents. It has covered the whole rural population since 2010. Provincial and county governments retain considerable discretion over the details of the pilots, including the placement of the pilot programme.

NCMS pilot counties were not randomly selected. A complex set of criteria, including local interest and capacity, level of economic development, and the status of the delivery system were considered. It allowed analysis of the effect of this health insurance programme on the diverse socio-economic conditions of the Chinese territory and thus to ensure its success.

Along with the NCMS, local governments provided some supporting policies, such as improvements in rural healthcare (delivery) networks and health service provision, the strengthening of pharmaceutical governance, and supply chain construction. These measures made it possible to improve the quality and delivery of healthcare service and also benefit families who choose not to participate the NCMS. Therefore, the adoption of the NCMS programme by the county had an effect on healthcare access for both the NCMS-insured and the NCMS-uninsured.

BRIEF CONCLUSION OF PUBLIC HEALTH INSURANCES LAUNCHED

By 2009, 94% of rural counties implemented the NCMS[19] and more than 94% of eligible rural residents (833 million people) were covered by the NCMS (China Statistical Yearbook 2010). In 2012, the medical insurance system (including the rural NCMS, the urban UEBMI and the urban URBMI) covered 1.34 billion participants.[20]

As the question of healthcare costs causing widespread poverty became a pressing issue, a rural public health insurance programme, the NCMS, was implemented at the beginning of 2003. The introduction of a public insurance system brought a momentary respite, although it did not resolve the issue in any lasting sense.[21] Furthermore, this health insurance system only made minor inroads into the healthcare network. In fact, if patients went to a hospital outside their local area, the rural public insurance system penalized them with a lower reimbursement (or none at all) for treatment.[22] Even now, repayments for consultations remain very low, meaning that patients and their families are usually prepared to relinquish them.

All this has meant that, in recent years, the very best hospitals in urban areas were, and still are, forced to deal with significantly higher demand than was intended.

MEDICAL (FINANCIAL) ASSISTANCE PROGRAMME

First piloted in some rural areas, the medical assistance programme aims at protecting rural households against poverty caused by serious illness. This programme was established with a focus on the estimated 5% of the population covered by the main social assistance programmes:

- *Wubao*: the five guarantees programme established in the mid-1950s with a minimum level of food, clothing, shelter, medical care and funeral expenses. In 2013, it was covering 5.37 million older people of whom 1.8 million were cared for collectively in homes for the aged and 3.5 million in their own homes in villages.[23]
- *Dibao*: for people under the poverty line, 2300 Yuan per person per year, close to the international level, was allocated. In 2013, the national average assistance standard for rural *dibao* was 203 Yuan per person per month with variability through the Chinese territory, from 100 Yuan to more than 300 Yuan, partially reflecting the local financial capacity (Leung and Xu 2015).

In 2003, the Ministry of Civil Affairs, the Ministry of Finance and the Ministry of Health jointly issued the Opinion on the Implementation of Rural Medical Assistance. This system provides cash assistance for poor people to cover expenses for inpatient services and treatment of major illnesses. Funds are also used to support poor households' participation to the NCMS. This system is funded by the central government and local government, from welfare lottery funds administrated by civil affairs departments and charity donations. Between 2003 and 2007, 22 out of 34 provinces received subsides from central government.[24]

As for the public health insurance system, implementation of the programme was delegated to county authorities, with considerable discretion over both policy design and execution. As a consequence, from one county to the other, there is variability in terms of funding eligibility, types of illness or services to be covered. In the same way, the levels of benefices and the payments methods differ from one place to the other.

In the end, the Medical Assistance System was less efficient than expected.[25] One reason could be that patients must spend money before being reimbursed. The audience for this programme, being the poorest of the poor, often cannot afford to pay for medical care even if they get a reimbursement for the expenditure. From 2007, some changes have occurred. Direct payments to hospitals by the civil affairs departments were adopted in some localities; eligibility for Medical Assistance was expanded to outpatient services; the ceilings and the reimbursement rates have been raised; and the fixed payment floors have been removed in some other areas, at least for the poorest part of the population.[26] By 2012, a total amount of 13.29 billion Yuan had been allocated for Medical Assistance by governments at different levels. Nationally, in 2010, reimbursement rates changed from 30% to 50% of the remaining healthcare expenditure after the NCMS payment.[27] Today, the population covered by the system stands at over 95%.[28]

CURRENT STATUS OF PUBLIC HEALTH INSURANCE SCHEMES

Before the "Open Door Policy", different types of programmes (as discussed above) were covering the population according to locality and residence permit. With the economic reforms, the social welfare system collapsed, leaving a large number of residents uninsured. In parallel, public hospitals have fostered the level of healthcare quality they provide, but this supply is located mainly in urban areas. From the early 2000s, extending the proportion of the population covered by public health insurance is one of the principal objectives declared by the Chinese government. From then on, three systems (the NCMS, UEBMI, URBMI) have been developed in both urban and rural areas, providing coverage for more than 90% of the population. The 12th Five Year National Healthcare Service System Plan 2015–2010 announced a universal "safe, effective and affordable basic healthcare services" for 2020. One of the five major issues pointed out was to expand basic medical insurance programmes. Between 2001 and 2013, the share of public and social funds in healthcare financing increased from 40% to 66.1% bringing out-of-pocket spending close to levels observed in OECD countries.[29,30]

The 13th Five Year Plan, released in 2016, aims at deepening the healthcare reform, focusing and strengthening the major points underlined in the12th Five Year Plan.

Behind this picture, the reality is more complex with widening rural versus urban disparities in health insurance coverage and related health-care services and costs, leading to tremendous variability in the out-of-pocket amount to be found. The conditions for healthcare expenses eligible for refunds also differ. All these differences combined to increase geographical inequality.

Differences Between the Three Systems of Public Health Insurance

There are two types of inequality. First of all, according to the public health insurance form, the coverage differs. Figure 6.1 displays the reimbursement rules in the three medical insurance systems. If the NCMS insurance form prioritizes reimbursement for outpatients, we observe that the UEBMI covers expenditure for inpatient as well as outpatient care, with a high level of reimbursement rate.

Migrant workers (from rural areas to cities) are eligible for the NCMS and URBMI programmes. In some localities, they are also eligible for specific programmes with additional advantages. As shown in Fig. 6.2, being covered by the URBMI provides overall a better reimbursement rate than with the NCMS. Specifically for drug expenditure incurred by outpatients, subscribers to the UEBMI are better covered than those covered by the NCMS.

Scheme	Urban Employees Basic Medical Insurance System (UEBMI)	Urban Residents' Basic Medical Insurance Program (URBMI)	New rural Community Medical System (NCMS)
Targeted population	Employees and retirees with regular employment in all institutions	Children, seniors, students, unemployed, underemployed and self-employed	Rural area residents
Type	Mandatory	Voluntary	Voluntary (family-based)
Inpatient reimbursement	80–95%	50–70%	50–70%
Outpatient reimbursement	Diseases : 100%	Diseases : 40–60%	Diseases : 50–60%
	Severe diseases : 80–95%	Severe diseases : 50–80%	Severe diseases : 50–80%

Fig. 6.1 Public healthcare insurance forms. Source: MOHRSS (2014); Citi Research (2012); Baidu Baike (2014)

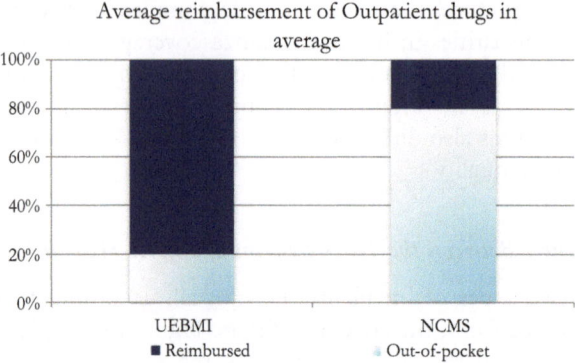

Fig. 6.2 Average reimbursement level of outpatient drugs under UEBMI and NRCMI. Source: Deloitte report, 2014

However, even for migrant workers, a very important feature of these public health insurance schemes is that there is no portability of rights. In other words, rights acquired are available only in specifically defined locations.

Until 2015,[31] each insurance programme was independently managed and operated. At present, Chinese authorities are planning to merge the NCMS and URBMI programmes. The inclusion of the UEBMI programme is still under debate. The major problem lies in the lack of consensus on the primary purpose, as different agencies and ministries are in charge of these public insurance programmes or parts of them, with very different agendas and priorities.

One of the purposes of this merger is an improvement in management efficiency. The statutory requirement set down that a policyholder of one programme cannot be eligible to any other public health insurance programme. However, some migrant workers subscribed to more than one public health insurance programme. That was a way to circumvent the lack of portability of rights[32] (available rights acquired in a restricted locality). As a result, this may reduce the coverage of part of the migrant/commuter population and, in the end, their healthcare access.

The Geographical Inequality

The second type of inequality is purely geographical, as shown in a study of the NCMS by Wang (2009).[33] He shows an important correlation between the NCMS package and local gross domestic product (GDP) per capita, with variability through the Chinese territory. Indeed, local governments provide the main part of the funding. Because of the huge GDP heterogeneity over the Chinese territory, the advantage offered by the NCMS package varies from one county to the other. There is variability not only in terms of funding eligibility, types of illness or services to be covered, but also in terms of levels of benefits and payment methods.

Overall, the basket of services covered by a given public health insurance programme varies across the Chinese territory. This basket depends on the level of funding that itself depends on the wealth of thelocality. It led to inequality in healthcare access from one county to the other.

Dong and Song (2009)[34] illustrate this phenomenon with an example, showing how it drives inequality to healthcare access.[35] They show that diabetes patients in Huangshui, Hubei province, face no deductibles, 75% reimbursement rates, and an annual reimbursement cap of RMB 1680 ($250). In contrast, diabetes patients in Shantou, Guangdong province, face a deductible of RMB 1000 ($150), a reimbursement rate of 50%, and a cap of RMB 6000 ($ 880).

The health risks are pooled at the county level, and this inequality is particularly strong between rural versus urban localities.[36,37] Figure 6.3 displays the difference in healthcare spending per person between urban and rural regions. It shows an increase in the difference over the past 20 years.

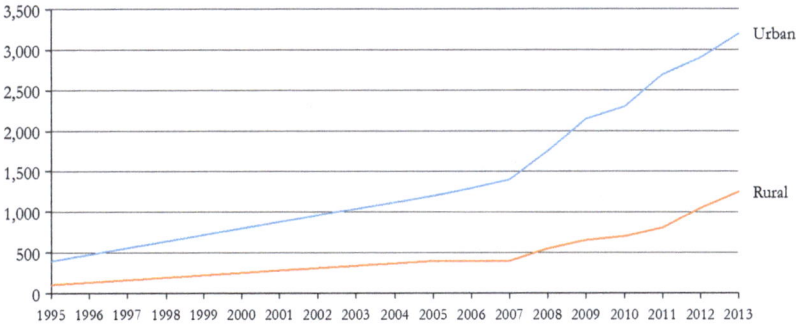

Fig. 6.3   Healthcare spending per person in urban and rural regions (in RMB). Source: Healthcare in China, A Kieger Report on the Chinese Healthcare Market, 2015. Figures from National Bureau of Statistics of China, 2015

Adverse Selection

It is said that adverse selection appears if people who do not participate in the public health insurance programme are those with excellent health and people who do participate are those with poor health.

Participation in NCMS or URBMI insurance systems is voluntary but the unit of participation is the household. There is reason to assume that household subscriptions are based on the average health status of the members of the household, but not that they are based on each member of the household having a poor health status: the system should theoretically reduce the adverse selection bias. However, although rural inhabitants are required to participate as household units in order to reduce adverse selection, the elementary conclusion drawn from previous studies is that the system does not totally prevent adverse selection.[38,39] Due to the voluntary nature of NCMS insurance or URBMI insurance, concerns about adverse selection remain, representing a threat to the financial sustainability of these programmes in the long run.

Those with the highest risk of getting ill are those that are the most likely to be early adopters of health insurance.[40] As a consequence, if the subscription ratio is low, the pool of subscribers will be composed of a population with a high risk of getting ill. In the case of private insurance, this means that the premium will be expensive, at it covers an event whose likeliness is high. In the case of public insurance, as for NCMS or URBMI, the insurance premium is fixed *ex-ante*, independently of the number of subscribers and their characteristics. It is then possible that the insurance premium that is charged may not be sufficient to cover the healthcare reimbursement level required for the pool of subscribers. This can explain the failure of previous attempts to set up public insurance at the local level prior to 2003. In addition, this shows the importance of having a large part of the population subscribing for the scheme to work successfully. One of the particularities of the Chinese model is that it is very decentralized, with insurance funds pooled and managed at county level. This explains why there is the need for a large number of subscribers in each municipality and not only at the global level. In other words, this implies a low variance in the subscription ratio between municipalities. This is a necessary condition to ensure the relatively homogeneous cost of this public insurance across the territory.

Impact of Insurance on Demand and Prices

The development of insurance schemes has an impact on the market equilibrium:

- It increases demand both by extending the pool of potential customers and through an induced demand mechanism;
- Ultimately, it tends to drive up prices.

Induced Demand

Following the definition of McGuire (2000),[41] under induced demand, a physician takes an action to shift the patient's demand curve in the direction of the physician's own interests. Physicians can affect such a shift, because they have more information regarding the patient's condition and treatment options than the patient. This is what is defined as *asymmetry of information*.

Given the way public hospitals currently operate (as described earlier), their doctors and staff can receive a supplementary income, via a series of opaque rules. This supplementary income is reliant on both the hospital activity, as a profit-making business, and public health insurance allowing patients to afford healthcare access.

It is therefore easy to understand why doctors might be encouraged to take steps to increase their most lucrative practices: increasing the number of appointments, over-prescribing and over-diagnosing. Consequently, the "operational objective" for treatment personnel and for doctors includes maximizing profits. Within this set-up, both hospital management and medical staff benefit from the increased activity. An occupation with a remuneration that was, until recently, disconnected from any profit-driven influence becomes a race for financial gain. Today, medication sales make up over 40% of the turnover of public health establishments. On the flip side, patients have to bear with the cost of healthcare increasing drastically in parallel with the over-consumption of treatment, creating a climate of ever-growing tension between medical staff, doctors and patients.

The Healthcare Price Increase

NCMS insurance programmes make healthcare services accessible to those who were previously unable to afford them due to not being covered by

Table 6.1 China GDP and healthcare spending (billion $)

Year	GDP	Healthcare spending (billion $)	Healthcare spending (% GDP)
2004	193	90.8	4.70
2009	4990	254.5	5.10
2014	10,355	590.2	5.70

any insurance scheme. As a result, providers have a greater population of potential patients. According to the theoretical literature, these healthcare providers may have an incentive to increase the price of their healthcare services to maximize profits to the greatest extent compatible with the continued financial viability of patients being treated in their facilities. Feldstein (1970)[42] showed that physicians raise their fees when insurance becomes more extensive—i.e., when a large part of the population becomes covered by health insurance. Chiu (1997)[43] uses a formal model to show that the introduction of insurance increases the equilibrium price of healthcare. In such cases, it is uncertain whether or not insurance will reduce the financial burden of ill people. Chiu (1997)[44] shows that if the supply of healthcare is sufficiently price inelastic, this increase in price always leads to a reduction in consumer welfare.

These mechanisms explain the tremendous increase in healthcare expenditure over the past decade (Table 6.1).

Out-of-Pocket Amounts

The out-of-pocket amount is the amount a patient has left to pay that is not covered by health insurance.

There is no full consensus in the literature on the impact of insurance schemes on out-of-pocket payments. Liu and Zhao (2014)[45] found that the Urban Resident Basic Medical Insurance (URBMI), designed for urban residents without a formal employment contract, has not reduced total out-of-pocket health expense but Babiarz et al. (2010)[46] found a reduction in the total out-of-pocket health expense. Wang (2005)[47] suggests that the government's financial support to the NCMS does not help rural inhabitants, as this support actually passes directly to healthcare providers via higher prices, over-prescription, and the over-use of high-tech equipment. However, the literature tends to find a positive effect for the low-income families total out-of-pocket expenses.

Overall, in both rural and urban areas, the introduction of various forms of public health insurance reduced the percentage of out-of-pocket charges for patients (without health insurance, this percentage is 100%). Between the 1990s and the present day, the percentage of out-of-pocket charges has decreased in relation to total expense. According to a report by the World Health Organisation (WHO),[48] in 1995 the figure was 46.4%, then rose to 59% in 2000, and now stands at 34.9% (Fig. 6.4). However, on one the hand, this figure does not take into account the significant geographical inequalities, particularly between cities and rural areas. On the other hand, at the same time there has been a considerable increase in expenditure, both as a percentage of GDP (from 4.55% in 2006 to 5.15% in 2011)[49] and per capita. This expenditure went up from RMB 178 in 1995 to RMB 362 in 2000, and now stands at RMB 1801.

As % of Total Healthcare Expenditure (THE)

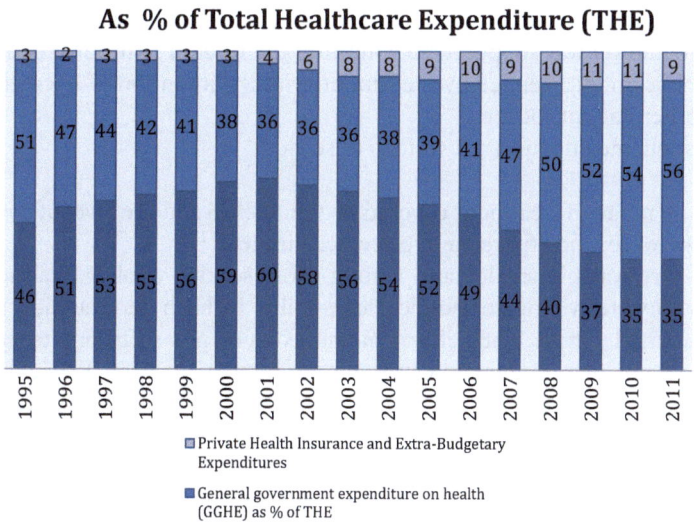

Fig. 6.4 Healthcare expenditure in China, 1995–2011. World Health Organisation (see http://apps.who.int//nha/database)

The result of this is that, despite an appreciable improvement in health insurance cover, out-of-pocket charges have risen considerably.

Public Health Insurance as a Response to a Concentrated Demand

A direct consequence of this concentrated demand on Level 3 hospitals was that they became over-burdened, leading to incredibly long queues and very short consultation times. The situation was exacerbated by the fact that these establishments were able to offer high-performance equipment and quality treatment. At the same time the primary care centres, along with Level 1 and a number of Level 2 hospitals, found their range of facilities, including their equipment, were being under-used. The proportion of beds in use was above 100% in the top-ranked hospitals, while it was at 80% in Level 2 establishments, and 55% in Level 1 establishments.[50] All this occurred at a time when a large proportion of the population was in a situation of financial instability. With expenditure increasing rapidly, making healthcare less financially accessible, this created a certain amount of tension between patients and medical staff at the top-ranked hospitals.

When public health insurance was introduced in rural areas in 2003, its implementation was supposed to condition the level of reimbursement to the establishment attended by the patient, with the intention of re-creating a smoother patient journey.

This scheme encountered various obstacles:

- The range of treatment covered by the NCMS and the level of coverage were, and still remain, extremely limited.[51]
- There was higher demand among those seeking quality treatment, who were willing to sacrifice accessibility in both geographical and financial terms. The reform measures were not sufficient to cope with the geographic upheavals among the patient base. Free clinics, primary care centres and Level 1 hospitals were shunned, in favour of Level 2 and especially Level 3 hospitals.

As a consequence, the launch of public health insurance programmes and in particular the NCMS programme, was not sufficient to force a new pathway of healthcare onto the patient, even with the huge increase in the reimbursement rate observed during the past decade.

First Results: Effect on Health
and Healthcare Access

Evidence in the literature on the effect of these public health insurance programmes on healthcare utilization is actually mixed. Wagstaff et al. (2009),[52] Lei and Lin (2009),[53] Liu and Zhao (2014)[54] have found that these programmes have significantly increased the utilization of formal medical services, including both outpatient and inpatient care. Liu and Zhao, (2014) also found that this programme has improved medical care utilization especially for children, members of low-income families and residents in the relatively poor western region.

Despite the fact that the main purpose of the NCMS is to improve the affordability of healthcare services, empirical evaluations have not found solid evidence of a decrease in out-of-pocket health expenditure (per visit) owing to the NCMS (Wagstaff et al. 2009; Lei and Lin, 2009). It has been suggested that suppliers may have exploited the benefit by increasing the price of healthcare services or increasing the number of visits or unnecessary tests or procedures for each patient, resulting in an increase in total healthcare expenses.

Besides, it is not clear whether more (less) healthcare utilization means better (worse) self-assessment of health status. On the one hand, more healthcare utilization can lead to a better objective and hence subjective health status; on the other hand, more healthcare utilization may lead to more awareness or anxiety of latent diseases (Koszegi, 2006).[55] Lei and Lin's (2009) found no significant improvement in self-reported health status or sickness or injury in the immediate four weeks after families acquired insurance coverage. Milcent and Wu (2015)[56] found a positive extensive margin: individuals feel better about their health status when covered by the NCMS. However, there is no intensive margin: an individual's self-assessed health status does not improve with the number of years enrolled in the programme. Secondly, they found a positive general equilibrium effect of introducing the NCMS programme on non-participants in NCMS counties. This effect accumulated over time.

In parallel, the government has to deal with two major issues:

- The increase in elderly people that restricts the share of public funding allocated to health expenditure, with the rising burden of chronic non-communicable diseases.
- The increase in medical healthcare costs due to local suppliers in a monopoly position, over-prescriptions and innovative treatments.

Private Health Insurance

Among the series of healthcare system reforms, the NDRC announced in March 2012 its clear intention to expand private health insurance.

A new regulation in 2014 enabled insurers, domestic and foreign, to invest and own more than one company in the same segment of the industry. Foreign companies (as well as domestic investors) may now own a stake in more than one insurance company that sells similar types of products. In addition, investors' stakes are now suppressed, alleviating foreign enterprises of the burden to rely on hard cash to finance acquisitions. In July 2015, newspapers articles including those in *China Daily* mentioned a press conference where Ma Xioawei, NDRC vice-minister, declared that the Chinese government supported commercial health insurance, particularly for older people, whose number had reached 202 million by 2013. This speech echoed the official document published by the State Council one year earlier.

What is the effect of private health insurance on the market? As we said, the reimbursement rate and the basket covered by public health insurance schemes are insufficient to fully satisfy healthcare demand. The Chinese population faces a contradictory situation. Even if 95% of the population is covered by one of the three major public health insurance schemes, the reimbursement rate is still insufficient leading to excessive out-of-pocket expenses. The important effort to increase the reimbursement rate by the central government was not enough to offset the increase in healthcare prices (in absolute value). Unlike public health insurance, private health insurance adjusts the premium according to willingness-to-pay and the intended healthcare basket covered taking into account the policyholder's characteristics. Private health insurance is more flexible in the healthcare package offered. Schemes can propose a supplementary share of reimbursement to healthcare covered by a public insurance scheme and cover additional packages of healthcare not covered by public health insurance.

The Rise of Private Health Insurance

In today's China, the rise of private health insurance is supported by the emergence of an upper middle class and self-employed workers. The upper middle class is defined by having a monthly disposable income of between RMB 10,000 and RMB 40,000.[57] They live mainly in urban areas and account for around 6% of the total urban households. They are the core target market for private insurance companies that reach out to them through direct marketing, as anyone travelling in Chinese cities will have experienced when receiving SMS adverts for health insurance policies on their mobile phone.

The market for personal insurance represented a turnover of RMB 1.02 thousand billion (or $167 billion) in 2012, and it reached RMB 1.3 thousand billion (or $210 billion) by 2014.[58] There are two predominant players in this market, Ping'an Life and China Life, with 40% of the market share.[59] However, this market includes life insurance and accident insurance as well. The healthcare insurance market itself is very recent and still remains quite small at RMB 79 billion in 2010[60] up to RMB 241 billion in 2015 (for total medical insurance premiums).[61]

Current Obstacles to the Rise

The first obstacles to the development of the private insurance market are quite structural: (1) the existence of universal coverage through the three main public insurance schemes; and (2) the lack of a unified reliable database covering the full patient population with their medical records, which creates major limits to forecasting health risk.

On top of this, it seems that services offered by insurance companies only partially meet demand. They are, to a large extent, designed mainly to ensure market solvency, when customers' expectations tend to become increasingly inclined toward healthcare quality. A study from McKinsey Consulting Group[62] shows that the biggest unmet need of upper-middle-class consumers (with yearly incomes above RMB 80,000) is quality of healthcare, of which more than two-thirds of respondents is not satisfied with.

Private healthcare insurance schemes sometimes enable a reduction in waiting time to visit a doctor (through services such as the green lane), direct billing and the provision of second opinions, but this is at a very early stage compared to customer expectations.

It seems that available products are still quite undifferentiated. Market leaders (such as PICC Health, Ping'an Health, Kunlun Health, Hexie Health) have very similar products addressing the same market segments. Hence they mainly compete on price, leading to profit margins that are too narrow to really develop the market.

Besides, private insurance healthcare is still often part of a more global package including critical illness insurance, disability insurance and elderly insurance for instance. As a consequence, consumers do not have a clear understanding of what their insurance subscription actually includes.

In summary, the market for private insurance has recently been booming but still falls short of expectations. Its offers are progressively getting more advanced and refined, but solely targeted at the urban upper middle class, which contributes to the increasing split of the Chinese healthcare market into different silos (see Chap. 10).

NOTES

1. D. Blumenthal and W.N. Hsiao, "Privatization and its Discontents—The Evolving Chinese Healthcare System," The New England Journal of Medicine, Vol. 353, No. 22, 2005, pp. 1165–1170.
2. Government insurance system. See further in this section.
3. Centre for Health Statistics and Information, 2004.
4. H. Wang, M. Gusmano, and Q. Cao, "An Evaluation of the Policy on Community Health Organisations in China: Will the Priority of New Healthcare Reform in China be a Success?" Health Policy, Vol. 99, No. 1, 2011, pp. 37–43.
5. The central government has considerably relaxed the residence permit system in order to encourage economic growth.
6. Therese Hesketh and Wei Xingzhu, "Health in China: From Mao to Market Reform," The British Medical Journal, No. 314, 1997, pp. 1543–1545.
7. Winnie Yip and William C. Hsiao, "What Drove the Cycles of Chinese Health System Reforms?" Health Systems & Reform, Vol. 1, No. 1, 2015, pp. 52–61.
8. Xingzhu Liu and Junle Wang, "An Introduction to China's Health Care System," Journal of Public Health Policy, Vol. 12, No. 1, 1991, pp. 104–116.
9. This *sanji zhi* system is often translated as "County-township-village Three-tier Healthcare System".
10. See Chap. 2 for more details.
11. John S. Akin, William H. Dow, Peter M. Lance, and Chung-Ping A. Loh, "Changes in Access to Health Care in China, 1989–1997," art. cit.
12. Chinese Ministry of Health, Research Report on China National Health Accounts, Beijing, 2004; Winnie Yip and William C. Hsiao, "The Chinese Health System at a Crossroads," Health Affairs, Vol. 27, No. 2, 2008, pp. 460–468. See the section on how the establishments were funded for further details.
13. Profit maximization under the nil profit constraint.
14. See Chapter 3, end of page 39
15. Liu Yuanli and Keqin Rao, "Providing Health Insurance in Rural China: From Research to Policy," Journal of Health Politics, Policy and Law, Vol. 1, 2006, pp. 71–92.

16. S.L. Barber and L. Yao, "Development and Status of Health Insurance Systems in China," The International Journal of Health Planning and Management, 2011.

17. Carine Milcent, "Healthcare-seeking Behaviour Changes in Rural China: The Situation of Farmers," Working Paper, PSE No. 201423, 2015; Gerald Bloom and Gu Xingyuan, "Health Sector Reform: Lessons from China," Social Science and Medicine, Vol. 45, No. 3, 1997, pp. 351–360; Therese Hesketh and Weixing Zhu, "Health in China: The Healthcare Market," The British Medical Journal, No. 314, 1997, pp. 1616–1618; Jun Gao, Shenglan Tang, Rachel Tolhurst, and Keqing Rao, "Changing Access to Health Services in Urban China: Implications for Equity," Health Policy and Planning, Vol. 16, No. 3, 2001, pp. 302–312.

18. The programme will also be offered in urban districts and county-level cities that include rural residents.

19. S.L. Barber and L. Yao, "Development and Status of Health Insurance Systems in China," The International Journal of Health Planning and Management, 2011.

20. MoHRSS, 2013.

21. In rural areas, the public health insurance scheme mentioned here is known as the NCMS, or New Co-operative Medical Scheme.

22. Here, we are referring to the period after the NCMS was introduced in the country.

23. Joe C.B. Leung and Yuebin Xu, China's Social Welfare: The Third Turning Point, ed. China Today, 2015.

24. China has 34 provincial-level administrative units: 23 provinces, four municipalities (Beijing, Tianjin, Shanghai, Chongqing), five autonomous regions (Guangxi, Inner Mongolia, Tibet, Ningxia, Xinjiang); and two special administrative regions (Hong Kong, Macau).

25. Y.B. Xu and X.M. Song, A Study on the Design and Implementation of the Rural Medical Assistance Program in China: Consultation Report to the Ministry of Health, unpublished, 2006.

26. Y.B. Xu and X.L. Zhang, "Rural Social Protection in China: Reform, Performance and Challenges," In J. Midgley and K.L. Tangs (eds.), Social Policy and Poverty in East Asia: The Role of Social Security, London: Routledge, pp. 116–127, 2010.

27. Ministry of Civil Affairs, 2012 Annual Statistical Report on Social Service Development, 2012.

28. Q. Meng and S. Tang, Universal Health Care Coverage in China: Challenges and Opportunities, Procedia—Social and Behavioral Sciences, Vol. 77, pp. 330–340.

29. J. Pan and D. Shallcross, "Geographic Distribution of Hospital Beds Throughout China: A County-level Econometric Analysis," International Journal for Equity in Health, Vol. 15, 2016.

30. M. Stabile and S. Thomson, "The Changing Role of Government in Financing Health Care: An International Perspective," Journal of Economic Literature, Vol. 52, No. 2, 2014.
31. Excluding pilot programmes.
32. The non-portability of rights is partially due to the decentralized level of the public healthcare system implemented.
33. H. Wang, "A Dilemma of Chinese Healthcare Reform: How to Re-define Government Roles?" China Economic Review, Vol. 20, No. 4, 2009, pp. 598–604.
34. C. Dong and Y. Song, Impacts of Different Insurance Schemes on Non-communicable Diseases Services Utilization, Beijing: World Bank, 2009.
35. H. Wang, "A Dilemma of Chinese Healthcare Reform: How to Re-define Government Roles?" China Economic Review, Vol. 20, No. 4, 2009, pp. 598–604.
36. H. Liu, S. Gao, and J.A. Rizzo, "The Expansion of Public Health Insurance and the Demand for Private Health Insurance in Rural China," China Economic Review, Vol. 22, No. 1, 2011, pp. 28–41.
37. H. Wang, M.K. Gusmano, and Q. Cao, "An Evaluation of the Policy on Community Health Organizations in China: Will the Priority of New Healthcare Reform in China be a Success?" Health Policy, Vol. 99, No. 1, 2011, pp. 37–43.
38. A. Wagstaff and S. Yu, "Do Health Sector Reforms have their Intended Impacts? The World Bank's Health VIII Project in Gansu Province, China," Journal of Health Economics, Vol. 26, No. 3, 2007, pp. 505–535.
39. Carine Milcent and Binzhen Wu, "How Do You Feel? The Effect of the New Cooperative Medical Scheme in China," The Journal of Development Studies, Vol. 51, No. 12, 2015.
40. Pour plus de détails, il faut se référer aux modèles d'assurance. L'un des premiers modèles sur la sélection adverse est le modèle d'Akerlof. G. Akerlof, "The Market for 'Lemons': Quality Uncertainty and the Market Mechanism," The Quarterly Journal of Economics, Vol. 84, No. 3, 1970.
41. T. McGuire, "Physician Agency," In A.J. Culyer and J.P. Newhouse (eds.), The Handbook of Health Economics, Vol. 1, pp. 462–536, Amsterdam: Elsevier, 2000.
42. M. Feldstein, "The Rising Price of Physicians' Service," Review of Economics and Statistics, Vol. 52, 1970, pp. 121–133.
43. W. Chiu, "Health Insurance and the Welfare of Healthcare Consumers," Journal of Public Economics, Vol. 64, No. 1, 1997, pp. 125–133.
44. Ibid.
45. H. Hong Liu and Z. Zhong Zhao, "Does Health Insurance Matter? Evidence from China's Urban Resident Basic Medical Insurance," Journal of Comparative Economics, Vol. 42, No. 4, 2014, pp. 1007–1020.

46. K.S. Babiarz, G. Miller, H. Yi, L. Zhang, and S. Rozelle, "New Evidence on the Impact of China's New Rural Cooperative Medical Scheme and its Implications for Rural Primary Healthcare: Multivariate difference-in-difference Analysis," British Medical Journal, 2010, pp. 341–350.
47. H. Wang, "Impacts of Medicine Price on New Cooperative Medical Scheme," China Price, Vol. 11, 2005, pp. 23–24 (in Chinese).
48. Shyama Kuruvilla, Julian Schweitzer, David Bishai, Sadia Chowdhury, Daniele Caramani, Laura Frost, Rafael Cortez, Bernadette Daelmans, Andres de Francisco, Taghreed Adam, Robert Cohen, Y. Natalia Alfonso, Jennifer Franz-Vasdeki, Seemeen Saadat, Beth Anne Pratt, Beatrice Eugster, Sarah Bandali, Pritha Venkatachalam, Rachael Hinton, John Murray, Sharon Arscott-Mills, Henrik Axelson, Blerta Maliqi, Intissar Sarker, Rama Lakshminarayanan, Troy Jacobs, Susan Jacks, Elizabeth Mason, Abdul Ghaffar, Nicholas Mays, Carole Presern, and Flavia Bustreo, "Success Factors for Women's and Children's Health Study Groups," Bulletin of World Health Organisation, Vol. 92, No. 7, 2014, pp. 533–544. www.who.int/pmnch/successfactors/en. Accessed 31 October 2016. The source data are drawn from the China Health Statistics Yearbook.
49. China Health Statistical Yearbook, 2012.
50. World Health Organization (see http://apps.who.int//nha/database) http://www.mckinsey.com/~/media/mckinsey/dotcom/client_service/healthcare%20systems%20and%20services/health%20international/hi10_china_healthcare_reform.ashx. Accessed September 2017.
51. Carine Milcent and Binzhen Wu "How Do You Feel? The Effect of the New Cooperative Medical Scheme in China," The Journal of Development Studies, Vol. 51, No. 12, 2015, pp. 1585–1602.
52. A. Wagstaff, M. Lindelow, J. Gao, L. Xu, and J. Qian, "Extending Health Insurance to the Rural Population: An Impact Evaluation of China's New Cooperative Medical Scheme," Journal of Health Economics, Vol. 28, 2009, pp. 1–19.
53. X. Lei and S. Lin, "The New Cooperative Medical Scheme in Rural China: Does More Coverage Mean More Service and Better Health?" Health Economics, Vol. 18, 2009, pp. 25–46.
54. H. Hong Liu and Z. Zhong Zhao, "Does Health Insurance Matter? Evidence from China's Urban Resident Basic Medical Insurance," Journal of Comparative Economics, Vol. 42, No. 4, 2014, pp. 1007–1020.
55. B. Koszegi, "Emotional Agency," The Quarterly Journal of Economics, Vol. 121, No. 1, 2006, pp. 121–155.
56. C. Milcent and B. Wu, "How Do You Feel? The Effect of the New Cooperative Medical Scheme in China," Journal of Development Studies, Vol. 51, No. 12, 2015, pp. 1585–1602.
57. China Yearbook, PwC Analysis 2015, www.pwccn.com. Accessed May 2016.

58. China Insurance Regulatory Commission, 2014.
59. S.L. Barber and L. Yao, Health Insurance Systems in China: A Briefing Note, World Health Report (2010), Background Paper 37, Geneva, Switzerland: World Health Organization, 2010.
60. China Insurance, Yearbook, 2010.
61. China Insurance, Yearbook 2014.
62. Ng Alexander and Süssmuth Dyckerhoff Claudia, "Private Health Insurance in China: Finding the Winning Formula," Health International is published by McKinsey's Healthcare Systems and McKinsey & Company, 2012.

Results from the 2012 McKinsey Patient & Physician Survey among more than 1000 upper-middle-class consumers (yearly income greater than RMB 80,000).

BIBLIOGRAPHY

Akerlof, G., "The Market for 'Lemons': Quality Uncertainty and the Market Mechanism," The Quarterly Journal of Economics, Vol. 84, No. 3, 1970.

Akin, John S., William H. Dow, Peter M. Lance, and Chung-Ping A. Loh, "Changes in Access to Health Care in China, 1989–1997," Health Policy, Vol. 20, 2005.

Alexander, Ng, and Süssmuth Dyckerhoff Claudia, "Private Health Insurance in China: Finding the Winning Formula," Health International is published by McKinsey's Healthcare Systems and McKinsey & Company, 2012.

Babiarz, K.S., G. Miller, H. Yi, L. Zhang, and S. Rozelle, "New Evidence on the Impact of China's New Rural Cooperative Medical Scheme and its Implications for Rural Primary Healthcare: Multivariate differencePinPdifference Analysis," British Medical Journal, 2010, pp. 341–350.

Barber, S.L., and L. Yao, "Development and Status of Health Insurance Systems in China," The International Journal of Health Planning and Management, 2011.

Barber, S.L., and L. Yao, Health Insurance Systems in China: A Briefing Note, World Health Report (2010), Background Paper 37, Geneva, Switzerland: World Health Organization, 2010.

Bloom, Gerald, and Gu Xingyuan, "Health Sector Reform: Lessons from China," Social Science and Medicine, Vol. 45, No. 3, 1997, pp. 351–360.

Blumenthal, D., and W.N. Hsiao, "Privatization and its Discontents—The Evolving Chinese Healthcare System," The New England Journal of Medicine, Vol. 353, No. 22, 2005, pp. 1165–1170.

Chiu, W., "Health Insurance and the Welfare of Healthcare Consumers," Journal of Public Economics, Vol. 64, No. 1, 1997, pp. 125–133.

Dong, C., and Y. Song, Impacts of Different Insurance Schemes on Non-communicable Diseases Services Utilization, Beijing: World Bank, 2009.

Feldstein, M., "The Rising Price of Physicians' Service," Review of Economics and Statistics, Vol. 52, 1970, pp. 121–133.

Gao, Jun, Shenglan Tang, Rachel Tolhurst, and Keqing Rao, "Changing Access to Health Services in Urban China: Implications for Equity," Health Policy and Planning, Vol. 16, No. 3, 2001, pp. 302–312.

Hesketh, Therese, and Wei Xingzhu, "Health in China: From Mao to Market Reform," The British Medical Journal, No. 314, 1997, pp. 1543–1545.

Hong Liu, H., and Z. Zhong Zhao, "Does Health Insurance Matter? Evidence from China's Urban Resident Basic Medical Insurance," Journal of Comparative Economics, Vol. 42, No. 4, 2014, pp. 1007–1020.

Koszegi, B., "Emotional Agency," The Quarterly Journal of Economics, Vol. 121, No. 1, 2006, pp. 121–155.

Kuruvilla, Shyama, Julian Schweitzer, David Bishai, Sadia Chowdhury, Daniele Caramani, Laura Frost, Rafael Cortez, Bernadette Daelmans, Andres de Francisco, Taghreed Adam, Robert Cohen, Y. Natalia Alfonso, Jennifer Franz-Vasdeki, Seemeen Saadat, Beth Anne Pratt, Beatrice Eugster, Sarah Bandali, Pritha Venkatachalam, Rachael Hinton, John Murray, Sharon Arscott-Mills, Henrik Axelson, Blerta Maliqi, Intissar Sarker, Rama Lakshminarayanan, Troy Jacobs, Susan Jacks, Elizabeth Mason, Abdul Ghaffar, Nicholas Mays, Carole Presern, and Flavia Bustreo, "Success Factors for Women's and Children's Health Study Groups," Bulletin of World Health Organisation, Vol. 92, No. 7, 2014, pp. 533–544. www.who.int/pmnch/successfactors/en. Accessed 31 October 2016. The source data are drawn from the China Health Statistics Yearbook.

Lei, X., and S. Lin, "The New Cooperative Medical Scheme in Rural China: Does More Coverage Mean More Service and Better Health?" Health Economics, Vol. 18, 2009, pp. 25–46.

Leung, Joe C. B., and Yuebin Xu, China's Social Welfare: The Third Turning Point, ed. China Today, 2015.

Liu, H., S. Gao, and J.A. Rizzo, "The Expansion of Public Health Insurance and the Demand for Private Health Insurance in Rural China," China Economic Review, Vol. 22, No. 1, 2011, pp. 28–41.

Liu, Xingzhu, and Junle Wang, "An Introduction to China's Health Care System," Journal of Public Health Policy, Vol. 12, No. 1, 1991, pp. 104–116.

McGuire, T., "Physician Agency," In A.J. Culyer and J.P. Newhouse (eds.), The Handbook of Health Economics, Vol. 1, pp. 462–536, Amsterdam: Elsevier, 2000.

Meng, Q., and S. Tang, "Universal Health Care Coverage in China: Challenges and Opportunities," Procedia—Social and Behavioral Sciences, Vol. 77, pp. 330–340.

Milcent, Carine, "Healthcare-seeking Behaviour Changes in Rural China: The Situation of Farmers," Working Paper, PSE No. 201423, 2015.

Milcent, Carine, and Binzhen Wu, "How Do You Feel? The Effect of the New Cooperative Medical Scheme in China," The Journal of Development Studies, Vol. 51, No. 12, 2015, pp. 1585–1602.

Ministry of Civil Affairs, 2012 Annual Statistical Report on Social Service Development, 2012.

Pan, J., and D. Shallcross, "Geographic Distribution of Hospital Beds Throughout China: A County-level Econometric Analysis," International Journal for Equity in Health, Vol. 15, 2016.

Stabile, M., and S. Thomson, "The Changing Role of Government in Financing Health Care: An International Perspective," Journal of Economy Literature, Vol. 52, No. 2, 2014.

Wagstaff, A., M. Lindelow, J. Gao, L. Xu, and J. Qian, "Extending Health Insurance to the Rural Population: An Impact Evaluation of China's New Cooperative Medical Scheme," Journal of Health Economics, Vol. 28, 2009, pp. 1–19.

Wagstaff, A., and S. Yu, "Do Health Sector Reforms have their Intended Impacts? The World Bank's Health VIII Project in Gansu Province, China," Journal of Health Economics, Vol. 26, No. 3, 2007, pp. 505–535.

Wang, H., "Impacts of Medicine Price on New Cooperative Medical Scheme," China Price, Vol. 11, 2005, pp. 23–24 (in Chineses).

Wang, H., "A Dilemma of Chinese Healthcare Reform: How to Re-define Government Roles?" China Economic Review, Vol. 20, No. 4, 2009, pp. 598–604.

Wang, H., M. Gusmano, and Q. Cao, "An Evaluation of the Policy on Community Health Organisations in China: Will the Priority of New Healthcare Reform in China be a Success?" Health Policy, Vol. 99, No. 1, 2011, pp. 37–43.

Xu, Y.B., and X.M. Song, A Study on the Design and Implementation of the Rural Medical Assistance Program in China: Consultation Report to the Ministry of Health, Unpublished, 2006.

Xu, Y.B., and X.L. Zhang, "Rural Social Protection in China: Reform, Performance and Challenges," In J. Midgley and K.L. Tangs (eds.), Social Policy and Poverty in East Asia: The Role of Social Security, London: Routledge, pp. 116–127, 2010.

Yip, Winnie, and William C. Hsiao, "The Chinese Health System at a Crossroads," Health Affairs, Vol. 27, No. 2, 2008, pp. 460–468.

Yip, Winnie, and William C. Hsiao, "What Drove the Cycles of Chinese Health System Reforms?" Health Systems & Reform, Vol. 1, No. 1, 2015, pp. 52–61.

Yuanli, Liu, and Keqin Rao, "Providing Health Insurance in Rural China: From Research to Policy," Journal of Health Politics, Policy and Law, Vol. 1, 2006, pp. 71–92.

CHAPTER 7

The Medical Drug Market and its Reforms

Abstract China is the second largest pharmaceutical market in the world. This sector grew by 21.4% between 2002 and 2012. In OECD countries, spending on medical drugs accounted for approximately 17% of total health spending or 1.5% of gross domestic product (GDP) in 2009. That same year, spending on pharmaceutical products in China represented 43% of the total healthcare expenditure. Aware of the issue, the Chinese government has reacted. A limitation on the hospital mark-up on drugs has been implemented and a list of key drugs that are considered essential has been set up. Drugs on this list have to be accessible to everyone, with a regulated price to be kept as low as possible. To keep prices low, procurement is made through centralized bidding at provincial level, pharmaceutical companies delivering directly to medical facilities. Yet, in the field, the reality remains at times complex, with different ways to circumvent these constraints.

Keywords Medical drug market • The essential medicines list • Over the counter (OTC) drugs • Prescribed drugs

In OECD countries, spending on medical drugs accounted for approximately 17% of total health spending or 1.5% of gross domestic product

(GDP) in 2009.[1] That same year, spending on pharmaceutical products in China represented 43% of total healthcare expenditure (Yip et al. 2012).[2]

Aware of the issue, the Chinese government has been trying to fix this problem. Its main tool has been to set up a list of key drugs that are considered essential, with the basic idea that these drugs must be accessible to everyone, with a regulated price to be kept as low as possible.

To keep prices low, procurement is made through centralized bidding; provinces purchase through the central level and pharmaceutical companies deliver directly to medical facilities. Yet, in the field, the reality remains somewhat complex. In this chapter, we will see that in the field, there are different ways to circumvent these constraints.

BACKGROUND

China is the second largest pharmaceutical market in the world. This sector grew by 21.4% between 2002 and 2012. China is also one of the heaviest users of antibiotics, with 70% of prescriptions containing antibiotics.[3] One of the reasons for this situation is the way hospitals are financed in China. Indeed, in a case of hospital admission, whatever the country, the patient is quite passive, rarely taking part in the decision to undergo a certain treatment. On the other hand, there is a strong difference between Asian and Western countries as far as outpatients are concerned. The physician is not consulted in his or her practice but within a hospital. Medicine is then supplied at the end of the consultation, the patient having no real choice as to whether to purchase it or not. The patient does not have to go to a separate pharmacy to buy medicines either. This empowers the physician with a dual role, both supplier of health services and supplier of health goods. At the end of the consultation, the invoice includes both, with a split that is often hard to make out.

As a consequence, there is an inverse relationship between the price asked for medical drugs and the funding for the hospital; when funding decreased the price of drugs increased. This phenomenon has been empirically described (Eggleston et al. 2008). A few years ago, drugs accounted for almost half of health spending. Over-prescription and over-use of high-tech diagnosis equipment is often pointed to as one of the main sources of soaring health costs.

The health system is usually considered costlier and more sophisticated than is medically justified. This triggered government actions which eventually led to a downward trend in the share of medicines in overall health expenditure. According to Ding et al. (2016),[4] over-prescription of antibiotics, injections and adrenal corticosteroids has been decreasing since the series of health reforms in 2009.

As part of this series of reforms, the central government limited the drug mark-up for public healthcare facilities. In hospitals, medical staff can now only charge 15% over the wholesale price for drugs. This limitation in the mark-up was initially introduced to reduce the healthcare cost burden on patients.

Public primary healthcare facilities were also obliged to prescribe and dispense drugs from the National Essential Medicines List (National EML) when possible. All public primary healthcare settings were required to stock only drugs from the EML for the common treatable diseases. They were also required to sell them at zero-profit (the zero-profit policy meant drugs on the EML have to be sold at cost).

As a compensation mechanism, public health insurance schemes that cover all essential medicines usually reimburse public health facilities at a higher reimbursement rate for drugs on the EML. Yet, because of the non-centralization and diversity of the Chinese healthcare system, the reimbursement rate still varies between Chinese provinces.

STRUCTURE OF THE MEDICAL DRUG MARKET

In order to permit drug prices to be determined by market forces, the National Development and Reform Commission (NDRC) removed Article 55 of the Drug Administration Law. From 1 June 2015, the Chinese administrative bodies ceased to set drug prices. Formally, the NDRC issued an "Opinion on the Promotion of Drug Price Reform".[5] This effort has been simultaneous in changing both the supply and distribution structures.

On the Supply Side: A Very Fragmented Market

The 12th Five Year plan pointed out as a weakness the fragmentation of the pharmaceutical and medical supply market in China. There are more than 6000 pharmaceutical companies in China today. The 10 biggest firms only account for 15% of the total market. For consumable medical suppliers, there are more than 15,000 different companies. The 30 biggest only account for 27% of the market.

The advantage of such a situation is a strong competitive environment, with no dominant player. On the flip side, it makes the control of this industry more difficult, creating risks about the quality of products that are offered to consumers. To counterbalance this, a round of directives and new norms has been implemented since 2009. For example:

- In October 2014, the China Food and Drug Administration (CFDA) defined four principles of good practice for factories manufacturing medical devices;[6] they were integrated into the New Good Manufacturing Practice (GMP), whose revised version was released during the seventeenth workshop of the CFDA on 12 December 2014 and implemented in 2015.[7]
- The new edition of *Pharmacopoeia* published in 2015 and implemented from 2016 increases the focus on the quality of drugs in China.[8]

In parallel, the 12th Five Year Plan has been encouraging the concentration of the industry and the creation of a handful of financially strong pharmaceutical companies. For instance, it is interesting to note that criteria from GMP include parameters such as the financial stability of the manufacturer. Larger firms also tend to receive a larger part of support and subsidies from provincial governments, such as support for research and development (R&D) for instance. As a direct consequence, smaller companies are being wiped out.[9] From 2010 to 2013, the number of pharmaceutical companies has shrunk from 7038 to 6525.

This evolution can be interpreted as a deliberate action to transform the market and concentrate the offer into a small number of larger firms. These companies would have significant assets and high R&D capabilities, with the ability to compete with international pharmaceutical giants in all markets. Smaller players would remain, active mainly on the local markets, to foster competition while offering quality that meets the new standards set by the latest norms.

An Evolving Distribution Landscape

As seen previously, China is a booming market for pharmaceutical products, creating a huge retail business. According to China's Ministry of

Commerce, the retail sale of drugs was 260.7 billion Yuan in 2013, representing 12% growth from the previous year.[10] Since 2010, China's pharmaceutical market has been the world's second largest.[11]

We will study in depth the online drug market in Chap. 9. In short, it has been booming over recent years but not in an orderly fashion. Officially, only over the counter (OTC) transactions are allowed for prescription drugs. Online prescription drugs are not allowed.[12,13,14] As a consequence, many online pharmacies do not comply with applicable Chinese laws and regulations. A study by the Alliance for Safe Online Pharmacies (ASOP)[15] and a LegitScript review[16] shows that 93% of China's online pharmacy market is operated illegally.

To improve the situation, the Chinese government has engaged in efforts since 2013 to crack down on online illegal drug sellers.[17] At that time, the CFDA partnered with China's largest internet search engine, Baidu, in a collaboration targeting rogue pharmacies and to combat illegal online drug sales. The CFDA gave Baidu, and then the other internet search engines, access to its database. This allows the internet company to provide detailed information and warning messages to consumers, empowering such companies with the mission of public service, with all the concerns this may raise.

The same year, the Ministry of Public Security also cracked down on illegal drug sales in an operation called "Operation Cloud". It was followed by other initiatives to curb the number of illegal manufacturers and online sale of drugs. Nowadays, such operations do not only focus on rogue internet pharmacies but also on certified internet OTC pharmacies that engage in unlawful prescription drug sales.

A medicine tracking platform has been implemented to screen for illegal manufacturers and online sales of drugs. Because of the technology mobilized to implement such systems, the tracking platform has been contracted out, to a division of the Alibaba group, Ali Health. This situation created a competitive advantage considered as unfair by rivals leading to some ups (developments) and downs (suspensions) in Ali Health's role as control tower of the drug market. The main grave concern is safety of national data.[18,19,20,21]

REGULATION OF THE MARKET THROUGH THE EML

The Origin of the EML

The World Health Organisation (WHO) initiated the concept of the EML in 1977. The aim is to define a list of drugs, medical devices and vaccines that satisfies the basic healthcare needs of the whole population. This definition, and as a consequence the list itself, can vary, depending on:

- Criteria definition and prioritization in terms of public health relevance, evidence of efficiency, safety and comparative cost-effectiveness;[22]
- Local specificities, for example in China, there is a national list alongside provincial lists.

The essential drugs on the list are supposed to be available at all times and everywhere, in adequate amounts, in appropriate dosage forms, with assured quality and sufficient information, and at a price affordable for the individual, the household and the community. This obviously requires a reasonably structured healthcare system to work. It also assumes appropriate national legislation for ensuring rational drug use.

- *A certain degree of structure to the healthcare system*: The distribution system is one of the keys for the efficient implementation of such an EML. It often appears to be a challenge across most countries and China is no exception.
- *Rational drug use*: The EML supposes a control of the demand. An explosion of the demand will jeopardize the availability of drugs on the list.
- *Role of patents and licensing medicines*: A patent can be a limit to the availability of a drug. With the generic drugs, licensing medicines may ensure the level of quality. In some countries like India or Indonesia, the government has imposed compulsory licensing and price control to ensure better affordability and availability.
- *Affordability*: Price is a key variable for the availability of the drugs on this EML. However, this constraint can be solved by health insurance. A low out-of-pocket amount ensures affordability, whatever the initial price and the level of reimbursement. In China, drugs on the EML are reimbursed by the three public health insurance schemes that cover 95% of the population.

The EML has now been adopted by numerous countries and international organizations (e.g. United Nations Children's Funds—UNICEF, Doctors Without Borders (Médecins sans frontière), etc.).[23]

In China, the Ministry of Health (MoH) initiated the first EML in 1982, including some traditional Chinese medicine recipes. In 2004, the

EML included 2033 products, including 1260 Chinese herbal preparations and 773 chemical and biological medicines. Since then, new versions of the EML have regularly been published,[24,25] with updates usually every two or three years. The integration of treatment for heavier pathologies is currently under study.

Similarly, medical devices have their own list, established by the MoH. The 2009–2011 National Class II Large-Scale Medical Device Allocation Plan has as an objective to regulate the number of medical devices.[26]

On top of this, the prices of some health products have also been capped. NDRC and its regional bureaus set a maximum authorized price for roughly 2700 products. For products that are also on the EML, the retail price is supposed to be below the maximum price fixed by the NDRC.

EML and Public Insurance Schemes

Until 2009, the EML was not taken into account in the reimbursement schemes of health insurance. At that time, a sublist of 307 drugs including 102 from Chinese traditional medicine was established. Drugs on that sublist were covered by public health insurance and their price was capped. From then onwards, the use of these EML drugs was imposed by the central government on public healthcare facilities.

This has a double objective: on one side, to improve the control of costs; on the other side, to give incentive to the population to subscribe to a public insurance scheme. Individuals covered by the Urban Employees Basic Medical Insurance or Urban Residents Basic Medical Insurance can buy medicines in hospitals with their insurance card. However, for patients without these policies, out-of-pocket payments for medicines are high, which impedes access, financial protection and equity for these patients.

Central and Local Responsibilities Regarding the EML[27]

Part of the 2009 reform regarding EML and its subsequent evolutions has been managed by different agencies under the leading group's supervision:[28]

- The Ministry of Health (MoH) is responsible for healthcare services delivery including drugs;

- The National Development and Reform Commission deals with pricing rules and regulations including the National Reimbursement Drug list;
- The Ministry of Human Resources and Social Security manages the government-funded health insurance that reimburses the EML sublist of drugs;
- The State Food and Drug Administration is responsible for health-related product safety;
- The China Insurance Regulatory Commission manages commercial health insurance.

The MoH is responsible for the selection of essential medicines for inclusion in the National EML. The MoH formed a committee consisting of experts in the field of medicine, pharmacy, health insurance, health management, and pricing. These experts are divided into two mutually exclusive groups, a consulting group and a review group.

- The consulting group: the experts evaluate drugs and give their opinions on the drugs. These opinions will be used to defined the candidate drugs list;
- The review group: these experts vote on which drugs have to be included in the draft list using the candidate list.

From the draft list, the government departments give approval and comment on each drug. Some suggestions and comments can be added from the public and other stakeholders. Only after that will the managing authority give the final approval.

Each provincial government has the authority to include more drugs on the EML at provincial level and to publish a provincial drug list. However, provincial governments do not have the authority to remove items from the national EML.[29]

In practice, provincial health administrations define province-specific essential drug lists relevant to the regional context. All the drugs on these lists are then compiled into the National EML. All government-sponsored primary facilities have been using EMLs since the end of 2011. Public insurance compensation for essential medicines is 10–15% higher than for non-essential ones. For Traditional Chinese Medicine (TCM), the compensation ratio is raised by 5–10%. The number of national essential medicines at the primary level in 2009 was 307 of which 102 were TCMs.

As a result of this complex process, a study over 22 provinces shows a positive correlation between the level of wealth of the province and the number of medicines added to the list.[30] This result highlights the inequalities that can exist due to the non-uniformity of the Chinese health system. Other decentralized systems, such as Switzerland for instance, have introduced equalization mechanisms between wealthier and poorer areas, but such a mechanism does not exist between the provinces of China.

The Reform of the EML

The EML and healthcare system in China is described in Table 7.1.

Impact of the EML in China

The implementation of the EML seems to have reached it goal. From 2008 to 2011, medicine expenditure as a percentage of the total health expenditure fell from 41.5% to 37.6%. Figure 7.1 displays the evolution of public healthcare expenditure, private healthcare expenditure and total expenditure on pharmaceuticals as a percentage of total health expenditure.

On the ground, results appear to be a bit more mixed. A study from Zhang et al. (2015),[32] realized in six different counties, shows this heterogeneous situation. For instance, the authors found that no non-essential drugs were used in the village clinics in the county of Changshu. In parallel, they observed that in Maiji district and Acheng district, non-essential drugs were still sold, and with a mark-up. They also noted that village doctors were earning an amount as compensation for using EML drugs in Changshu whereas this amount was only a few hundred RMB in Maiji. Hence, the amount of funds and allocation largely differed from one location to the other. Besides, according to the same study, it was shown that the supply of drugs differs depending on the type of geographical location. Resupplying remote or mountain areas is not worth the effort in terms of cost, so supply is often insufficient.

The way the EML policy is perceived by patients has been studied in detail in an article from Song et al. (2016).[33] Usually speaking, patients have little awareness of the ongoing reform. Nonetheless, they tend to notice a decrease in price and increase in quality of medicines that are listed on the EML.

Table 7.1 EML and the healthcare system in China

Area of reform	Impact on essential medicines
Social security and insurance	• Large-scale in the number of people covered under formal insurance programmes (93.0% coverage in 2011). Insurance reimbursement lists are required to incorporate the medicines on the EML at central and provincial levels, at higher reimbursement rates compared with medicines not on the EML • Inpatient insurance reimbursement rates rose steadily, averaging 46.9% in 2011, including medicines and service fees • Per capita premiums for basic health insurance programmes to increase to 360 Yuan (US$57) per person by 2015, from about US$32 in 2010 → *Essential medicines available at cost* → *Inpatients are reimbursed for essential medicines at **higher** rates than non-essential medicines*
Service delivery	• Reconstruction of the primary care system, including some 2200 county hospitals and 33,000 urban and rural primary care facilities. • In government-run primary care facilities, comprehensive financing reform underway to replace revenue from medicine sales to fund operational costs, through increased insurance and government subsidies • At all government-run primary care facilities, essential medicines are provided at cost (zero profit mark-up): – in urban areas, – in rural areas • Zero mark-up has been expanded as a pilot programme to **selected**: – village clinics, – non–government run primary care facilities, – county hospitals • Link between volume of prescriptions and profit: prescribing and physician remuneration have been disconnected in many primary care facilities. The expected effect is to reduce the incentives for over-prescription. • Centralized procurement and bidding platforms implemented at provincial level, including online purchasing: – Efforts are made to reduce the number of distributors and mark-ups in the distribution chain; – The two-envelope system: the supplier has to submit two sets of documents. One is for the quality and performance standards of the pharmaceutical product; the other is for the pricing proposal. The commercial bid cannot be considered if the document on the drug's quality is not validated by local authorities; – This two-envelope system supposes that authorities have the ability to evaluate the drugs and resources in terms of staff qualification, time and available information; – The implementation at provincial level may introduce geographical disparities in the quality of drugs offered on the market;

(continued)

Table 7.1 (continued)

Area of reform	Impact on essential medicines
	– However, this process ensures at least a certain level of quality, under the tendering system prior to consideration of the commercial bid; – Release of pricing data to foster price transparency. • Digital as an efficiency tool: – Online bidding platforms have been set up to facilitate the purchase of medicines from the EML at the best cost possible. The objective is to circumvent the *de facto* monopoly situation of some wholesalers at local level. These platforms make it possible to regroup all sellers and buyers in one market when they were previously scattered, increasing the level of competition. • Limit of the competition: – In a static context, the bidding process allows the most efficient provider to be selected: the one proposing the lowest possible price at a level of quality required by the performance standards. The two-envelope system allows local authorities to ensure quality standards; – This principle supposes that supply is in adequate quantity and that the number of suppliers remains sufficient to ensure the sustainability of the competitive situation; – In a dynamic process, the different rounds of bidding tend to decrease the competitive market and reduce the number of producers. The result is often an oligopolistic market situation or, in some cases, a monopolistic one. Besides, fewer firms may imply a decreased supply. The consequence may be an insufficient quantity of the EML drugs. For instance, in Fujian province, 42 products on the EML could not be easily procured and according to the authors one of the main reasons is the shortage in the number of producers at the proposed price.[31]
Public health	10 categories of basic public health services have been implemented, including expanded access for Hepatitis B vaccines and cervical and breast cancer screening, through a per capita subsidy (RMB 40) to primary care facilities. The public health subsidy replaces to a large extent the revenue lost through the zero mark-up policy for essential medicines, and covers a large share of operational costs at township hospitals, village clinics and community health service centres.
Public hospital reform on a pilot basis	17 municipalities and 37 provincial cities were designated to undertake hospital reform on a pilot basis, to reduce the reliance on medicine sales as a major source of revenue. The main activities include provider payment reform (mainly Diagnostics Related Groups and case-based payments) and clinical pathways, setting fixed prescription fees, and setting up independent pharmaceutical distribution networks. In 300 county hospitals in 2012, it was proposed to eliminate completely the medicines bonus policy, whereby staff are rewarded for over-prescription.

Source: http://www.jogh.org/documents/issue201301/V3_Barber.pdf. Accessed September 2017

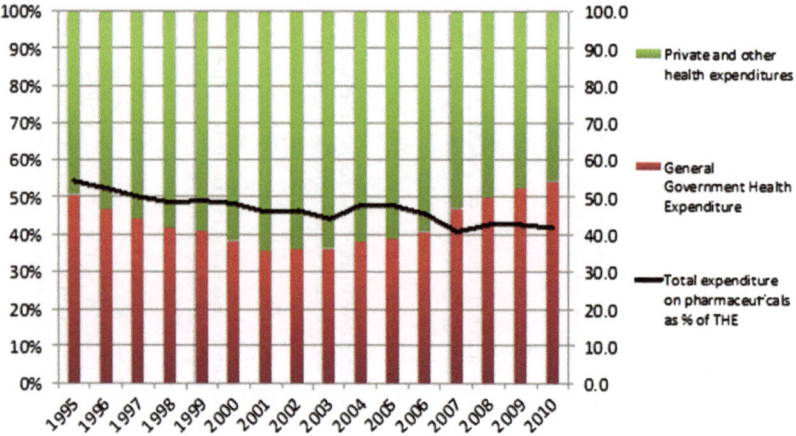

Fig. 7.1 Private and general government health expenditure, and percentage of total health spending devoted to pharmaceuticals, 1995–2010. Source: China National Health Economics Institute. National health accounts report 2012. Beijing: Ministry of Health, People's Republic of China, 2012. http://www.jogh. org/documents/issue201301/V3_Barber.pdf. Accessed September 2017

According to another study from 2015,[34] the EML caused village doctors' satisfaction about their employment to reduce. The reasons given in the study is that integrated management of village doctors' activities by township-level staff has reduced their independence, and different counties' economic status and health reform processes have also led to inconsistencies in village doctors' billing and revenue.

On top of allowing universal access to essential drugs, another goal of the EML is to improve rational drug use, especially in primary healthcare facilities. According to the WHO, worldwide in 2002, more than 50% of all drugs prescribed, dispensed or sold were inappropriate. More than 50% of patients failed to take their medicines correctly. A 2014 study of township health centres providing healthcare services for a large rural population showed that this EML tends to improve rational medicine use in China. However, the over-prescription of antibiotics and injections remains common.[35] What about pricing: how has it been affected by the EML? According to the authorities, the price of drugs on the list has been decreasing.[36] This seems to be supported by other studies.[37] According to Song et al.'s (2014b) study,[38] imposing the use of the drugs from the national EML led to a price reduction for essential medicines.

However, more-expensive drugs were often preferred in the post-reform period. Besides, most public primary healthcare facilities started to earn less after the mandatory implementation of the EML, as compensation mechanisms from public health insurance were insufficient. Some centres saw their debts pile up. In July 2011, the State Council, the National Development and Reform Commission and the MoH took official steps to address this and instructed provinces to set up plans to put the financial situation of health institutions on a sounder foot.

To conclude, it is possible to say that the implementation of the EML is widely approved by consumers for its impact on both price and quality. It is also usually quite well supported on the supply side. Yet, sufficient supply seems to be a key variable for the stability of a health system that is increasingly reliant on the medicines from the EML.

BEYOND THE EML

Since the mid-1980s, hospitals have tried to modernize, to improve their level of equipment and quality, while suffering from decreasing financial support from central and local authorities. The sale of medical drugs and other medical supplies has gradually become one of the main sources of revenue for public hospitals. Margin rates between cost and resale prices have rocketed. All policies implemented since 2009 are aimed at reducing this mark-up.

Beyond EML, hospitals must now keep their margin levels below 15% of the wholesale price, which has heavily affected their financial stability. The compensation has been delegated to provincial governments, whose wealth levels can be very different. This raises an issue of inequality in healthcare access or inequality in the quality of healthcare.

Hospitals also tend to set up other self-funding strategies. One of them is the increase in the turnover of health services through a larger number of diagnoses and procedures per patient. Although this strategy is more difficult to detect than medicine price increases, even before 2009 some empirical studies[39] were showing that the Chinese health system's consumption of certain actions and procedures was already excessive. Another strategy is over-prescription. In 2009, the cost of medical drugs accounted for 41% of total medical costs. One of the ways to contain such strategies is to implement a prospective payment system based on pathologies. Specifically, for hospital stays, a Chinese version of the DRGs may be an answer. Each stay is associated with a DRG and a specific fee is associated with a specific DRG. The result is that, at any given time, the fee payment is disconnected from the actual procedures and diagnosis performed on the patient during his or her stay. This scheme of payment is widely used in OECD countries, but is at a pilot stage in China.

NOTES

1. OECD, Value for Money in Health Spending, Paris: OECD Health Division, 2010.
2. Winnie Chi-Man Yip, William C. Hsiao, Wen Chhen, Shanlian Hu, Jin Ma, and Alan Maynard, "Early Appraisal of China's Huge and Complex Health-Care Reforms," The Lancet, Vol. 379, No. 9818, 2012, pp. 833–842.
3. L. Reynolds and M. McKee, "Factors Influencing Antibiotic Prescribing in China: An Exploratory Analysis," Health Policy, Vol. 90, No. 1, 2009, pp. 32–36.
4. D. Ding, Q. Pan, L. Shan, C. Liu, L. Gao, Y. Hao, J. Song, N. Ning, Y. Cui, Y. Li, X. Qi, C. Liang, Q. Wu, and G. Liu, "Prescribing Patterns in Outpatient Clinics of Township Hospitals in China: A Comparative Study Before and After the 2009 Health System Reform," International Journal of Environmental Research and Public Health, Vol. 13, No. 7, 2016.
5. http://www.linklaters.com/Insights/AsiaNews/LinkstoChina/Pages/Challenges-pharmaceutical-companies-under-China-new-drug-pricing-regime.aspx. Accessed September 2017.
6. http://eng.sfda.gov.cn/WS03/CL0757/131483.html. Accessed September 2017.
7. http://eng.sfda.gov.cn/WS03/CL0757/112570.html. Accessed September 2017.
8. http://eng.sfda.gov.cn/WS03/CL0757/122060.html. Accessed September 2017.
9. UBS research, 2013. http://pg.jrj.com.cn/acc/Res/CN_RES/INDUS/2013/10/2/ee2e6a3a-afcc-457b-a634-3a8827d20585.pdf. Accessed September 2017.
10. http://sczxs.mofcom.gov.cn/article/dyplwz/bh/201406/20140600639859.shtml. Accessed September 2017.
11. http://sczxs.mofcom.gov.cn/article/dyplwz/bh/201305/20130500145831.shtml. Accessed September 2017.
12. http://www.scmp.com/news/china/policies-politics/article/1858097/just-what-doctor-ordered-chinas-e-tailers-await-end. Accessed September 2017.
13. http://www.reuters.com/article/us-china-pharmaceuticals-iduskbn-0ki0y220150109. Accessed September 2017.

14. http://www.chinadaily.com.cn/business/2015-04/03/content_19992944. htm. Accessed September 2017.
15. The Alliance for Safe Online Pharmacies (ASOP) is a global non-profit dedicated to protecting patient safety online. Learn more at www.safeonlinerx.com.
16. LegitScript is a company that monitors healthcare products and internet pharmacy websites with a focus on patient safety. Learn more at www. legitscript.com.
17. https://www.nytimes.com/2015/06/22/world/asia/in-china-illegal-drugs-are-sold-online-in-an-unbridled-market.html?_r=0.   Accessed September 2017.
18. http://www.reuters.com/article/us-china-pharmaceuticals-ali-health-idUSKCN0VX0UX. Accessed September 2017.
19. https://www.wsj.com/articles/ali-health-swallows-bitter-pill-as-china-halts-drug-monitoring-system-1456144563. Accessed September 2017.
20. http://www.scmp.com/business/companies/article/1897939/alibaba-health-care-unit-stumbles-2016-deal-online-pharmacy. Accessed September 2017.
21. http://www.marbridgeconsulting.com/marbridgedaily/archive/article/92367/alihealth_to_launch_new_third_party_drug_tracking_platform. Accessed September 2017.
22. www.who.int/topics/essential_medicines/en/. Accessed September 2017.
23. S. Shekhar Kar, H. Sekhar Pradhan, and G. Prasad Mohanta, "Concept of Essential Medicines and Rational Use in Public Health," Indian Journal Community Medicine, 2010.
24. S. Barber, B. Huang, B. Santoso, R. Laing, V. Paris, and C. Wu, The Reform of the Essential Medicines System in China: A Comprehensive Approach to Universal Coverage, WHO, 2013.
25. D. Wang and X. Zhang, "The Selection of Essential Medicines in China: Progress and the Way Forward," Southern Med Review, 2011.
26. Christine Kahler, "China's Healthcare Reform: How Far Hat it Come?" China Business Review, 1 January 2011. http://www.chinabusinessreview. com/chinas-healthcare-reform-how-far-has-it-come/. Accessed September 2017.
27. Institute for Healthcare Informatics—IMS, "Understanding the Role and Use of Essential Medicines Lists," 2015.
28. As explained in a previous chapter, the State Council established the leading Group for Coordination Healthcare System Reform, an interagency team headed by Vice Premier and administrated by NDRC.
29. L. Wang, E. Ma, and W. Xu, Comparative Analyses of China National & Twenty Two Selected Provincial Essential Medicines Lists to the WHO 2011 Model List, WHO, 2011.

30. D. Wang and X. Zhang, "The Selection of National Essential Medicines in China: Progress and the Way Forward," Southern Med Review, Vol. 4, 2011, pp. 22–28.
31. S. Barber, Baobin Huang, Budiono Santoso, Richard Laing, Valerie Paris, and Chunfu Wu "The Reform of the Essential Medicines System in China: A Comprehensive Approach to Universal Coverage," Journal of Global Health, Vol. 3 No. 1, June 2013.
32. S. Zhang, W. Zhang, H. Zhou, H. Xu, Z. Qu, M. Guo, F. Wang, Y. Zhong, L. Gu, X. Liang, Z. Sa, X. Wang, and D. Tian, "How China's New Health Reform Influences Village Doctors' Income Structure: Evidence from a Qualitative Study in Six Counties in China," Human Resources for Health, Vol. 13, No. 26, 2015.
33. Y. Song, Y. Bian, and L. Li, "Current Perspectives on China's National Essential Medicine System: Primary Care Provider and Patient Views," BMC Health Services Research, Vol. 16, No. 30, 2016.
34. S. Zhang, W. Zhang, H. Zhou, H. Xu, Z. Qu, M. Guo, F. Wang, Y. Zhong, L. Gu, X. Liang, Z. Sa, X. Wang, and D. Tian, "How China's New Health Reform Influences Village Doctors' Income Structure: Evidence from a Qualitative Study in Six Counties in China," Human Resources for Health, Vol. 13, No. 26, 2015.
35. Y. Song, Y. Bian, M. Petzold, L. Li, and A. Yin "The Impact of China's National Essential Medicine System on Improving Rational Drug Use in Primary Healthcare Facilities: An Empirical Study in Four Provinces," BMC Health Services Research, Vol. 14, 2014, p. 507. http://www.biomedcentral.com/1472-6963/14/507. Accessed September 2017.
36. Zhang Xiang, "More Measures Needed to Deepen Healthcare Reform in China: Vice Premier," Xinhua English News, November 11.
37. Y. Li, C. Ying, G. Sufang, P. Brant, L. Bin, and D. Hipgrave, "Evaluation, in Three Provinces, of the Introduction and Impact of China's National Essential Medicines Scheme," Bulletin of the World Health Organization, Vol. 91, 2013, pp. 184–194; L. Yang, C. Liu, J.A. Ferrier, W. Zhou, and X. Zhang, "The Impact of the National Essential Medicines Policy on Prescribing Behaviors in Primary Care Facilities in Hubei Province of China," Health Policy Plan, 2012.
38. Y. Song, Y. Bian, M. Petzold, and A. Yin, "Effects of the National Essential Medicine System in Reducing Drug Prices: An Empirical Study in Four Chinese Provinces," Journal of Pharmaceutical Policy and Practice React-text: 15, Vol. 7, No. 1, p.12, /react-text react-text: 18/react-text react-text: 19 September 2014a.
39. K. Eggleston, L. Li, Q. Meng, M. Lindelow, and A. Wagstaff, "Health Service Delivery in China: A Literature Review," Health Economics, Vol. 7, 2008, pp. 149–165.

BIBLIOGRAPHY

Barber, S., Baobin Huang, Budiono Santoso, Richard Laing, Valerie Paris, and Chunfu Wu, "The Reform of the Essential Medicines System in China: A Comprehensive Approach to Universal Coverage," Journal of Global Health, Vol. 3 No. 1, June 2013.

Ding, D., Q. Pan, L. Shan, C. Liu, L. Gao, Y. Hao, J. Song, N. Ning, Y. Cui, Y. Li, X. Qi, C. Liang, Q. Wu, and G. Liu, "Prescribing Patterns in Outpatient Clinics of Township Hospitals in China: A Comparative Study Before and After the 2009 Health System Reform," International Journal of Environmental Resource of Public Health, Vol. 13, No. 7, 2016.

Eggleston, K., L. Li, Q. Meng, M. Lindelow, and A. Wagstaff, "Health Service Delivery in China: A Literature Review," Health Economics, Vol. 7, 2008, pp. 149–165.

Institute for Healthcare Informatics—IMS, "Understanding the Role and Use of Essential Medicines Lists," 2015.

Kahler, Christine, "China's Healthcare Reform: How Far Hat it Come?" China Business Review, 1 January 2011. http://www.chinabusinessreview.com/chinas-healthcare-reform-how-far-has-it-come/. Accessed September 2017.

Li, Y., C. Ying, G. Sufang, P. Brant, L. Bin, and D. Hipgrave, "Evaluation, in Three Provinces, of the Introduction and Impact of China's National Essential Medicines Scheme," Bulletin of the World Health Organization, Vol. 91, 2013, pp. 184–194

OECD, Value for Money in Health Spending, Paris, OECD Health Division, 2010.

Reynolds, L., and M. McKee, "Factors Influencing Antibiotic Prescribing in China: An Exploratory Analysis," Health Policy, Vol. 90, No. 1, 2009, pp. 32–36.

Shekhar Kar, S., H. Sekhar Pradhan, and G. Prasad Mohanta, "Concept of Essential Medicines and Rational Use in Public Health," Indian Journal Community Medicine, 2010.

Song, Y., Y. Bian, and L. Li, "Current Perspectives on China's National Essential Medicine System: Primary Care Provider and Patient Views," BMC Health Services Research, Vol. 16, No. 30, 2016.

Song, Y., Y. Bian, M. Petzold, L. Li, and A. Yin "The Impact of China's National Essential Medicine System on Improving Rational Drug Use in Primary Health Care Facilities: An Empirical Study in Four Provinces," BMC Health Services Research, Vol. 14, 2014a, p. 507. http://www.biomedcentral.com/1472-6963/14/507. Accessed September 2017.

Song, Y., Y. Bian, M. Petzold, and A. Yin, "Effects of the National Essential Medicine System in Reducing Drug Prices: An Empirical Study in Four Chinese Provinces," Journal of Pharmaceutical Policy and Practice React-text: 15, Vol. 7, No. 1, p.12, /react-text react-text: 18/react-text react-text: 19 September 2014b.

UBS research, 2013. http://pg.jrj.com.cn/acc/Res/CN_RES/INDUS/2013/10/2/ee2e6a3a-afcc-457b-a634-3a8827d20585.pdf. Accessed September 2017.

Wang, L., E. Ma, and W. Xu, Comparative Analyses of China National &Twenty Two Selected Provincial Essential Medicines Lists to the WHO 2011 Model List, WHO, 2011.

Wang, D., and X. Zhang, "The Selection of National Essential Medicines in China: Progress and the Way Forward," Southern Medical Review, Vol. 4, 2011, pp. 22–28.

Xiang Zhang, "More Measures Needed to Deepen Healthcare Reform in China: Vice Premier," Xinhua English News, November 11.

Yang, L., C. Liu, J.A. Ferrier, W. Zhou, and X. Zhang, "The Impact of the National Essential Medicines Policy on Prescribing Behaviors in Primary Care Facilities in Hubei Province of China," Health Policy Plan, 2012.

Yip, Winnie Chi-Man, William C. Hsiao, Wen Chhen, Shanlian Hu, Jin Ma, and Alan Maynard, "Early Appraisal of China's Huge and Complex Health-Care Reforms," The Lancet, Vol. 379, No. 9818, 2012, pp. 833–842.

Zhang, S., W. Zhang, H. Zhou, H. Xu, Z. Qu, M. Guo, F. Wang, Y. Zhong, L. Gu, X. Liang, Z. Sa, X. Wang, and D. Tian, "How China's New Health Reform Influences Village Doctors' Income Structure: Evidence from a Qualitative Study in Six Counties in China," Human Resources for Health, Vol. 13, No. 26, 2015.

CHAPTER 8

The Rise of Violence as a Result of Inefficiency in the Healthcare System

Abstract China is currently experiencing an over-utilization of university hospitals and hospitals with high-tech equipment, usually located in main cities. Even though they have a large capacity, they are faced with congestion leading to long queues. In parallel, there is under-utilization of smaller institutions. The Ministry of Health estimates that 70% of patients treated in university hospitals of a higher level (Level 3) could have received adequate treatment in hospitals of a lower category, closer to their home. In 2009, the Chinese government published a large-scale development plan for the health sector, with over RMB 770 billion to be invested. Four years later, RMB 620 billion was already spent, with a public insurance scheme set-up and a network of Community Health Centres created. Yet, this key issue of the Chinese health system, that is, the concentration of demand on a small number of hospitals, still remains, eventually leading to a tense relationship between doctors and patients, and to increasingly common acts of violence. The origin of such violence as well as possible directions to restore trust, respect, and understanding between patients and medical staff is examined. The decentralization of quality care seems to be the key, but there are different ways to achieve this goal. Obviously, digital tools such as connected health object and other online services are likely to play a growing role in addressing this issue.

Keywords Inefficiency in the healthcare system • *Yi nao* • Waiting lists • Internet and web platforms

© The Author(s) 2018   171
C. Milcent, *Healthcare Reform in China*,
https://doi.org/10.1007/978-3-319-69736-9_8

In 2009, the Chinese government published a large-scale development plan for the health sector, with over RMB 770 billion to be invested. Four years later, RMB 620 billion has already been spent, with a public insurance scheme set up and Community Health Centres (CHCs) created. Yet, the key issues for Chinese health systems have remained, leading to tense relationships between doctors and patients, with increasingly common acts of violence.

Indeed, China is currently experiencing an over-utilization of university hospitals and hospitals with high-tech equipment, which are usually located in main cities in spite of them having an important capacity. This also true for admissions, with an occupancy rate above 100%, which is as much as for outpatient activity.

According to the Ministry of Health (MoH),[1] level 3 hospitals represents 2% of the total number of hospitals but 37% of consultations. For instance, every day 700,000 patients come from other hospitals to be treated in Beijing.[2]

The MoH estimates that 70% of patients treated in Level 3 hospitals could have received adequate treatment in hospitals of a lower category, closer to their homes.

Yi nao or Hospital Violence

Yi (medical) *nao* (dispute/violence): different forms of violence have been developing over the years in Chinese hospitals. This can take quite a passive form, such as exposing the body of the defunct in front of the hospital to very active forms like vandalism or even direct physical altercations with hospital staff, up to involving organized gangs.[3] The key words "hospital/violence/China" in any search engine will deliver scores of press articles covering cases of physicians being assaulted and sometimes even killed by patients.

Each year, more than 10,000 physicians are said to be assaulted one way or another. The number of reported incidents was 17,243 in 2010, up 70% from 2004. According to a 2012 report,[4] the number of conflicts between medical personnel and patients and their families is increasing by 22.9% per annum. A survey covering 10 Chinese provinces shows that half of Chinese doctors have been verbally assaulted at least once and one-third have been physically assaulted.[5] This is consistent with the conclusion of the 2012 national forum of Chinese hospital presidents, estimating that about 30% of medical personnel have had conflicts with their patients.[6]

In February 2014, a doctor in northeast China's Heilongjiang province was beaten to death by a patient. In January 2015, in Zhengzhou, a doctor and a patient died following a fight in a central China hospital.[7] In July 2015, the *China Daily* reported that an online petition demanding a crackdown on violence against hospital personnel had collected the signatures of more than 600,000 doctors.[8] This petition was started after the attack on a physician by a patient at Longmen County People's Hospital, in Guangdong province. In May 2016, still in Guangdong province, the death of a retired doctor after being stabbed in a knife attack by a former patient was reported by the *China Daily*.[9]

Overall, the Chinese national media have covered roughly 30 medical-related violent disputes (including fatal stabbings) from October 2013 to June 2015. Besides this, there were thousands of small disputes happening in hospitals across China every day that did not make it into national news media.[10]

We have seen earlier in this book how the hierarchy of the Chinese healthcare system progressively eroded and drove demand to concentrate on certain hospitals. How did this affect the efficiency of the entire system and lead to a situation where some patients see violence as their only option? The key elements to answer this question are:

- The changes in healthcare supply:

  - The shift in the way hospitals are financed and manage their staff;
  - Conditions of consultation and admission in Level 3 hospitals tainted by waiting list tickets sold on the black market and bribes to jump queues;
  - The low social recognition of medical careers and overall lack of consideration for medical staff;
  - The lack of legal recourse in case of suspected medical malpractice.

- The changes in healthcare demand:

  - Spatial changes in healthcare demand including urbanization and occupational changes;
  - The easier dissemination of information with the development of the internet and web platforms, improving the level of knowledge of patients and their relatives.

THE ORIGIN OF SUCH VIOLENCE

Changes in Supply

Hospital Financing and Personnel Management

The uniqueness of the Chinese hospital system is that hospitals abruptly shifted from offering care almost independently from any financial consideration to operating like for-profit entities, through investment choices and pricing policies, while still retaining the governance of a public institution (for instance, medical personnel with *bianzhi* status have safety of employment and other benefits, as described in Chap. 5). Additionally, hospitals are, to a large extent, in a monopoly situation in their local area, which creates a lack of regulation in price setting by the market. The hospital can increase its revenue by offering more costly care and has all the incentives to do so.

Due to this necessity for public hospitals to finance themselves, they distribute all sorts of income supplements to doctors and medical staff, often in a non-transparent way, with the objective of boosting activity and revenue. It is useful to break down the sources of income for physicians into four categories:

- Basic salaries as hospital employees;
- Productivity-based bonuses paid by the hospital;
- Drug rebates, consisting of payments from drug companies and hospitals, related to the physicians' prescribing behaviour;
- Gifts from patients, known as *hongbao* or "red envelopes".

The last two sources of revenue are considered as bribery and totally forbidden but are still widespread. They have widely contributed to patient distrust.

The second source of revenue comes from the incentive for medical staff to increase the profit of public hospitals by increasing the number of patient visits, and to over-prescribe. This behaviour creates what is called *induced demand.* The objective function of medical personnel and physicians then includes profit maximization as a parameter. A search for profit then becomes central to an activity whose remuneration was until then totally disconnected from it. As a case in point, we can quote the sales of medical drugs that now account for more than 40% of the turnover of public hospitals, with some abuse. According to the World Health

Organisation (WHO), the situation is such that antibiotics are prescribed at twice the rate recommended and anti-inflammatory drugs at more than three times the rate found in similar countries. The victims of this situation are patients, for whom the cost of care dramatically increases, with a lot of unnecessary prescriptions. All of this contributes to an ever-tenser relationship between medical personnel and patients.

To study the doctor–patient relationship, a survey was carried out in Shenzhen in December 2013. The data containing 504 licensed medical doctors was drawn by random sampling. To explain the over-prescription behaviour, a critical predictor is the low basic salaries of hospital employees. However, this study shows that over-prescription is also driven by doctors' intention to avoid disputes with patients.

In a 2016 qualitative study, Tucker et al. [11] proposed to better understand the determinants of the current patient–physician mistrust and violence in Guangdong province. This study is based on 160 patients, their family members, physicians, nurses and hospital administrators in seven hospitals. According to the authors, "the blind pursuit of financial profits at a systems level has eroded patient-physician trust in China".

On the medical staff side, these additional sources of revenue are justified by the very low level of basic salaries for hospital employees (see Chap. 5). Medical staff prefer to remain in the public sector because of the advantage tied with their *bianzhi* status. At the same time, according to a 2011 Chinese Medical Association survey, only 20% of responding doctors are satisfied with their medical practice environments.

Consultation and Admission Conditions in Level 3 Hospitals in the Congestion Context
The number of Community Health Centres (CHCs) have rocketed over the past few years, making it possible to consult without having to wait in long queues. Yet demand is little adapted to this new organization of supply. These newly set-up structures remain under-used by patients who still prefer Level 3 hospitals. For Level 3 hospitals, the occupancy rate is above 100%, when it is only around 80% for district hospitals and between 50% and 60% in CHCs.[12]

Level 3 hospitals continue to have increasing numbers of outpatient consultations and all the more so for inpatient admissions. Between 2007 and 2011, the number of consultations soared by 33% and admissions by 56%. It has been estimated that 30% of admissions are unnecessary.[13] For some analysts, this situation has been exacerbated by the official classification of public hospitals based on their level of equipment and training of physicians, as it has objectivized patients' preference for these hospitals. Similarly, Shanghai's Fudan University has released a list of mainland China's top 100 hospitals. The goal was to encourage hospitals to do better. An external effect was to encourage patients to go to hospitals from this list (i.e. the already over-crowded elite institutions). According to the *South China Morning Post*, "the rankings garnered plenty of coverage in the media, leading micro-bloggers to say they would save the list and use it as a reference if they ever needed to go to hospital".[14]

In summary, it is fair to say that public hospitals represent almost all medical consultations and hospital admissions. Over the entire Chinese territory, they represent 89% of the total number of hospital beds, 91.6% of the admissions and 91.7% of outpatient consultations.[15,16] According to a study, 20% of outpatients are treated for colds or gastroenteritis (Lim et al. 2002).[17]

As a result of this concentration of demand, the more that public hospital have a high level of equipment and trained physicians, the more they are congested. On the Beijing Hospital's website, it is said that 4500 medical consultations are performed there every day. Depending on the source, the number of consultations per physician is between 60 and 80 per day.

In the end, consultations end up being prone to tension:

- Physicians are overwhelmed by demand, having very little time for each patient (as little as 2 minutes in certain, not uncommon, cases), both because of the long queues and because they are financially incentivized on the number of consultations they perform;
- Physicians are also incentivized to over-diagnose and over-prescribe, while giving little explanation to patients, due to the lack of time, in a context of asymmetry of information where the patient cannot appreciate the relevance of the diagnosis and prescriptions.

Queues Tainted by a Black Market and Bribery
One of the consequences of the current congestion situation is the development and of a black market in queue tickets. Indeed, as a first step, patients usually wait in a queue to take a number just to be allowed to make an appointment. Scammers run a thriving practice trading numbers outside hospitals. Even if the ticket itself is not free, its cost is too low to prevent this traffic, in particular for Level 3 hospitals. As a case in point, in one of the best-equipped hospitals in Beijing, the Peking University

Renmin Hospital, each waiting tickets costs RMB 5, with the total tickets distributed per day being a closed number. On the black market, their price can rapidly grow to RMB 200 and sometimes even higher, increasing the total cost of consultation.

The Difficulty of Getting Referred to the Right Specialist
A visit to public hospitals is quite instructive about the management of outpatients. Hospital are divided in two sectors. The sector dedicated to outpatients usually starts with a huge entry hall with a reception desk in the middle, attended by nurses. Their role is to direct patients toward the specialty they need. Yet, this desk is usually under-staffed, making it difficult to address all the requests for information from patients.

A researcher from CASS explains:

The number of nurses at the reception desk doesn't make it possible to treat all the requests. As a result, the patient himself must often chose the specialty to consult. He must take a waiting number and is then registered as an outpatient. He then goes to the prepayment desk to validate his place on the waiting list. This system generates a vast array of frustrations.[18]

One has to be reminded that the status of general practitioner (GP) is a very recent addition to the Chinese health system and that there are little, if none, in Level 3 hospitals.

This lack of information does not make it possible for the patient to know with certainty which specialist to consult. His waiting time first to get a ticket and then for the consultation is turned into a bigger burden due to the uncertainty of having made the right choice.

What with queues that can last for days, consultation times that are shrinking, costs that are going up amidst widespread over-diagnosis and over-prescription, one can understand the frustration of patients. If you add the commonly practised black market of waiting tickets or "red envelopes", bribes to medical personnel to cut through queues, this is how the situation degenerates into violent acts in some cases.[19]

The Low Social Recognition of Medical Careers and Lack of Consideration for Medical Staff
According to a 2011 survey by the Chinese Medical Doctors Association, 78% of respondents did not want their own children to become doctors. As described earlier in this book (Chap. 5), recruitment of students with

high potential is getting increasing difficult for medical schools, except the most prestigious ones.[20]

This is to be seen in parallel with the little satisfaction medical personnel have with their current situation. Xinhua news agency reported that nearly 40% of medical personnel surveyed at 316 hospitals nationally from December 2012 to July 2013 said they plan to give up their profession because of increased violence in hospitals.[21]

In March 2012, an online survey was carried out by the *People's Daily* after a physician was savagely murdered by a patient, gaining national coverage and strong condemnation from authorities. This survey was inquiring about the emotion this event triggered in the respondents. An overwhelming 65% of them answer "joy", against only 14% for "anger" and 7% for "sadness". Given its very disturbing results, the study was quickly withdrawn from the newspaper's website. Among the numerous comments this incident generated, Xu Xialong, a human resources consultant from Beijing, reckoned that these results echoed patients' feelings of frustration and that the violence shown by respondents was against the system and not really symptomatic of the tragedy itself.[22]

On a lighter note, in November 2015, an article from the *Chinese Medical News* praised the training of nurses by flight attendants to adopt a more outgoing and customer-friendly attitude in order to improve the public's negative image of them.[23]

In summary, all these anecdotes point to a lack of respect towards medical staff. This fuels the vicious circle of violence, as trust and respect are absolutely mandatory.

Lack of Legal Recourse in Cases of Suspected Medical Malpractice
According to many press articles and academic research, the problem of violence is also tied to an inefficient legal mechanism allowing patients to address issues during their medical process.

Indeed, China's judicial system was widely improved since the economic reforms. Until the early 1980s, there was no legislation to deal with medical liability or medical malpractice.[24] In 1985, the municipal government of Shanghai and the provincial government of Shanxi established an experimental form of "administrative" system for handling civil liability in medical malpractice claims in their local administrative regulations.

These experiments provided an administrative institutional path for addressing medical complaints. In 1987, the MoH drafted the Medical Accident Rules that were promulgated by the State Council. For "harm" caused by a direct medical accident, a patient or patient's family/relatives can seek redress. The term "harm" referred to death, disfigurement, disability or serious dysfunction. The burden of proof was upon the plaintiff to prove causation.

The law further subdivides "medical accident" into "technical accidents" (negligent treatment) and "malpractice accidents" (breach of duty, violation of rules or regulations) with the latter having more serious punishments.[25] This law was highly criticized as being too restrictive.[26] In response to criticism of the 1987 Rules, the State Council promulgated in 2002 the Medical Accident Regulations. These Regulations broadened the scope of liability regarding medical practitioners. Hospitals had a greater obligation, at least on paper, to maintain good medical records. The burden of proof remained on patients.

Rapidly after 1987, civil malpractice suits became more common than criminal ones. A 2011 Chinese Hospital Management Association survey reported that the number of malpractice lawsuits in China has been increasing at an average rate of 23% a year since 2002.[27]

Improving the rights of patients to seek redress, the 2009 Tort Liability Law came into effect in 2010. One of the important changes is that it increased attention on the "standard of care".[28] This law also made clear that medical institutions are liable for their staff.[29]

Even if China's government is improving its judicial system, there are still a lot of grey zones where patients or relatives may experience an absence of justice. Most laws and regulations are quite recent and some points of confusion still exist. According to Rossner (2014):[30] "Liability for medical errors took many decades to be formally established in the People's Republic of China, and the use of administrative 'appraisal panels' and mediation reflect a continued preference for reducing litigation and limiting compensation for medical liability."

Changes in Demand

Spatial Changes in Healthcare Demand

Including Urbanization

With the improvement of the transport and communication network, people have become more mobile, including in rural areas. They no longer hesitate to travel long distances for treatment in major hospitals in cities, even sometimes out of their home province.

The constraints imposed by public insurance to get reimbursement do not seem to give enough incentive to curb this phenomenon. As explained in Chap. 6, the three main public insurance schemes cover a remarkable share of the population, but the level of coverage remains quite limited, especially for outpatient consultations. Out-of-pocket payments are high for the patient who has to decide between:

- Consult in a hospital with high-quality standards, with little or no reimbursement; or
- Go to a local health centre to get better but still limited treatment.

The data showing congestion in Level 3 hospitals tend to show that a major part of the population chooses the first option, except those in the direst poverty.

For migrants and commuters, the obligation to go back to their registered place of residence in case of health troubles has been considerably reduced. It is increasingly common for companies to have agreements with hospitals covering medical consultations for their employees, including migrant workers.

Occupation Changes
One factor that cannot be neglected is the importance of having family or a social network close to the place of hospitalization. Indeed, in Chinese hospitals, family and relatives of patients play a crucial part in the care and healing process. The non-medical services supplied by the hospital, such as catering, are minimal and the family needs to be very present to support the patient:

- For his or her meals, as glass or cutlery can be missing and food itself is very basic;
- But also to get full attention from medical personnel: the presence and monitoring of relatives has an influence on the way the patient is treated, not to mention the *hong bao* or red envelopes filled with money to encourage the engagement of staff with the patient.

The presence of family or a social network living close the hospital is thus a key element. EY,[31] a consulting group, surveyed consumers who are employed and whose incomes fall solidly into mainland China's mid-to-upper middle class bracket: annual incomes of RMB 60,000–229,000.

Some 79% of survey respondents indicated that they have to return to the place of their household registration to get healthcare. Of this group, 49% would return home for any health problems, and 30% would return for only serious medical issues.

Studies from Milcent (2015) show that access to healthcare is all the more difficult for rural inhabitants with agricultural activity compared to rural inhabitants.[32] When people commute on a regular basis to cities, travelling long distances to go to a Level 3 hospital is not that much of a hurdle. In addition, they are more likely to have some kind of network in cities. As the share of the really sedentary population in rural areas is shrinking, this explains why this factor cannot prevent the congestion in the best hospitals in cities, partially due to the inflow of patients from other areas.

The Dissemination of Information: Internet and Web Platforms

For the Public
The internet also plays an important part in the appeal of big public hospitals, acting as a sounding board to disseminate information. It makes it possible for individuals to have private or semi-private discussion forums, or at least appear to do so, in which speech and criticism can be more direct. It is very common for families to use such forums to protest against the quality of care. Conversely, the list of elite healthcare institutions published by Shanghai's Fudan University was singled out by many microbloggers, who have stated that the information on this list ensured a certain level of quality.

According to Wei Zhong, Professor at the Chinese Academy of Social Sciences (CASS):

Ten years ago, there already were conflicts between patients and medical personnel, sometimes involving violence. Cases of medical malpractice leading to anger and frustration on the patient side were already out there. Yet, they seldom gained coverage in printed newspapers. There was the case of the coffin of a deceased child that the family had placed at the entrance of the hospital, which was widely commented on across China and considered quite unique, even though it wasn't. Today, it is possible to find all kinds of similar stories every day all across the internet. Families living thousands of kilometres apart can share their pain and frustration with the healthcare system. This undoubtedly fuels violence.

Hospitals sometimes try to disconnect the physician from the aftermath of care that does not turn out as expected. For instance, the patient can be transferred to another hospital, with the family being notified only afterwards. In such cases, they cannot materially "seek justice" (*tao gongdao*), but can digitally post their complaints and criticism. It is possible that sharing these types of experiences reduce the sense of powerlessness *vis-à-vis* the asymmetry of information between the family and medical personnel. The internet enables patients and their relatives to better understand their rights[33], it corrects the asymmetry of information and elevates the level of expectations in terms of quality of care.

For the Authorities
For China's Ministry of Public Security, the use of microblogs is also a tool to interact with the public. It can be a way to release "correct and authorized information to dispel misunderstandings, and serve the people" as explained by Huang Ming, the Vice- Minister of Public Security.[34]

The Medical Literacy Level of Patients and their Relatives
As exposed by Zhong Nanshan in his speech at China's National People's Congress in March 2014, violence against health-workers can be explained by low medical literacy among the public.

Some reckon that, due to their lack of education, patients fail to understand the difficulty or impossibility of treating certain pathologies, which explains in the end why they resort to violence.[35] Yet, literacy levels and superstition are comparable to what is found in neighbouring countries, even though they do not have to face the same violence phenomenon. Thus, these do not appear to actually be key criteria.

HOW TO RESTORE TRUST, RESPECT AND UNDERSTANDING BETWEEN PATIENTS AND MEDICAL STAFF?

Improvements in Physician Qualification and Mobility

The training of physician in China is both complex and very diverse depending on each geographical area. Yet, overall it is insufficient. In 2013, only 28.5% of the healthcare in hospital was provided by personnel with a Bachelor's degree or above. This figure is on the increase, since it was only 26.7% the previous year.[36] In rural areas, the situation is even worse with 70% of medical personnel having only junior high school training.[37,38]

The low professional mobility of doctors: In theory, a physician having graduated as a "rural doctor" will not be able to consult in urban areas, even though seniority can make up for the diploma in certain cases.

Within each area, mobility is also low. The professional registration number of each doctor is attached to the hospitals he or she works for. Globally speaking, the doctor cannot work elsewhere, even part-time, even though some pilot experiments are currently being tested. As a consequence, recruitment of highly qualified doctors is extremely difficult for a private hospital, as most graduates from renowned medical universities will chose to work in a Level 3 hospital.

As there is a strong correlation between highly trained medical personnel and Level 3 hospitals, competition in each geographical area to work in these hospitals is high. Only such hospitals are really attractive for patients, thanks to the training and skills of their staff.

More details are provided in Chap. 5 regarding medical staff and their incentives.

Police Presence as Short-term Fix

As a first solution to this phenomenon, the government reacted by increasing security in hospitals.

The attack described earlier, against a physician in Guangdong, led to this security response. The Health and Family Planning Commission requested the implementation of a police post in each hospital with regular patrols for swift intervention in case of incident. Surveillance cameras and alarms were also installed.

At the national level, the Ministry of Public Security (MoPS) advised in October 2013 that hospitals with 2000 beds should have at least 100 security guards. The Vice Minister of Public Security, Huang Ming, said at the end of March 2016 that "Chinese police would crack down on hospital-related crimes and show zero tolerance to perpetrators who assault and injure medical personnel".[39]

This answer to violence through increased security can only be a short-term fix. It contributes to the mistrust towards the healthcare system and cannot really improve the situation as long as the root causes are not addressed.

In the Mid-term, Family Doctors are Seen as the Way to Re-build Trust

In China, it is not yet common for physicians to enter into a dialogue with their patients, to explain the diagnosis and discuss treatment. Patient–doctor communication plays a very small part in the consultation. In a recent conference, Bo Tang,[40] Secretary General, Physician Commission of District Healthcare, compared consultations held in Hong Kong versus those in mainland China. He pinpointed this lack of dialogue as one of the main differences, contributing to the poor relations between patients and doctors.

To solve this situation, one of the objectives of the reform introducing CHCs is to enable a long-term relationship between patients and their doctors. All CHCs are supposed to have a pool of GPs who would be able follow their patients in the long term. Close both geographically and in terms of relationship, they could restore patient trust.

In fact, what is often used as a benchmark is the relationship that could exist between "barefoot doctors" and their patients, in spite of their very sparse training. The characteristics of this relationship were:

- *Proximity*, making it possible to avoid misunderstandings;
- *The absence of pecuniary factors*, made possible by the financing;
- *The consultation time*, that had little constraint.

To rebuild this type of relationship, a pilot experiment was carried out, setting up family doctors whose revenue is totally disconnected from volume of consultation and prescription.[41] Yet, this can only be a mid-term solution, since it requires a large cohort of GPs that today does not exist, since specific training for GPs is fairly new (see Chap. 5).

Insurance Schemes as a Tool to Streamline Demand

The implementation of public insurance schemes is an opportunity to recreate a patient's care pathway and ease the congestion in public hospitals, by conditioning reimbursement to the place where the consultations happens. Yet, public insurance coverage of medical consultations remains low and the basket of care covered is limited.[42] In reality, this gives little financial incentive to patients, who still opt for a perceived quality of care versus its geographical or financial accessibility. This is one of the main reasons why dispensaries, primary care centres and Level 1 hospital have so far failed to fully find their place.

To solve this, better coverage of consultations in CHCs and township centres is seen as one of the potential solutions to redirect demand from public hospitals. With a real incentive to make the first step of the patient's pathway in less-congested establishments, a real patient pathway could be recreated, improving the efficiency of the overall system. Yet, on top of the financial incentives, a strong policy to improve the training of physicians and quality of these establishments needs to be carried out to really shift the demand from public hospitals.

In parallel, the implementation of private insurance, including private health structures, is encouraged. This integrated system is called Managed Care in the United States. So far, the lack of mobility of medical personnel has been an obstacle to the development of such schemes, as well as the remaining administrative hurdles that make this type of investment quite complicated for investors.

The Internet as a Tool for Healthcare Efficiency
Digital tools can also play a role in addressing the issue of concentration of demand. As will be shown in Chap. 9, they enable a more efficient system, by supporting the new policies, such as the implementation of family doctors.

One of the potential benefits of internet tools is to solve the issue of incredibly long queues in hospital entrance halls. Patients can make appointments and pay online to avoid physically queuing. In Beijing, it is now mandatory to use such tools, even though an alternative phone number has been put in place for the elderly to make appointments.

Internet and mobile apps thus appear as an instrument to regulate demand and reduce congestion in Level 3 hospitals. Yet, if they make it possible to reduce the time spent in a queue, they cannot reduce the total lead time to actually get a consultation. In the end, patients are waiting at home instead of waiting in the hospital. This already has had some benefits, as it makes it possible for medical personnel to work in a much less tense environment, without the pressure of other patients actually waiting. It also eliminates, to a large extent, the black market in queuing tickets.

The internet can also to offer innovative tools for medical practice itself, such as telemedicine and teleconsultation. If at least part of the demand currently turning to public hospitals could be redirected to online consultations, it would ease the congestion phenomenon, eventually leading to reduced waiting times and longer consultation times, restoring dialogue and trust between patients and medical personnel. But why do people trust the online consultation services? This virtual consultation is provided by qualified and trained doctors working in high-tech hospitals. A grey zone in the Chinese legislation makes it possible for a physician to offer online consulting services.

It also introduces a form of competition between normal consultations and online consultations, potentially curbing the trend of increasing prices for patients. Yet, solutions brought about by digital tools are not without drawbacks. They raise issues such as the confidentiality of medical data, the responsibility in terms of medical malpractice and the control of quality standards.

NOTES

1. MoH, China Health Statistical Yearbook, 2012.
2. Source: National Health and Family Planning Commission, Figures Estimated in 2013. http://europe.chinadaily.com.cn/opinion/2017-05/04/content_29194712.htm. Accessed September 2017.
3. J. Tu, "Yinao: Protest and Violence in China's Medical Sector," December 2015, Berkeley Journal of Sociology. http://berkeleyjournal.org/2014/12/yinao-protest-and-violence-in-chinas-medical-sector/. Accessed September 2017.
4. Zhongming Wang and Jianhua Li, "Yiliaojiufen fasheng de yuanyin ji yingduicuoshi" ("The Reason and Countering Measures of Medical Disputes"), Zhongguo Shequ Yishi (Chinese Community Doctor), No. 12, 2012, pp. 409–410.
5. "Every Year Ten Thousands Doctors were Attacked, the Fragile Doctor-Patient Relationship could not Stand the Heavy Burden of Attacks, When could the Violence Stop?" ("Meinian yiwan yisheng bei ouda, cuiruo yihuan jinbuqi zhongya, baoli shang yisheng heshixiu").
6. Kai Cao, "Hospitals' Return to Public Service Key to Tackle Doctor-Patient Disputes," Xinhua, 19 November 2011. Web. 30 September 2013.
7. http://www.chinadailyasia.com/nation/2015-01/26/content_15219326.html. Accessed September 2017.
8. "600,000 Chinese Doctors Sign Petition Against Hospital Violence," China Daily, 19 July 2015. http://www.chinadaily.com.cn/china/2015-07/19/content_21326495.htm. Accessed September 2017.
9. http://www.chinadailyasia.com/nation/2016-05/07/content_15429118.html. Accessed September 2017.
10. http://www.whatsonweibo.com/new-law-combats-chinas-yinao-phenomenon/. Accessed September 2017.

11. J.D. Tucker, Y. Cheng, B. Wong et al., "Patient–Physician Mistrust and Violence Against Physicians in Guangdong Province, China: A Qualitative Study," BMJ Open, Vol. 5, No. 10, 2015.
12. Source: MoH, China National Health Yearbook 2009. http://www.mckinsey.com/~/media/mckinsey/dotcom/client_service/healthcare%20systems%20and%20services/health%20international/hi10_china_healthcare_reform.ashx. Accessed September 2017.
13. Urban China: Toward Efficient, Inclusive, and Sustainable Urbanization Par the World Bank; Development Research Center of the State Council, Source MoH, 2011.
14. http://www.scmp.com/news/china/article/1094805/fudan-universitys-top-hospitals-list-blamed-worsening-bed-crunch. Accessed September 2017.
15. Source: Chinese Health Statistical Yearbook, 2012.
16. S. Barber, M. Borowitz, H. Bekedam, and J. Ma, "The Hospital of the Future in China: China's Reform of Public Hospitals and Trends from Industrialized Countries," Health Policy and Planning, Vol. 29, No. 3, 2014, pp. 367–378.
17. M. Lim, T. Yang, Z. Zhang, F. Zhao, W. Feng, and Y. Chen, "The Role and Scope of Private Medical Practice in China," Final Report to the World Health Organization and the United Nations Development Program, UNDP, WHO and MOH China, 2002.
18. Interview in Beijing, November 2015 (translated from Chinese).
19. C. Shun Ching Chan, "A Market of Distrust: Unofficial Payments for Hospital Care in China," The 12th Conference of the European Sociological Association (ESA 2015), 2015.
20. http://www.ft.com/cms/s/35a081ae-2653-11e3-8ef6-00144feab7de.html#axzz3dqYRbv78. Accessed September 2017.
21. Ibid., note 26.
22. http://www.bloombergview.com/articles/2012-03-29/violent-crimes-in-china-s-hospitals-spread-happiness. Accessed September 2017.
23. http://www.chinesemedicalnews.com/2015/11/medical-news-from-china-7-stories-that.html. Accessed September 2017.
24. Zhu Wang and Ken Oliphant, "Yangge Dance: The Rhythm of Liability for Medical Malpractice in the People's Republic of China," Chicago-Kent Law Revue, Vol. 87, 2011, pp. 26–30.
25. Statute on Handling Medical Accidents, published 29 June 1987. For a translated copy, see: "1987 Rules on Handling Medical Accidents in China," http://www.china.org.cn/english/2002/Jun/35661.htm. Accessed September 2017.

26. Dean M. Harris and Chien Chang Wu, "Medical Malpractice in the People's Republic of China: The 2002 Regulation on the Handling of Medical Accidents," The Journal of Law, Medicine & Ethics, Vol. 33, No. 3, 2005, pp. 456–477.
27. Jessie Jiang, "In Some Chinese Hospitals, Violence is Out of Control and It's Doctors Who are at Risk," Time Magazine, 11 October 2011. Web. http://www.time.com/time/world/article/0,8599,2096630,00.html. Accessed September 2017.
28. S. Wang, Annotations of the Tort Liability Law of the People's Republic of China, China Legal Press, 2010, pp. 274–268 (in Chinese); Xi and Yang, "Medical Liability Laws," 72.
29. Article 54, 2009 Tort Liability Law of the P.R.C.
30. Ryan Rossner's Report (2013), http://chinamedicalboard.org/sites/chinamedicalboard.org/files/rossner30sept13.pdf. Accessed September 2017.
31. EY, the Rise of Private Health Insurance in China—Consumer Demand Presents Huge Opportunities and Risks 2016. http://www.ey.com/Publication/vwLUAssets/EY-the-rise-of-private-health-insurance-in-china/$FILE/EY-the-rise-of-private-health-insurance-in-china.pdf. Accessed September 2017.
32. C. Milcent, "Industrialization and Inequalities: Healthcare in Chinese Rural Areas," C. Milcent, Under Revision for Revue Economique, 2015.
33. New Law Combats the "yinao" Phenomenon, December 2015, What's on Weibo. http://www.whatsonweibo.com/new-law-combats-chinas-yinao-phenomenon/. Accessed September 2017.
34. http://www.chinadaily.com.cn/china/2011-09/27/content_13796619.htm. Accessed September 2017.
35. They are often referred to as "ignorant people" on forums and social networks such as Sina Weibo.
36. That year, the number of registered doctors reached 2.06 per 1000 inhabitants, the number of nurses was 2.05 and the number of beds 4.55.
37. 初級中學.
38. K. Eggleston, L. Li, M. Qingyue, M. Lindelow, and A. Wagstaff, "Health Service Delivery in China: A Literature Review," Health Economics, Vol. 9, No. 2, 2008.
39. http://english.sina.com/news/2016-05-07/doc-ifxryahs0466505.shtml. Accessed September 2017.
40. Bo Tang, Secretary General, Physician Commission of District HealthCare, during his presentation "How Doctors Establish New Rules and Consensus in the Internet Era" during the conference "New Era of Internet+ Health: Value Discovery and Ecological Restructuring" held by CASS on 21 November 2015 in Beijing.

41. This point was already described in Chap. 5.
42. C. Milcent and B. Wu, "How Do You Feel? The Effect of the New Cooperative Medical Scheme in China," Journal of Development Studies, Vol. 51, No. 12, 2015, pp. 1585–1602.

Bibliography

Barber, S., M. Borowitz, H. Bekedam, and J. Ma, "The Hospital of the Future in China: China's Reform of Public Hospitals and Trends from Industrialized Countries," Health Policy and Planning, Vol. 29, No. 3, 2014, pp. 367–378.
Cao, Kai, "Hospitals' Return to Public Service Key to Tackle Doctor-Patient Disputes," Xinhua, 19 November 2011. Web. 30 September 2013.
Eggleston, K., L. Li, M. Qingyue, M. Lindelow, and A. Wagstaff, "Health Service Delivery in China: A Literature Review," Health Economics, Vol. 9, No. 2, 2008.
EY, The Rise of Private Health Insurance in China | Consumer Demand Presents Huge Opportunities and Risks, 2016. http://www.ey.com/Publication/vwLU-Assets/EY-the-rise-of-private-health-insurance-in-china/$FILE/EY-the-rise-of-private-health-insurance-in-china.pdf. Accessed September 2017.
Harris, Dean M., and Chien Chang Wu, "Medical Malpractice in the People's Republic of China: The 2002 Regulation on the Handling of Medical Accidents," The Journal of Law, Medicine & Ethics, Vol. 33, No. 3, 2005, pp. 456–477.
Jiang, Jessie, "In Some Chinese Hospitals, Violence is Out of Control and It's Doctors Who Are at Risk," Time Magazine, 11 October 2011. Web. http://www.time.com/time/world/article/0,8599,2096630,00.html. Accessed September 2017.
Lim, M., T. Yang, Z. Zhang, F. Zhao, W. Feng, and Y. Chen, "The Role and Scope of Private Medical Practice in China," Final Report to the World Health Organization and the United Nations Development Program, UNDP, WHO and MOH China, 2002.
Milcent, C., "Industrialization and Inequalities: Healthcare in Chinese Rural Areas," C. Milcent, Under Revision for Revue Economique, 2015.
Milcent, C., and B. Wu, "How Do You Feel? The Effect of the New Cooperative Medical Scheme in China," Journal of Development Studies, Vol. 51, No. 12, 2015, pp. 1585–1602.
Shun Ching Chan, C., "A Market of Distrust: Unofficial Payments for Hospital Care in China," The 12th Conference of the European Sociological Association (ESA 2015), 2015.
Tang, Bo, Secretary General, Physician Commission of District HealthCare, during his presentation "How Doctors Establish New Rules and Consensus in the

Internet Era" during the conference "New Era of internet+ Health: Value Discovery and Ecological Restructuring" held by CASS on 21 November 2015 in Beijing.

Tu, J., "Yinao: Protest and Violence in China's Medical Sector," December 2015, Berkeley Journal of Sociology. http://berkeleyjournal.org/2014/12/yinao-protest-and-violence-in-chinas-medical-sector/. Accessed September 2017.

Tucker, J.D., Y. Cheng, B. Wong et al., "Patient–Physician Mistrust and Violence Against Physicians in Guangdong Province, China: A Qualitative Study," BMJ Open, Vol. 5, No. 10, 2015.

Urban China, Toward Efficient, Inclusive, and Sustainable Urbanization Par The World Bank, Development Research Center of the State Council, Source MoH, 2011.

Wang, S., Annotations of the Tort Liability Law of the People's Republic of China, China Legal Press, 2010, pp. 274–268 (in Chinese); Xi and Yang, "Medical Liability Laws," 72.

Wang, Zhongming, and Jianhua Li, "Yiliaojiufen fasheng de yuanyin ji yingduic-uoshi" ("The Reason and Countering Measures of Medical Disputes"), Zhongguo Shequ Yishi (Chinese Community Doctor), No. 12, 2012, pp. 409–410.

Wang, Zhu, and Ken Oliphant, "Yangge Dance: The Rhythm of Liability for Medical Malpractice in the People's Republic of China," Chicago-Kent Law Revue, Vol. 87, 2011, pp. 26–30.

CHAPTER 9

Digital Healthcare

Abstract This chapter addresses the increasing role of digital healthcare in the overall Chinese healthcare system. As described in previous chapters, the healthcare system faces many issues, such as the confrontational relationship between doctors and patients, the poor access for populations in rural areas, the significant mark-up throughout distribution channels, a financially heavy burden for chronic diseases, poor quality of healthcare supply and inefficient hospital operation except Level 3 hospitals that have to deal with an over-demand. Many solutions have been proposed, such as the multiplication of healthcare suppliers, the establishment of general practitioners as gatekeepers for hospital admissions, the implementation of public health insurance schemes or the government support for reforms in favour of private health insurance and private healthcare providers. However, they have not proven sufficient to solve all problems yet. Digital healthcare is likely to play an increasing part in addressing these issues. One of the strengths of e-health is the quick and widespread adoption of mobile platforms. This may help solve access challenges, through online appointment registration systems, models of online-offline services, two-communication platforms between patients and physicians, sharing information through the Electronic Health Record (EHR) and Electronic Medical Record (EMR) systems, the generalized implementation of a DRG-based payment system, making patients more increasingly active actors in maintaining the health status, and improving the online drug market. On the flip side,

© The Author(s) 2018
C. Milcent, *Healthcare Reform in China*,
https://doi.org/10.1007/978-3-319-69736-9_9

this also raises many concerns regarding the confidentiality of personal medical data and the monopoly situation of some internet companies.

Keywords Digital healthcare • Online appointment • E-health • Cloud computing and big data • Three internet giants

As described in different chapters of this book, the Chinese healthcare system faces many issues such as the confrontational relationship between doctors and patients, lack of access in rural areas, the significant mark-up throughout distribution channels, the financial heavy burden for chronic diseases, poor quality of healthcare supply and inefficient hospital operations except at Level 3 hospitals that have to deal with an over-demand. So far, solutions have been proposed as more healthcare suppliers, the establishment of general practitioners (GPs) as gatekeepers for hospital admission, the implementation of public health insurance schemes and government support with reforms in favour of private health insurance and private healthcare providers. However, they have not yet proven sufficient to solve all problems.

In this chapter, I show how digital health may be part of the response to inefficiencies in the healthcare system. One of the strengths of e-health is the mass adoption of mobile platforms. In 2011, there were already 500 million internet users, 180 million online buyers and 300 million users of social networks. In 2014, $700 million was invested in e-health firms. A McKinsey Global Institute report (2015) gave other figures shedding light on the rapid growth of the mobile health sector in China. Some 83% of internet users are mobile phone internet users. The number of active smart devices was 700 million in 2014, with around three hours per person spent on smartphones every day,[1] making the potential for e-health huge. According to the Boston Consulting Group, the market is expected to be worth over $110 billion by 2020. This market is wide in scope as it covers, on top of smartphone applications, *cloud computing*, as well as applications using *Big Data*. There are over 2000 healthcare-related smartphone applications on the market. Some of these applications are targeted at physicians and healthcare institutes, while others are aimed at patients. For patients, the most frequently used applications are for tele-medical consulting, teleconsultation, diagnosis services and treatment services. These services are modifying the behaviour of each of the four actors: patients, physicians/medical staff, insurers, and pharmaceutical companies.

The government accelerated its support for e-health services and devices in the 2009 reforms. With the 12th Five Year plan, regarding the medical equipment industry, the Ministry of Commerce (MoC) stated that "the latest technologies in digitalization, internet, and cloud will be the key for electronic healthcare development". The Ministry of Health (MoH), in the Strategic Report on Healthy China 2020, planned a $9.8 billion budget to standardize information technology (IT) systems in major hospitals, building a public Electronic Medical Record (EMR) system and regional medical information platform. The Guideline for Remote Medical Service from the National Health and Family Planning Commission (NHFPC), published in August 2014, allowed online service providers to offer medical suggestions but so far, only healthcare institutions can provide remote medical treatment. In January 2015, telemedicine pilot programmes were launched in five provinces in the most remote areas of China (Ningxia, Yunnan, Inner Mongolia, Guizhou and Tibet).

INFORMATION CONTEXT

Smartphone Usage and Apps

In China more than anywhere, smartphones have totally transformed the way people communicate and consume. To access digital services, a vast majority of Chinese consumers use their mobile phones. One of the essential and vital apps is WeChat. Everyone communicates via this free app (phone, video, messages). It can be a one-to-one communication or a group of people chatting together simultaneously. They disseminate information with files, pictures, photos and audios. They exchange opinions through private or semi-private networks. They can buy products and services (the bank details can be linked) but also use virtual money that is used to reimburse a friend for dinner or group gifts. The key success of this app is the personal QR code that can be scanned as easily as taking a photo. The publisher of this app, Tencent, has turned into a major player in the industry and has diversified its activities.

Alibaba and Baidu are also widely present through different apps. Their apps focus on specific areas, which is the main difference between them and WeChat. Below, we will see how Alibaba provides a booking registration system that allows streamlining the hospital queuing process. We also look at Baidu apps that make online consultation as easy as a phone call to a friend. Other apps allow access to information on a patient's health status. If some apps help medical staff to follow-up a health condition, others provide information to the individual patient to help him or her achieve better health through lifestyle changes.

Institutional Changes
The National Health and Family Planning Commission of the People's Republic of China (NHFPC) published, on 29 August 2014, its opinions regarding telemedicine services. This document promoted a more intensive use of telemedicine throughout China. Yet, support for telemedicine from the Chinese authorities had appeared as early as 1999, with a notice from the former Ministry of Health (MoH).[2] If the definition was quite restrictive in the earlier part of the first decade after 2000, the new notices since then were more inclusive. The 2014 notices widely expanded the telemedicine definition to procedures, diagnoses, patient follow-up and doctor communication.

In 2013, according to the official published statistics of NHFPC, more than 2057 medical institutes called on telemedicine to treat patients. Since 2010, the financial authorities of the central government have invested 84.28 million Yuan, in supporting 22 midwestern provinces in setting up telemedical systems.[3] This reflects the Chinese government's endeavour to make the adoption of telemedicine by medical institutions more widespread. Remote healthcare access can be interpreted as an alternative used by the Chinese authorities to deal with geographic disparities observed over the territory. Its goes hand in hand with the wide development of public health centres, which can be interpreted as a mixed solution involving both physical resources (extensive networks of health centres) and digital resources (online telemedicine).

Since the first notices on telemedicine, the provincial Health and Family Planning Commissions obtained a certain degree of flexibility, with little strong direction from the central government. As a result, each Chinese province has defined its own standards for content and implementation. The consequence is a wide disparity in the internet platforms that are implemented. Hospitals are then poorly connected between provinces. In addition, the reimbursement rule differs from one location to the other. Ultimately, this brings about a paradox in which telemedical systems are entrenched in different geographical silos that cannot connect, creating a physical barrier for a digital system.

To solve this paradox, a new notice was published on 15 January 2015 to define the broad outline of a unified telemedical system over the Chinese territory. Each province is only in charge of the executive part of this telemedical network.[4] In this document, the condition of privacy and confidentiality of information is also stated, but remains quite general.

SOLVING ACCESS CHALLENGES

Recall that the Chinese population is covered mainly by three public health insurance schemes. In most cases, these schemes do not cover outpatient expenses. Even when these expenses are covered, the percentage of patients' out-of-pocket expenses remains high. Therefore, the price of an outpatient visit is a determinant variable for healthcare access.

Online Appointment Registration Systems

As explained earlier in this book, one of the most common complaints voiced by the Chinese population about the health system is the time spent in queuing for outpatient registration. Some patients or relatives of patients have to wait in line for long hours, even overnight sometimes, to ensure registration. The black market of tickets to jump the queues has spread over the country. Online appointment registration systems are viewed as easing this situation, providing easier access to hospital medical services.

Several advantages can be listed:

- Avoid the long queues symptomatic of the traditional registration system, eventually leading to an increase in the satisfaction level of patients;
- Limit the black market of registration tickets;
- Reduce the risk of cross-infection developing during the registration process;
- Share medical information before and after the appointment or the admission-discharge process. The patient can share any preanalysis made through connected devices or in other ways and is able to share his or her medical information obtained on the internet or any other devices. The physician can follow up with the patient after consultation or discharge;
- The system may enhance the consistency and continuity of patient medical records. A kind of historical medical record could in theory be available for each patient;

- For hospitals, appointment systems can optimize medical procedures, prevent outpatient bottlenecks and reduce economic costs.[5,6,7,8,9,10,11,12,13]

The Beijing Municipal Commission of Health and Family Planning took a bold approach in December 2015: all Level 3 and 3A hospitals in this province-level municipality offer an online registration system, with a mobile phone app, since the end of 2017. This move aims at accelerating a trend that had already started well. Some Level 3A hospitals, for instance the Beijing Children's Hospital had already introduced such online systems. Others had WeChat-based registration systems, including advanced functionalities, such as sharing blood test results or other diagnoses with patients. According to many doctors, this system of registration has already improved the atmosphere at hospitals entrances. A doctor from Beijing Anzhen Hospital, Nie Xiaolu, explains[14]: "It used to be common to see more than 1000 patients and family members queuing up in the hospital early in the morning". This hospital received 3.37 million outpatients in 2014.

GuaHao is now the largest online platform in China. Founded in 2010, it is part of the Weiyi group that is linked to the Tencent group. GuaHao has an information-sharing system and its well-designed, easy-to-use online platform allows patients to access their personal calendars, local hospitals and physicians, and helps them make appointments within minutes. In 2011, eight hospitals participated and 7 million appointments were registered. Today, 1600 hospitals are listed on its platform, with 190,000 specialists and 100 million registered users. The services offered have now extended to online services to Chinese hospitals, doctors and patients who can make hospital appointments and payments using its mobile app and web portal. The name was eventually changed to WeDoctor,[15] to make the link with WeChat clearer for customers.

Competition is heating up in this lucrative market. While several online scheduling system providers have popped up in China during the past decade, GuaHao stands out. It has been endorsed by the NHFPC, thus providing it with a quality and accreditation status. Consumers are influenced in their choice of online providers so this accreditation gives GuaHao a dominant position on the market.

Amongst the many competitors, Baidu also offers an app for patients to access physician networks and make online registration, search for healthcare-related information let patients ask doctors questions and provide feedback.

Access to Online Healthcare

Online consultation is highly developed in some countries such as in the United States with 5 million users per month and 35% of the population using the internet for self-diagnosis.

Online access to healthcare can be divided into three market segments. The first segment aggregates information from various sources, including patient reviews, while the second directly proposes services. This second segment focuses on personal services without medical staff intervention and the third proposes online medical consultations.

The first segment focuses on healthcare advice. The app compiles a mass of data, information that would be time consuming and expensive to obtain otherwise. The success of such apps is obviously based on the subjective judgement of consumers. So far, neither a public authority nor an external authority without a conflict of interest guarantees the objective quality of the service offered. Today, consumers are increasingly requiring a form of accreditation.

The second segment is better described through concrete examples of apps that are massively used. Among the "success stories" is Dayima, introduced in 2012 and the most popular menstruation record application in China. The basic function of this app includes recording and predicting periods. Each day more than 3.2 million active visitors use the app, with 45 million registered users.

Another popular app is Gengmei, a networking app dedicated to beauty in general and cosmetic surgery in particular. This app offers services in the second and third segments. Users can use the app to consult with cosmetic surgeons free of charge, and obtain professional advice regarding procedures they may be considering. Advice and consulting is given by more than 3000 physicians online. For consumers, this is free and quick access to cosmetic physicians in a country where healthcare access is time consuming and expensive. Online users are then incentivized to consume cosmetic products purchased online via the app. For instance, laser treatment for acne is widely available to be booked online, with a cost ranging between RMB 5000 and 10,000.[16] Launched in 2013, there were more than 20 million Gengmei users in 2016.

The third segment: Faced with overcrowded Level 3 hospitals the healthcare market has developed a new offering of a virtual consultation by a highly qualified physician. This offering has several advantages: the delay in consultation is drastically reduced, the price of the consultation is lower, the time in consultation is significantly longer and complementary information can be provided with no delay by the physician. All these elements may explain the incredibly success of this new offering.

Besides, teleconsultation is also used to get a second medical opinion after a first diagnosis. The patient can send photos, scans or files of medical information obtained during the first medical visit. This information then helps and guides the physician making the online consultation. For chronic diseases where the patient has to return regularly to consult in order to get adequate medication, the teleconsultation is clearly seen as an improvement in the healthcare process.

From the physicians' point of view, online consultation allows them to extend their activity without wasting time travelling. From the legal and administrative standpoint, the physician belongs to a definite healthcare institution. He cannot work in a different place at the same time. However, the online consultations are considered "consulting activities" and are tolerated as such. This activity sits in a legally grey area. According to a researcher in Law at CASS, the current legal status of "consulting" gives flexibility to Chinese authorities to observe how things go before fixing a stricter framework.[17] However, it leaves many questions unanswered, one of which is who takes responsibility when a medical error occurs?

Online consultation and the implementation of family doctors are parallel solutions to address the same issue, namely the congestion in Level 3 and above hospitals. First, online consultations bring an additional healthcare supply. In contrast to the community health centres (CHCs), Level 1 hospitals and some Level 2 hospitals, the demand for online consultations is massive and increasing. The supply is judged by consumers as offering a sufficient level of quality. Secondly, the online solution enables electronic information on patients, to keep track of the historical medical health status of the patient, to be stored and shared. This information is available instantaneously to all online physicians of the website and, if needed, can be simultaneously accessed by several physicians. With a conventional consultation, the medical file can be on paper or in electronic form but the availability of the information may be less immediate. This advantage, however, has a drawback: the risk of mishandling confidential information. The information disclosed by the patient in his or her consultation might be disseminated and used for other purposes. Strong regulations have to be implemented to avoid any potential misuse. Finally, there is a disconnect between hospital inpatient activity and outpatient activity. Indeed, inpatient activity cannot be done without the physical presence of a physician.

Depending on the app, the cost of an online consultation is a flat fee, whatever the diagnosis, or monthly or annual contributions. The physician determines the pathology according to the symptom described by the patient and any medical information provided by the patient.

Amongst the most popular apps are Chunyu yisheng, founded in 2011. Originally, this app was only a remote physician consultation platform. Today, the range of medical services provided has been extended. The app provides physicians with access to their patients' medical records. Furthermore, it enables patients to communicate and schedule appointments with doctors. In addition, it offers reservation line treatment services to its users. In terms of pricing, various plans are offered, with either an annual fee, a monthly fee or fixed fee per online consultation. For instance, the delay in getting an answer to an inquiry ranges from 3 to 30 minutes. This app has 50,000 visits/requests per day, more than 40 million registered users and 40,000 certified physicians?[18,19]

Public institutions have also started to test remote care models. In January 2015, the NDRC approved pilot programmes in five provinces. Hospitals from Beijing make medical resources available for remote care in the provinces of Ningxia, Guizhou, Tibet, Inner Mongolia and Yunnan. In Shenzhen, the Second People's Hospital was authorized to adopt a rare disease diagnosis platform where patients can upload information and have access to experts around the county; an expert consultation is given within two days. Patients can get access to online video conferencing in communities, village healthcare centres and pharmacies, thereby remotely getting medical advice from highly qualified doctors.

Remote consultation appears as a solution to geographical disparities in healthcare access in a context where disparities between urban areas and rural areas are deep and widening. In 2011, the ratio of urban to rural healthcare expenses per capita was around 2.8.[20] This gap is due to the difference in healthcare price increases over the past two decades. If healthcare expenditure has been increasing 17 times in rural areas, it has increased 33 times in urban areas. As a comparison, this ratio is about 4 for the income per capita. Online consultation removes the physical topography constraint of healthcare access. Internet users get access to the same level of quality whatever the inhabitant's location and at the same price. This is in contrast to the past situation with a level of quality depending on the healthcare facilities' level and a drastic variation in healthcare prices. Today, healthcare system pricing is completely decentralized. The internet may unify the pricing policy of healthcare suppliers, at least for outpatient consultations.

Besides, online consultations emerge as an alternative entry point into the healthcare system versus a visit to a doctor in a Level 3 hospital. Earlier in this book, we presented reforms to push for referral to family doctors to become the standard entry point as a means to redefine the patient's pathway through the healthcare system, in order to limit the demand for Level 3 and 3A hospitals. Up until now, this reform has largely failed to enforce a new patient's pathway, as it meets reluctance in demand. The level of qualification of such doctors has not yet met expectations. On the other hand, the digital path seems to succeed where the traditional solution has failed. Many patients seem quite open about getting a first diagnosis online by a qualified physician at an affordable cost, prior to physically going to the hospital.

However, the question of data confidentiality is a crucial issue. All medical information flows and is stored in systems managed by private, for-profit, internet firms that may be tempted to monetize such information. Wechat, the Tencent group star app, is an example, as it is widely used for all purposes in many e-health situations, without much control over the usage of data. So far, regulation is insufficient to guarantee complete personal data confidentiality as well as prevent the use of these data for screening purposes. But is it realistic to imagine that such regulation can be implemented?

Besides, these remote consultations have other drawbacks. By definition, the patient is not physically seen by a doctor. Some information that cannot be detected by a virtual observation of the patient (e.g. it could be a gesture, some medically noticeable marks on skin) may be relevant for the medical diagnosis. In case of medical error, the legal responsibility of the physician is not clearly defined. There is no clear regulation on remote doctor consultation. Another point relates to the prescription of drugs. In China, delivering drugs is part of the consultation. For a physical medical consultation, the patient gets the drug prescription from the physician during the visit. For an online medical consultation, it is not possible for patients to get their drugs during the consultation and so they have to go to a sometimes distant pharmacy. This raises the question of online sales of prescription drugs. Until now, only over-the-counter drugs are allowed to be sold online.[21]

Integrated Model of Online–Offline Services

Moving beyond simply offering, on the one hand, online services and on the other, physically located healthcare services, internet companies are exploring a new scheme where these two services are integrated into the same model.

Alibaba Group is one of China's internet giants, initially specializing in online retail, similar to Amazon in the United States. It is a very good example in the sense it has a comprehensive and integrated strategy concerning health.

Alibaba Health Information Technology Ltd. or Alihealth was set up as a trading brand, offering online-based healthcare services. It has progressively widened its scope. In the course of 2014, Alibaba Group transferred the transactions of Tmall Online—an online pharmacy—to Alihealth. In October 2014, Ant Financial (formerly known as Alipay, a privately owned bank) was established by Alibaba as a financial affiliate of Alibaba Group.[22]

The "Future Hospital" programme was launched in May 2014 by Alihealth. It proposes a platform between patients and hospitals, where hospitalizing activities are online. Alipay is key to this integrated model.

On the patient side: It allows patients to register online and to pick up medical reports. If they have an Alipay account then they can link it to the hospital's service, to pay using their Alipay wallet. This service enables patients to avoid queues at the hospital cash desk. Two years after its release, this programme accounts for 400 hospital partners nationwide that offer reservation and payment services and has served over 50 million people. The registered users are mostly rural inhabitants.

On the hospital side: First, hospitals must pay an entry fee for them to get this service set up. Once available, the "Future Hospital" healthcare platform stores medical records at the individual level on behalf of the hospital. It sorts out patients according to the estimated degree of severity, allowing the hospital to propose some patients have remote consultations. This way, the medical staff can quickly deal with patients that do not genuinely need to come in to see a doctor. It also allows them to identify patients that need services that will make the hospital money. These services lead to less pressure on Level 3 hospital queues and crowding. In addition, they generate a new source of revenue through online consultation. The programme may ease the transition away from the current profit model heavily reliant on hospital drug sales. Indeed, revenue directly stemming from online consultations as well as indirect revenue from patient selection can ease this reliance on medicine sales. The Central Hospital of Wuhan is a vivid example of this move to a hospital profit model based on medical services. The IT system of this hospital is now completely dependent on the "Future Hospital" health-care platform.[23]

In a showcase programme, Alibaba demonstrated its vision of the future for mobile healthcare. The firm proposes an integrated model of online–offline services. A villager, who lives in a remote fishing village of Hubei province, called a hospital several hundred kilometres away, and spoke to a doctor. The doctor wrote an online prescription, which the villager purchased at an Alibaba-affiliated online pharmacy. The drugs arrived the next day and the villager paid the delivery person. There was no long bus ride, no standing in line to make an appointment, no waiting for the doctor. This view will revolutionize the way rural communities everywhere access healthcare services.[24]

This flow allows a much improved efficiency of the healthcare system. It may succeed where health authorities still struggle, despite repeated attempts over at least three decades, to change a hospital's profit model based on drug sales to an alternative but profitable one. Besides, it represents one of the first cross-hospital consolidated patient databases in many Chinese provinces.

However, there are downsides, such as:

- A possible systematic selection of patients;
- Concerns about private data collection, especially in the Chinese context where public services have been relatively slow to digitize their databases. How to preserve public interest when this public mission is delegated to a for-profit enterprise?

Improving Communication Between Patients and Physicians

The Chinese population has, generally speaking, a great appetite for IT and social media, and this is particularly the case for medical staff. For example, most physicians run a microblog and 50% of them are Weibo users.[25]

On the patients' side, a 2013 study from the McKinsey consulting group showed that 17% of patients were using the internet to choose their hospital, this percentage reaching 28% for those under 25. This creates an impetus to improve communication between patients and medical staff, using these digital tools.

Restoring the Basics of Communication

There is a growing number of apps allowing patients to get information on healthcare facilities or doctors. Here, we can cite the "Care Voice", an app based on patient peer reviews and recommendations on medical health services and GBi with "Reframe Health", introduced in 2015, and the first clinical evaluation app allowing mobile intervention. The focus is on chronic disease and on post-acute care.

Mobile Nurse Stations

E-health proposes ways to improve the quality of care delivery by improving communication between medical staff and patients regarding their health status. Mobile nurse stations are one of them. First, when admitted to hospital, patients are braceleted with a unique QR code. This allows them to be accurately identified and reduces medical accidents caused by patient misidentification. Secondly, before examining patients, nurses can access the QR code with all its digital health information on any mobile device. Nurses are then able to examine the patient and directly note information about the patient on their mobile devices. The second phase allows the storage and sharing of patient data more efficiently. Thirdly, the patient is connected to the mobile nurse station. If a clinical event occurs or the patient needs help, nurse staff are alerted. This mobile nurse station also allows the evaluation of nurses' performance based on reaction time documented by the mobile nurse station.

Such mobile nurse stations are already in place in some local areas. For instance, in Hong Kong Special Autonomous Region (SAR), this type of station is used in all public hospitals. Yet, the cost for the hospital remains an obstacle to its widespread adoption.

So far, there is little or no scientific study fully analyzing the effects of mobile nurse stations on medical staff and patient communication or on the assessment of the healthcare provided versus the risk it bears regarding the mishandling of confidential information.

Electronic Health Records (EHRs)

Electronic Health Records (EHRs) are now in use in over 80% of developed markets and they are quickly becoming commonplace in China as well.[26] An EHR enables physicians to record, manage and share health information at patient level in a very convenient way, using photos and audios.

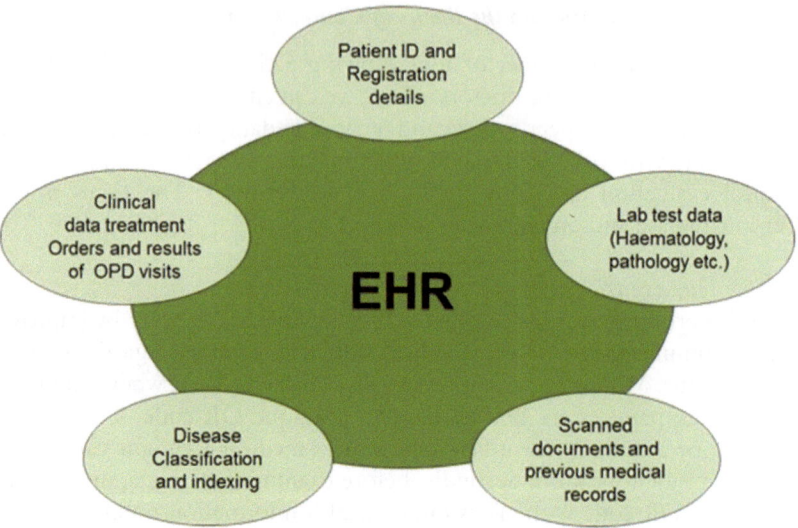

Fig. 9.1 Electronic Health Records according to the WHO. Source: Electronic Health Records: Manual for Developing Countries by WHO

According to Pacific Century Ventures, as of 2014, half of all tertiary hospitals in China use their own EHR system, as do 30% of urban health centres and 20% of rural hospitals (Fig. 9.1). This growth is only expected to continue, with experts predicting 80% participation in tertiary hospitals by 2020. Government officials also hope to implement EHRs in at least half of urban clinics and rural hospitals by 2020.[27]

Xingshulin (Apricot Forest) is a mobile app that provides EHR services where doctors can photograph, store, and organize patient records, and Medical e-pocket (reference materials and medical Journals)—a content that includes frequently used clinical guidelines, lab handbooks, pharmacopeia and medical literature with a bilingual medical literature library containing more than 300 scientific journals. So far, this application has failed to make a profit. Most revenue is from advertising. However, it still covers a small part of Chinese physicians (around 20%). They expect to take advantage of the EHR resources in the future to generate a profit.

Communication Between Physicians

Digital is also a useful tool to support the activity of physicians. The Clinical Decision Support System alerts physicians to the secondary effects of the drugs they may prescribe, any allergies as well as undesirable effects. Introduced in the early 1990s, it remains marginally used, as some apps offering the same services are actually easier to handle.

The behaviour of physicians is also modified by using the internet. It fosters rapid dissemination of new technologies and innovative procedures, changing the way patients are cured.

DXY (DingXiangYuan) company is the leading online community for physicians, healthcare professionals, pharmacies and facilities. It provides a biomedical trade platform, job posting, medical knowledge—with medical information, academic journals, drug guides—social media, a survey platform, and data services. Launched in 2000, this healthcare information sharing website has more than 4 million registered users—most of them are medical professionals.

Tencent invested in DXY in 2014. For this internet giant, this investment is aimed at exploring possible services to integrate into WeChat, the now essential app in China. With DXY, Tencent has access to drug information and connects with millions of health professionals.[28]

PATIENTS ARE INCREASINGLY ACTIVE ACTORS OF THEIR HEALTH

The topology of the Chinese territory explains that some areas are less populated than others. For obvious profitability reasons, the density of healthcare centres can be very different and the network is scarce is some areas. Connected devices are then an option to support the follow-up of patients.

Wireless Heart Health is an example of this tendency. Smartphones and cardiac sensors have been provided to 11,000 patients. The information collected is then sent to physicians for follow-up. When the data reveal a potential problem, the patient is contacted and in some cases admitted to a Level 1 hospital for additional tests (96 healthcare centres have been selected). DuLife, a division of Baidu, offers similar services and products.

These types of programmes promote e-health as a tool for more equal healthcare access. To cite Xiaohui Yu from the China Academy of Telecommunication Research of MIIT–CATR during the Brookings Institution conference in March 2014[29], "Our research shows that mobile technology can provide a means for China to meet challenges and achieve equal access to medical care." During this conference, Daryl West, vice president of the study department of Brookings Institution, reported the figure of 40,000 healthcare apps available on mobile phones.

mHealth[30] and Connected Devices

Baidu has developed mHealth (mobile health devices) and other connected devices. In 2014, it clearly stepped into the connected devices medical market with Dulife. The intelligent Bluetooth sports bracelet developed by Dulife, a fully owned subsidiary of Baidu, is a wearable health device. It collects and analyzes users' physiological indexes, such as blood pressure, body fat percentage, cholesterol level and other medical information. From this information, some advice can be given on adapted physical exercises and proper nutrition. In addition, nutritional training for customers can be proposed.

Another example is iHealth, a leader in mobile medical devices. It proposes to monitor not only activities such as sleeping or steps but also life signs (glucose, weight, body hydration, body fat, body mass, pulse rate via pulse sensor). It provides historical health documents available on smart devices. All the information can be shared automatically remotely.

These examples of connected devices can be compared to Fitbit, another wearable health device launched in 2007, in its updated version.

There are also connected devices specifically dedicated to chronic disease management. The most common usage is for diabetes management and there are around 500 apps in this area. For instance, "Control Diabetes" is an app that proposes a monitoring, documentation and reminder function, help to inform about the disease, and online consultation services. There are around 200 physicians working for this app. "D space" or "D nurse" are also other apps used for diabetes monitoring.

Cloud Computing and Big Data Initiatives

Since the SARS epidemic, Chinese authorities have been very eager to set up a unified medical information system. Such a database would allow them to monitor the prevalence of infectious diseases. It may also ensure controlling the health condition of the population and forecasting health problem events as well as the early detection of unusual health problems.

Various initiatives have been taken, for instance, a public agency whose mission is to launch Cloud-based health platform has been created. The Regional Health Information Networks (RHIN) is an information system linking hospitals to CHCs. Within this network, each hospital can create its own information system and share it with other healthcare centres in their network. This programme, however, remains mostly at the experimental stage, including a trial in Beijing starting from 2008, and has not been widely duplicated.

Another initiative is a joint venture between Baidu and the Beijing municipal government—the Beijing Health Cloud or *Jiankangyun*. It provides prediagnosis assessments for patients or medical staff using Big Data technology. There are three steps: monitoring, analyzing and advising for personalized (at the individual level) healthcare support.

- *Monitoring*: From smart connected devices such as wristbands, medical information on, among other aspects, weight or blood pressure, is collected at the individual level and stored in the "Cloud";
- *Analysis*: From this Big Data, with information at the individual level stored on a Cloud-computing platform, analysis screen the population and evaluates very precisely the risk of healthcare expenses for each individual. Prediagnosis assessments will be available on request at the individual level. It can be used to prevent illness or to plan and anticipate the public cost of healthcare demand;
- *Advising*: From this analysis, it is possible to offer consultancy health services. Personalized healthcare products or services could be proposed to help people remain healthy. Personalized advice and coaching could be provided with a specific and individualized programme on how to better one's health condition. With connected devices, additional offers may allow a follow-up on the individual, for instance through remote electrocardiogram monitoring.

Baidu gave a glimpse of the ultimate with the presentation in November 2016 of its virtual medial assistant called "Melody". This technology is designed to be the first port of call for a person feeling sick at home. A patient poses a health query to Melody, which responds in real time with further questions, and compares responses with Baidu's database of medical information. All that data is crunched, and Melody then poses a possible diagnosis to a doctor who can then recommend the next steps.[31] Here is the ultimate use of Big Data stored on the Cloud platform.

Here, the analysis of the Big Data on medical information supported on a Cloud is supposed to be a tool for the regulator to accurately forecast healthcare expenses through Big Data analysis. The population can be accurately screened according to their propensity to illness and the cost associated. It can also be viewed as a tool to help prevent illnesses and the spread of epidemics. As claimed by Li Mingyuan, vice-president of Baidu, the objective of this health Cloud platform is to better social well-being.[32] However, this health Cloud is also highly valuable in terms of differentiation of customers to monetize healthcare service products, in terms of assessing health insurance premiums for patients. The question is then what happens to the non-profitable group of consumers?

Electronic Medical Records (EMRs)

Electronic Medical Records (EMRs) and Electronic Health Records (EHRs) are at the individual level but they do not share the same focus. The EHR collects information on the historical health status of the patient. This information allows health information about the patient to be shared over the time and enables a clinical follow-up of the patient by different doctors. The EHR collects information about the hospital admission and this information focuses on the hospital's medical activity. It answers the question: what was done by the hospital's medical staff in terms of health-care and for whom? It provides population characteristics defined by diagnosis and co-morbidity but also in terms of demographic variables.

In 2012, the MoH invested $9.5 billion in the development of medical data and the improvement of information systems in public Chinese hospitals.[33] The main goal is the creation of a standardized database on patients' characteristics https://www.bcgperspectives.com/content/articles/biopharmaceuticals-medical-devices-technology-chinas-digital-health-care-revolution/?chapter=2 accessed 12/12/2017:

- With a unified electronic format of the health information collected at the individual level;

- Yet, details of the information may still be different between local bureaus of health and from the national level;
- Collection and storage of electronic medical records (EMR).

In some provinces such as Beijing, Jiangsu and Fujian, pilot programmes have been initiated to collect data following this newly defined protocol.[34] Yet, the development of Big Data-enabled solutions and a Cloud system to improve the quality of healthcare is limited by geographical differences in hospital IT systems.

As a consequence, the focus is currently on building e-platforms to improve access and efficiency of the healthcare system. One of the major targets is to reach, by 2020, a personal healthcare information system that covers the entire population. Different hospitals, counties and provinces have established digital databases for EHR and patient information. The objective is to build robust health information platforms at four levels (national, provincial, city and county) and to achieve integration.

Diagnosis Related Groups (DRGs) and Reimbursement

To curb the increase in the cost of healthcare and improve the inefficiencies in healthcare access, one of the solutions is to change the reimbursement methods for hospitals. Until now, hospitals are reimbursed on a fee-for-service basis, but the development of IT makes it possible to develop alternative schemes, based on the pathology and not the act, in order to control costs more strictly.

Such schemes have been implemented in the United States from the beginning of the 1980s and are now widespread across OECD countries. A categorization of pathologies, diagnoses and acts is set up. Each group defined is called a Diagnosis Related Group (DRG).

Each DRG is defined by a subpathology as well as associated diagnoses and acts and procedures to be performed. This way, each patient can be linked to a DRG. Then, to each DRG is attributed a lump sum, based on the cost the hospital will have to bear for this precise type of patient. The advantage of this lump sum is that it is not correlated to the care actually performed but to what is theoretically necessary for each specific DRG. The creation of the different groups requires elaborate IT systems, collecting at patient level information regarding all acts, procedures, diagnoses and co-morbidities.

China is currently testing such schemes, through pilot experiments carried out in Beijing among other locations.

ONLINE DRUG MARKET

China's online retail market is the largest in the world, exceeding the US market since 2013, and this market is growing ever faster. Since 2012, the MoH and the NHFPC published directives in favour of the development of online pharmacies. China has become the world's second largest online pharmaceutical market in less than five years, and there are already around 180 websites approved to sell over-the-counter (OTC) drugs online.[35]

So far, the most consumed products are vitamins and dietary supplements (VDSs). Indeed, until 2016, the pharmaceutical laboratories were not authorized to sell prescription drugs online. That year it was announced that authorization was imminent, but as of late 2017 it has not been given. In newspapers or from consulting group interviews (carried out in Beijing, Shanghai and Hong Kong, from 2015 to 2017), the big internet groups are all anticipating that the lift of this ban on prescription drug e-commerce is just a matter of time, and all that is needed is to overcome the reluctance of some stakeholders.

This has to be put in the context where, today, 80% of drug sales take place in public hospitals and are essential to their financial model. A fully fledged online drug market, including prescription drugs, is direct competition to in-hospital drug sales to patients. In the United States, by comparison, 30% of the OTC and prescribing drug sales are carried out on the internet. This explains the opposition to open the online market to prescription drugs.

For the consumer on the other hand, this move should result in lower drug prices, but with questions regarding the quality of the product, in a context of proliferation of fake medical drugs reaching the marketplace. The level of quality and the trust in any online market will depend on the level of guidelines and regulation set up by the authorities. Indeed, it is more difficult to control drug sellers on the internet than those with a shop on the street corner.

The government has sought to implement a platform that would authenticate and track pharmaceutical products. In 2005, the State General Administration of Quality Supervision, Inspection and Quarantine (AQSIQ) first promoted and then enforced the use of an electronic quality control system named Product Identification Authentication and Tracking System, or PIATS. This system was developed by a structure co-owned by AQSIQ and Citic 21CN. By mid-2008, around 68,500 firms were using this system. It codes all the drugs listed in the national basic medicine categories as well as imported medicines. The target is to fight fake medical drugs, by enabling both retailers and consumers to easily check the authenticity of the products they intend to purchase.

Later, Citic 21CN obtained approval from the China Food and Drug Administration (CFDA) to sell drugs on a third-party website. In 2014, Alibaba and Yunfeng bought control of Citic 21CN[36] on the Hong Kong stock exchange, with a 51.3% stake. Alibaba's objective is to develop a pharmaceutical product information and selling platform. It can use the large pool of pharmaceutical product data obtained by CITIC 21CN, combined with Alibaba's knowledge of e-commerce, Cloud computing and Big Data analysis. Besides, Alibaba's Yao.Tmall is the Alibaba marketplace that aggregates diverse online pharmacy vendors.

As a result, PIATS is today outsourced by the China Food and Drug Administration (CFDA) to Ali Health, the health division of Alibaba. The managing structure has been renamed Alijiankang. This situation has raised criticism, due to potential conflicts of interest by both entities taking part in the regulation of pharmaceutical sales while simultaneously operating within that market. Nineteen big pharmaceutical companies, including the two most powerful (Sinopharm Group Co. Ltd and Laibaixing Pharmacy Chain), took action to sue the CFDA over the monitoring system. These firms alleged that the arrangement concerning PIATS gave an unfair advantage to Ali Health.[37,38] In February 2016, the CFDA decided to freeze PIATS. After a few months, PIATS resumed with new conditions: participation of pharmaceuticals is now on voluntary basis and no longer mandatory as was previously planned. Besides, to placate the other operators in the sector, it was announced that pharmaceutical companies would be exempt from drug tracking fees for a period of three years. But what lies in store after that?[39]

Beyond the questions raised by a private, profit-driven enterprise collecting personal medical data, the company appears to be embroiled in a conflict of interest, in the sense that the company itself sells medication online. This gives Ali Health a major role in regulating healthcare products and in giving access to privileged information on those very same products.[40]

New Models of Drug Purchase

If the online market opens to prescription drugs, hospitals will lose their monopoly situation and the advantage of being both the prescriber and the seller. Different scenarios can be imagined. The patient could visit a doctor and then buy the prescribed drugs online. Another scenario could be that the patient consults a doctor online and then, after a competitive bidding process, purchases through increased competition.

The online to offline prescription drug sale pilot model of Ali Health is based on such a bidding process. First tested in 2014 for Shijiazhuang and Hangzhou, it is now available in major cities such as Beijing, Shanghai and Guangzhou. The patient can send a picture of a prescription drug script and then chooses a pharmacy after a bidding process. The selected pharmacy will sell the drugs and deliver them offline. A direct payment can also be made on Tmall's drugstore (a division of Alibaba). The drug's scanned electronic code allows the patient to acquire information on the drug product purchased. Prescription drug scripts can also be sent directly from hospitals that partner with Ali Health.

The online to offline (O2O) prescription drug sale model has also attracted other companies. For instance, the insurance giant Pingan has a division called Yihaodian that is accredited to sell OTC list A drugs. GSK, the British pharmaceutical company, opened an official shop on Tmall, while some apps (such as Ehaoyao and Qumaiyao) have launched their O2O drug sale platforms.

Justification of Government Intervention

How to ensure competitive conduct in the market? Under which circumstances is state intervention desirable? The public interest approach may justify state intervention. There are three mains reasons:

- *The asymmetric information between consumers and providers.* The implementation of PIATS is a way to compensate for this lack of information for the consumer. However, it places a private firm in a dominant position;
- *The externality that happens when costs or benefits affect agents other than those directly concerned by the transaction.* Pollution is an easy to understand example. The drug market is another good example. The

control of drug quality ensures a positive externality in a public health perspective;

* *The concept of public good.* Goods and services defined as pure public goods need to have specific properties. National defence, education (at least at the basic level) and healthcare access (for a defined basket) are established as examples of universal access.

THE UPCOMING CHALLENGES FOR E-HEALTH

Constraints of Data Collection

To collect and process information, medical staff have to dedicate part of their time to administrative tasks. If digitalization has many advantages, on the flip side the time dedicated to it comes at the expense of pure medical attention. For instance, nurses, in addition to their usual tasks, now have to scan the bracelets of their patients to check their identity (via a QR code) and then check the tag on the drugs before giving them to patients. Lili Hua, a nurse in a Level 3 hospital in Beijing, explained the cumbersome administrative procedures since the implementation of the electronic medical system. She said that the time spent with patients is even less than before, even if this new constraint leads to reduced medical errors.[41] Overall, these changes lack scientific studies to assess the global effect on the healthcare provided to patients.

Figure 9.2 displays the tasks to be done by the nurse at each visit to a patient.

Confidentiality of Data and Patient Privacy

How to deal with the confidentiality of the data? This question is central to the development of e-health, not only in China but elsewhere.

Figure 9.3 shows the results from a survey carried out by the Economist Intelligence Unit think tank regarding e-health. It involved interviewing 144 CEOs, managers and strategy managers of healthcare institutions, both public and private, pharmaceutical companies as well as medical device producers, in 23 countries. Surprisingly, for interviewees from the public sector, patient privacy is the main obstacle to the development of e-health.

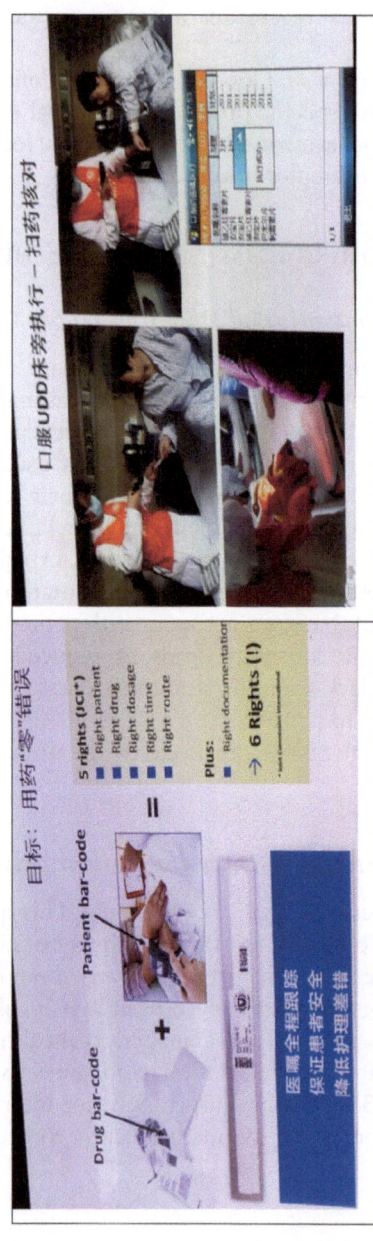

Fig. 9.2 Tasks to be done by the nurse at each visit control to a patient

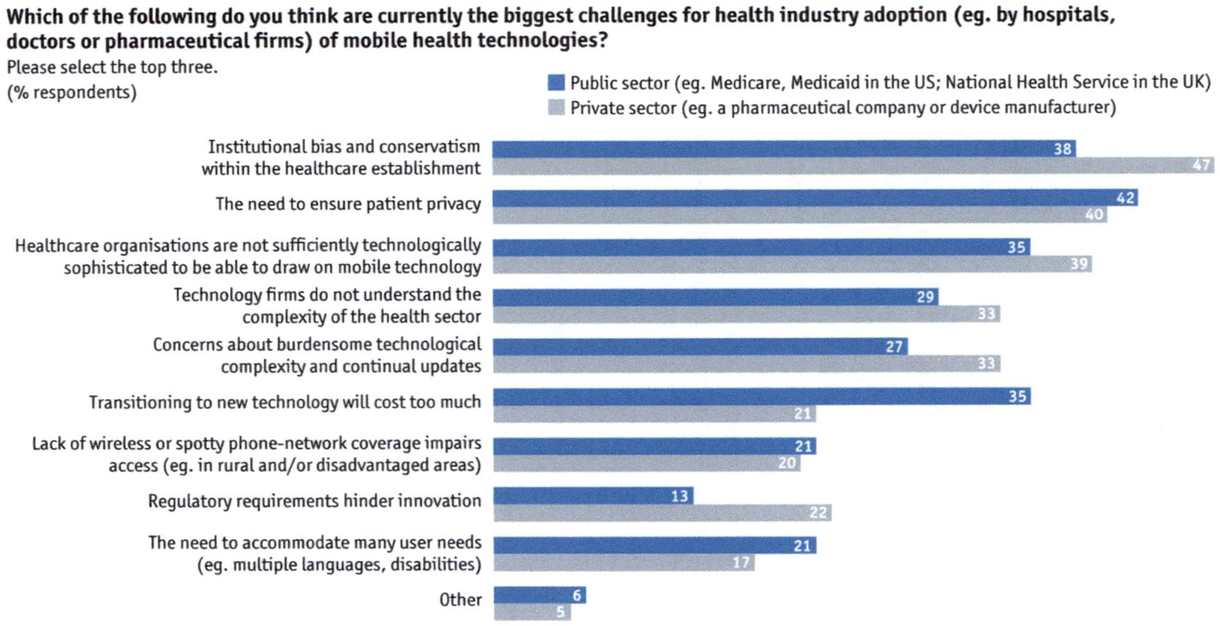

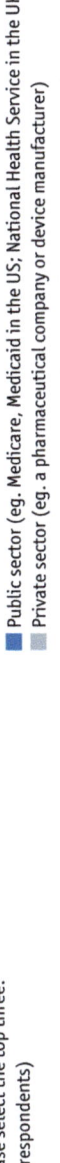

Which of the following do you think are currently the biggest challenges for health industry adoption (eg. by hospitals, doctors or pharmaceutical firms) of mobile health technologies?

Please select the top three.

(% respondents)

■ Public sector (eg. Medicare, Medicaid in the US; National Health Service in the UK)
■ Private sector (eg. a pharmaceutical company or device manufacturer)

Institutional bias and conservatism within the healthcare establishment — 38 / 47

The need to ensure patient privacy — 42 / 40

Healthcare organisations are not sufficiently technologically sophisticated to be able to draw on mobile technology — 35 / 39

Technology firms do not understand the complexity of the health sector — 29 / 33

Concerns about burdensome technological complexity and continual updates — 27 / 33

Transitioning to new technology will cost too much — 35 / 21

Lack of wireless or spotty phone-network coverage impairs access (eg. in rural and/or disadvantaged areas) — 21 / 20

Regulatory requirements hinder innovation — 13 / 22

The need to accommodate many user needs (eg. multiple languages, disabilities) — 21 / 17

Other — 6 / 5

Fig. 9.3 Survey result / challenges to health industry adoption of mobile technologies

According to Robert B. McCray, president and CEO of Wireless-Life Sciences Alliance:[42] "If people won't use the technology because of data breaches, we run the risk of losing the benefits of these technologies." The president and strategy director of Samsung Electronics, Young Sohn, added that[43] "privacy is probably the single biggest issue of our time".

Another point is the inequality generated by connected objects. If the financial dimension is a minor issue, the demographic dimension is central (Fig. 9.4), with the older generation less prone to be comfortable with digital technologies.

Without being totally excluded, the elderly population is the least exposed to e-health and mHealth. Even if the healthcare system reform is putting the emphasis on digital tools, they still need to be duplicated in a more traditional fashion for the elderly. For instance, for the online registration system, a phone service has been implemented as well as a simplified app. However, the voice speed on automated answering machines with pre-recorded instructions is not always easily understood by senior citizens. In some areas, "real-world" help desks have opened to help the elderly to navigate this digital environment. But what about the areas without this help?

Conflicts of Interest

Concerns about possible conflicts of interest have become increasingly prominent in the light of recent scandals. Below are examples focusing on the three internet giants (Baidu, Alibaba and Tencent), with an emphasis on the implications for the Chinese health system.

The Baidu Tieba Forum, part of Baidu, is an internet forum administrator. It contains more than 10,000 subforums, including those aimed at exchanging healthcare information. In recent months, a number of scandals have erupted[44] over the ability of private companies to take control of these non-commercial forums, allowing adverts for medical products of dubious quality. The flashpoint for this was the case of a forum on haemophilia (a blood disorder). It was displaying advertisements that extolled the virtues of healthcare providers that turned out to be unlicensed and of poor quality. More recently, in May 2016, a student who died of cancer published a long post where he placed the blame squarely on Baidu for irresponsibly exaggerating the capabilities and quality of the hospital where he chose to have his treatment.

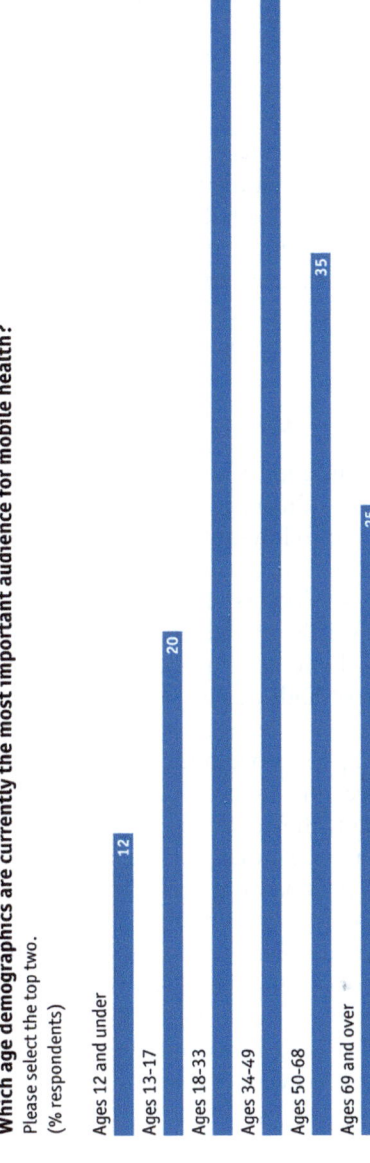

Fig. 9.4 Survey result / most important audience for mobile health

As explained above, PIATS was outsourced by the CFDA to Ali Health, a division of Alibaba. Beyond the questions raised over a private, profit-driven enterprise collecting personal medical data, the company appears to be embroiled in an array of conflicts of interest, in the sense that the company itself sells medication online (Alibaba announced that the running of online pharmacy Tmall Online would be transferred to Ali Health).[45] This gives Ali Health a major role in regulating healthcare products and privileged information on those very same products.

In conclusion, we can say that digital healthcare offers many sources of improvement but is not in itself a fully-fledged solution to fix all the inefficiencies of the Chinese healthcare system. It needs to be integrated into a strong-willed set of policies, including a redefined patient journey and clear monitoring of private actors carrying out missions of public service. This is obviously still a work in progress.

CONCLUSION

One solution to the inefficiency of the Chinese healthcare system may be to foster the development of managed care organizations. Integrated core services from diagnosis to follow-up could be provided and managed by private insurance schemes. The e-consultations would be a way to offer a very high quality panel of doctors. These doctors, working otherwise in government-owned hospitals, would provide their services remotely. So far, the main barrier is the level of quality provided by private hospitals. The slow development of high-quality private hospitals is an obstacle, as well as the government controlled status of high-quality Level 3 and Level 3A hospitals. Currently, pilot programmes have been launched to encourage co-operation between private health insurers and Level 3 or Level 3A hospitals. For the patient, the advantage is rapid access to healthcare for benign illnesses to severe pathology. For the supply side, the advantage is total control of the patient's pathway and complete knowledge of the historical medical file owing to Big Data.

Up to now, according to private investors, the public simply lacks trust in Big Data initiatives concerning their health. The health Cloud, though, is valuable in terms of social well-being improvement. Privacy concerns build a social barrier that has to be overstepped for the health Cloud to fully thrive. However, is that what is desired by the population? In terms of health prevention and control of healthcare expenses, Big Data is a really powerful tool. However, in terms of equality, the answer is not straightforward. A healthcare system based on an intensive screening of the population will disclose and uncover those with a high probability if incurring major healthcare expenses. The question of private insurance cover for this disadvantaged population will be even more acute. With a pooling population of patients, without information on their health condition, the healthcare system could be based on a percentage of wages. With the development of the health Cloud and its increasing use, such a financing scheme becomes less and less plausible. Could we say that the veil of ignorance has certain virtues in this case?

NOTES

1. China Mobile Internet 2013 Overview, Umeng Insight Report, March 2014.
2. "Notice on Reinforcing the Administration of Telemedicine," Health Office Issue, No. 2, 1999.
3. The original notice from NHFPC with an English translation can be found at following address https://www.healthcarelawtoday.com/wp-content/uploads/sites/15/2014/09/China-Telemedicine-Opinions-Aug-29-2014.pdf. Accessed September 2017.
4. http://www.nhfpc.gov.cn/ewebeditor/uploadfile/2015/01/20150115100526329.pdf. Accessed September 2017.
5. Y. Su, J.L. Liu, Y., and X.M. Yi, "The Idea About the Mode of a Patient-Centered Modern Clinic," Journal of Medical Postgraduates, Vol. 19, No. 1, 2006, pp. 74–78.
6. R. Guo, Z.M. Miao, G. Wei, S.C. Xing, and Y. Zhang, "The Present Situation and Suggestions of the Domestic Appointment Registration of Hospital," Progress in Modern Biomedicine, Vol. 12, No. 7, 2012, pp. 1357–1360.
7. M. Huang, "Exploration and Practice about Outpatient Appointment Registration Service Mode," Gansu Journal of Traditional Chinese Medicine, Vol. 24, No. 1, 2011, pp. 59–60.
8. X.Q. Yin, Z.Z. Huang, and L.J. Huang, "Design and Research on Appointed Outpatient Registration System in Modern Hospital," Hospital Digitalization, Vol. 31, No. 12, 2010, pp. 48–53.
9. Y.X. Xu and H.X. Ding, "Current Situation Analysis of the Hospital Outpatient Appointment Services," Clinical Medical Engineering, Vol. 19, No. 1, 2012, pp. 105–106.
10. X.Q. Yin, Z.Z. Huang, and L.J. Huang, "Design and Research on Appointed Outpatient Registration System in Modern Hospital," Hospital Digitalization, Vol. 31, No. 12, 2010, pp. 48–53.

11. J.H. Chen, S.G. Tu, H. Xiong, and N.Z. Xu, "Practice of Mobile Phone Real-Name System Appointment Registration," Chinese Nursing Research, Vol. 26, No. 1, 2012, pp. 170–171.

12. M. Huang, "Exploration and Practice about Outpatient Appointment Registration Service Mode," Gansu Journal of Traditional Chinese Medicine, Vol. 24, No. 1, 2011, pp. 59–60.

13. W. Yu, X. Yu, H. Hu, G. Duan, Z. Liu, and Y. Wang, "Use of Hospital Appointment Registration Systems in China: A Survey Study," Global Journal of Health Sciences, Vol. 5, No. 5, 2013, pp. 193–201.

14. "No More Long Queues in China's Smart Hospitals," China Daily, 8 December 2015.

15. McKinsey Analysis, 2015. https://fr.slideshare.net/fle864/20150402-chic-mc-k-e-health-in-china-vf. Accessed September 2017; http://www.iamwire.com/2015/09/practos-chinese-counterpart-guahao-raises-394m-1-5b-valuation-led-hillhouse-goldman/123356. Accessed September 2017; http://www.sramanamitra.com/2016/06/17/billion-dollar-unicorns-guahao-targets-chinas-healthcare/. Accessed September 2017.

16. "A New Face for China's Plastic Surgery Industry," South China Morning Post, May 2015. http://www.scmp.com/news/china/society/article/1799127/new-face-chinas-plastic-surgery-industry. Accessed September 2017.

17. Interviews in Beijing, October and November 2015.

18. China Mobile Health Market Research Annual Report 2012–2013, published by iiMedia Research Consulting. http://eng.hi138.com/computer-papers/internet-research-papers/201305/439592_20122013-annual-report-of-china-mobile-healthcare-market.asp#.VnENmtATH8s. Accessed September 2017.

19. "Digital Diagnoses: A Remedy for the Mainland's Healthcare Ills," September 2013. http://economists-pick-research.hktdc.com/business-news/article/International-Market-News/Digital-diagnoses-a-remedy-for-the-mainland-s-healthcare-ills/imn/en/1/1X000000/1X09U8HV.htm. Accessed September 2017.

20. China National Health Development Researcher Center.

21. See details on online purchase drugs below in the chapter.

22. https://www.wsj.com/articles/alibaba-affiliate-wins-approval-to-start-private-bank-1411970203. Accessed September 2017.

23. https://healthintelasia.com/alihealth/. Accessed September 2017; http://technode.com/2015/04/24/alibaba-affiliates-future-hospitals-can-access-chinese-medical-data/. Accessed September 2017.

24. http://www.chinabiotoday.com/articles/20160219. Accessed September 2017.

25. McKinsey/DXY, 2012 Physician Survey, June 2011.
26. https://www.clinicalleader.com/doc/overview-of-ehr-systems-in-bric-nations-0001. Accessed September 2017.
27. http://paccentury.com/electronic-health-records-in-china/. Accessed September 2017.
28. https://www.forbes.com/sites/ywang/2014/09/02/tencent-buys-minority-stake-in-chinese-healthcare-website/#6026ea662e99. Accessed September 2017.
29. From the report, "Power to the Patient: How Mobile Technology is Transforming Healthcare," The Economist Intelligence Unit, 2015.
30. mHealth is an abbreviation for mobile health, a term used for the practice of medicine and public health supported by mobile devices. Definition from Wikipedia: https://en.wikipedia.org/wiki/MHealth.
31. http://www.cnbc.com/2016/10/11/chinese-baidu-unveils-ai-health-chatbot-for-patients-and-doctors.html. Accessed September 2017.
32. http://www.chinadaily.com.cn/beijing/2014-07/31/content_18221458.htm. Accessed September 2017.
33. General Office of MOH of China: The Notice of the General Office of the Ministry of Health on the Promotion of Pilot Program of Building Electronic Medical Records as the Core Hospital Information. http://wenku.baidu.com/view/e098b6020740be1e650e9a9f.html. Accessed September 2017 (in Chinese); General Office of MOH of China: The Notice of the General Office of the Ministry of Health on the Issuance of the Second Batch of Electronic Medical Records Pilot Cities and Pilot Hospitals. http://wenku.baidu.com/view/e6226d0ebb68a98271fefae6. html. Accessed September 2017 (in Chinese); J. Lei, P. Sockolow, P. Guan, Q. Meng, and J. Zhang, BMC Medical Informatics and Decision Making, Vol. 13, 2013, p. 96.
34. "China's Health Care Reforms, " Health International, 10 Number 2010.
35. http://daxueconsulting.com/e-pharmacy-in-china/. Accessed September 2017.
36. Alibaba, Yunfeng Bought Control of Citic 21CN for $171 Million. https://www.bloomberg.com/news/articles/2014-01-23/alibaba-yun-feng-to-buy-control-of-citic-21cn-for-171-million. Accessed September 2017.
37. http://fortune.com/2016/02/21/cfda-ali-health-drug-monitoring/. Accessed September 2017.
38. http://www.wsj.com/articles/ali-health-swallows-bitter-pill-as-china-halts-drug-monitoring-system-1456144563. Accessed September 2017.
39. "Ali Health to Launch New Third-party Drug Tracking Platform," Marbridge Daily, 10 May 2016.

40. "China Pharmacies Urge Abolition of Alibaba Health Drug Tracking Platform," Reuters, 24 February 2016. http://mobile.reuters.com/article/idUSKCN0VX0UX. Accessed September 2017.
41. Interview in Beijing, November 2015. Name has been modified.
42. From the report, "Power to the Patient: How Mobile Technology is Transforming Healthcare," The Economist Intelligence Unit, 2015.
43. "Power to the Patient: How Mobile Technology is Transforming Healthcare," The Economist Intelligence Unit, 2015.
44. Zhou Dongxu, "Baidu Backtracks on Letting Private Firms Run Popular Forums," CaixinOnline, 13 January 2016. http://english.caixin.com/2016-01-13/100899054.html; Belinda Cao and Stephen Stapczynski, "Baidu Retreats on Chinese Private Hospital Advertising Boycott," Bloomberg, 6 April 2015.
45. The Relationship between the Branches of the Alibaba Group and Ali Health have been simplified here.

BIBLIOGRAPHY

Cao, Belinda, and Stephen Stapczynski, "Baidu Retreats on Chinese Private Hospital Advertising Boycott," Bloomberg, 6 April 2015.
Chen, J.H., S.G. Tu, H. Xiong, and N.Z. Xu, "Practice of Mobile Phone Real-Name System Appointment Registration," Chinese Nursing Research, Vol. 26, No. 1, 2012, pp. 170–171.
Dongxu, Zhou, "Baidu Backtracks on Letting Private Firms Run Popular Forums," CaixinOnline, 13 January 2016. http://english.caixin.com/2016-01-13/100899054.html
Guo, R., Z.M. Miao, G. Wei, S.C. Xing, and Y. Zhang, "The Present Situation and Suggestions of the Domestic Appointment Registration of Hospital," Progress in Modern Biomedicine, Vol. 12, No. 7, 2012, pp. 1357–1360.
Huang, M., "Exploration and Practice about Outpatient Appointment Registration Service Mode," Gansu Journal of Traditional Chinese Medicine, Vol. 24, No. 1, 2011, pp. 59–60.
Lei, J., P. Sockolow, P. Guan, Q. Meng, and J. Zhang, BMC Medical Informatics and Decision Making, Vol. 13, 2013, p. 96.
McKinsey Consulting Group Analysis, 2015. https://fr.slideshare.net/fle864/20150402-chic-mc-k-e-health-in-china-vf. Accessed September 2017.
Su, Y., J.L. Liu, and X.M. Yi, "The Idea About the Mode of a Patient-Centered Modern Clinic," Journal of Medical Postgraduates, Vol. 19, No. 1, 2006, pp. 74–78.
Xu, Y.X., and H.X. Ding, "Current Situation Analysis of the Hospital Outpatient Appointment Services," Clinical Medical Engineering, Vol. 19, No. 1, 2012, pp. 105–106.

Yin, X.Q., Z.Z. Huang, and L.J. Huang, "Design and Research on Appointed Outpatient Registration System in Modern Hospital," Hospital Digitalization, Vol. 31, No. 12, 2010, pp. 48–53.

Yu, W., X. Yu, H. Hu, G. Duan, Z. Liu, and Y. Wang, "Use of Hospital Appointment Registration Systems in China: A Survey Study," Global Journal of Health Sciences, Vol. 5, No. 5, 2013, pp.193–201.

CHAPTER 10

Conclusion and Discussion

Abstract As a conclusion to this book, the Chinese population is categorized into three subgroups that are likely to represent the demand side of
three very different healthcare markets in the future:

- A very disadvantaged population with a very low income that cannot
  afford healthcare access, even for basic healthcare, without the support and intervention of the state. This population is composed of
  those who benefit from Medical Assistance but also who are eligible
  for the two main public insurance schemes, namely the New Rural
  Cooperative Medical Insurance scheme and the Urban Residence
  Basic Medical Insurance scheme. This population is mainly from
  rural areas but with a growing element from urban locations;
- An intermediate level of population with income sufficient to afford
  access to basic healthcare but who cannot afford the whole package
  of healthcare offered. This population has, over the past three
  decades, experienced an amazing change in their healthcare quality
  preference. The level of quality required to satisfy their demand has
  increased highly. In the 1980s, considered here as the initial context,
  they were satisfied with a poor level of quality for almost free access.
  Nowadays, they look for qualified and trained physicians working in
  well-equipped hospitals. This population is willing to pay a substantial healthcare cost to get the level of quality it rates as necessary. For

© The Author(s) 2018   225
C. Milcent, *Healthcare Reform in China*,
https://doi.org/10.1007/978-3-319-69736-9_10

this population, severe pathology or chronic disease can lead to impoverishment and deterioration in the quality of life;

• A high-income population able to subscribe to a private insurance policy. This population mostly lives in urban locations. On the one hand, the level of quality requested to satisfy this audience is high. On the other hand, this population can afford to access a certain level of healthcare without the support of public health insurance. This population is the one targeted by commercial private insurance companies. These firms offer them supplementary insurance in addition to the public health insurance package.

Keywords Disadvantaged population • Income inequity • Urban/rural locations • Healthcare access • Health insurance package • Willingness-to-pay • Future healthcare markets

Today, China's public hospitals manage 90% of consultations for what English-speakers would call ambulatory care or outpatient care,[1] and 90% of hospital inpatient admissions. As such, public hospitals deal with the demand for treatment by consultation just as they must deal with inpatient treatment.

China is in the midst of a paradoxical situation. There has been a spectacular upward surge in health indicators, matching a similar increase in economic indicators. It is also a colossal market, with healthcare expenditure reaching $511.3 billion in 2013.[2] That is equivalent to 5.6% of gross domestic product (GDP).[3] On the other hand, the health system has officially been described as inefficient, and there is a toxic atmosphere between medical staff and patients.

In July 2015, an article in *China Daily* reported a 600,000-strong online petition by doctors calling for an end to attacks on medical staff.[4] This petition came in the wake of a patient's violent attack on a doctor during his shift at a Tier III hospital (*Longmen xian renmin yiyuan* 龙门县人民医院) in Guangdong Province. The local health and family planning commission responded by demanding that a police branch be set up inside the hospital, and regular patrols carried out, in order to facilitate swifter intervention in the event of violence. Surveillance cameras and alarms were also installed.[5]

The healthcare system has been through several phases of development. The major series of reforms[6] were announced in March 2009 by the State

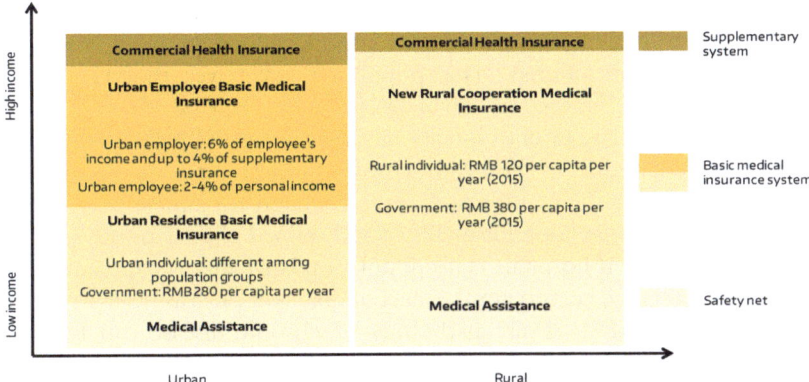

Fig. 10.1 Segmentation of the population. Source: Citi Research (2010); Ministry of Health (2014); UBS Research (2014)

Council of the People's Republic of China and the Central Committee of the Chinese Communist Party. They were followed by the 12th Five Year Plan (2012–2016), and now by the 13th Five Year Plan (2016–2020), which set out new directions for the future.

Along with healthcare reforms, demographic changes and increase in wealth inequalities have modified the demand for healthcare. Different types of insurance have been implemented according to the population location and income level (Fig. 10.1).

I propose to consider a categorization of the Chinese population into three subgroups.

As a conclusion to this book, the Chinese population is categorized into three subgroups that are likely to represent the demand side of three very different healthcare markets in the future:

- A very disadvantaged population with a very low income that cannot afford healthcare access, even for basic healthcare, without the support and intervention of the state. This population is composed of those who benefit from Medical Assistance but also who are eligible for the two main public insurance schemes, namely the New Rural Cooperative Medical Insurance scheme and the Urban Residence Basic Medical Insurance scheme. This population is mainly from rural areas but with a growing element from urban locations;

- An intermediate level of population with income sufficient to afford access to basic healthcare but who cannot afford the whole package of healthcare offered. This population has, over the past three decades, experienced an amazing change in their healthcare quality preference. The level of quality required to satisfy their demand has increased highly. In the 1980s, considered here as the initial context, they were satisfied with a poor level of quality for almost free access. Nowadays, they look for qualified and trained physicians working in well-equipped hospitals. This population is willing to pay a substantial healthcare cost to get the level of quality it rates as necessary. For this population, severe pathology or chronic disease can lead to impoverishment and deterioration in the quality of life;
- A high-income population able to subscribe to a private insurance policy. This population mostly lives in urban locations. On the one hand, the level of quality requested to satisfy this audience is high. On the other hand, this population can afford to access a certain level of healthcare without the support of public health insurance. This population is the one targeted by commercial private insurance companies. These firms offer them supplementary insurance in addition to the public health insurance package

In this book, I have shown that patients' expectations have become higher over time. They have been increasingly demanding about what a "trained and qualified" doctor should mean. As a consequence, the actual, addressable supply has been shrinking, creating longer and longer queues coupled with shorter and shorter consultation times. In parallel, the price of treatment has spiralled upwards due the financial autonomy of hospitals, as the government has withdrawn its support and doctors have been incentivized to generate revenue through over-diagnosis and over-prescription.

What with rocketing costs, extreme waiting times, consultation times reduced to a bare minimum, added to rampant bribery throughout the system, the patient–doctor relationship has progressively become more conflictive.

To address this situation, measures haven been taken to increase the number of public primary health centres and to encourage the development of the private sector in order to fuel competition among providers, or even to limit profit margins, for example by implementing "zero mark-up" policies on a list of essential medicines. Yet, all of these have had limited impact. Digital technologies offer a promising route to develop innovative solutions to fix the current inefficiencies in the health system in China. Among others, apps can be used as tools to streamline demand and orient it better to avoid, or at least limit, the congestion in Level 3 hospitals. We have also seen how the internet can be used by the authorities, public or private insurers or hospitals themselves to improve the efficiency of the healthcare system.

On the flip side, digital solutions also have their shortcomings. One of them is that this market is entrusted to a handful of giant private players. In order to achieve certain specific goals, the Chinese government made the decision to outsource certain public service tasks to profit-driven companies. There are therefore questions being raised about the potentially dominant position in which these firms could soon find themselves.

Based on recent reforms and innovative pilot programmes that are currently tested, three main models are emerging and might well be cohabiting in the future.

- *A model run by private insurance companies:*

    - Integrating digital healthcare, geographically located healthcare facilities (whatever their ownership: public, private for-profit or private non-profit);
    - This model may merge public health insurance schemes into the package offered;

- *A model run by internet companies:*

    - Primarily based on digital but integrating geographically located healthcare facilities (whatever their ownership: public, private for-profit or private non-profit):
    - With a banking service ensuring individual solvency;

- *A model run by public authorities at a local level:*

    - with a family doctor as gatekeeper of the healthcare system access;
    - with public health insurance and universal access to a basic basket of healthcare including drugs.

Thus, the main player could be the group of private insurance companies, the group of three internet giant companies or the public authorities at a local level. As we will see here, the same ingredients may give different results according to the main player driving the healthcare system.

A MODEL RUN BY PRIVATE INSURANCE COMPANIES

The Evolution

The basic medical insurance scheme covers a large majority of the population. However, an individual's out-of-pocket health expenditure is far from being negligible and it keeps increasing over the years.

Going back to the past for a quick reminder of the context, government and social health expenditure decreased dramatically and patients' out-of-pocket payments increased significantly as a result of the 1990s reforms. With the 2009 reform, the share of out-of-pocket payments decreased from 53% in 2005 to 38% in 2010.[7] According to Yip et al. (2012),[8] the enrolment rate in the public health insurance scheme (Urban Employee Basic Medical Insurance—UEBMI) reached nearly 93% in 2010 for urban residents without formal employment. The same year, 96.6% of rural residents had enrolled in the public medical insurance scheme there (the New Cooperative Medical System—NCMS).[9] However, the high proportion of out-of-pocket expenditure still remains one of the major problems of the current healthcare system.[10] In 2010, inpatient care expenses were reimbursed at a rate of 68.2% and all outpatient expenses were paid using the individual's medical account. For chronic diseases (such as diabetes) that are primarily treated in an outpatient setting, reimbursement rates are even lower. Actually, out-of-pocket payments for outpatient treatments can exceed 90% of the bill.

As a consequence, although a comprehensive public medical health insurance scheme is present, there are opportunities for commercial private insurance. Holders of public insurance cannot tailor their insurance coverage according to their needs and their willingness to pay when this can be offered by a private health insurance package. For instance, single-room inpatient care can be included in the package offered by private health insurance. These private health insurance packages are a form of supplementary insurance for consumers who already benefit from the public medical insurance scheme.

These packages are obviously mainly targeted at the most affluent part of the Chinese population. But, China's consumers are increasingly willing to pay for private health insurance and, in turn, look for access to better healthcare in the form of private healthcare services in private as well as public hospitals and extended service offerings. Thus private health insurance companies have proposed innovative models integrating physically located healthcare as well as digital health.

The presence of public health insurance can be seen as a limit to the development of such a scheme, but this assertion is only partially true. In Europe, different countries such as Switzerland and France provide evidence that supplementary insurance can be a highly developed market under the presence of a public health insurance scheme covering the whole population.

The more the system is integrated, the easier it is to pay bills. Up until now, the ability of insurance companies to tailor packages is hampered by their lack of data. Yet, there are ongoing discussions with the Ministry of Human Resources and Social Security (MoHRSS) in order to use some existing databases, even though there is no unified data system across the Chinese territory. At present, it is not possible to properly estimate the cost of treatment based on the pathology and the characteristics of the individual. As the insurers have little idea of the cost they might bear, they pass on the risk to their customers in the price of insurance policies.

To mitigate this risk, some insurance companies offer packages covering care up to a certain threshold, with or without co-payment, meaning consumers still bear their health risk directly by themselves to a large extent.

A diagnosis related group (DRG)-based payment method is also an alternative to control the cost in the context of lack of health information for insurers. The insurer reimburses the hospital for each subscriber's stay according to the fee set up *ex ante* and that depends on the pathology, the co-morbidity but also on the procedures performed. However, this mode of payment implies a unified healthcare database on the pathologies, co-morbidities, diagnostics and procedures as well as the details of the cost. Moreover, it implies an amount of the fee acceptable to the supplier (the hospital) and the payer (the insurance company).

Another direction is vertical integration, with health structures being part of the insurance. On the market there is an increasing number of packages based on the US managed care model. The most integrated schemes leave the insurer to decide the provider. According to the patient's pathology, he or she will be directed to a specific structure either belonging to the insurance company or at least an approved supplier of the insurance company. This delegation of choice of provider to the insurance company is compensated by an out-of-pocket payment that necessarily has to be lower and a quality of healthcare above the standards of the rest of the population. A good case in point is Cigna and CMC Life Insurance Company, a joint venture between Cigna and China Merchants Bank, which has been building a controlled network with a large number of health suppliers since 2010.

To address the main challenges of the Chinese healthcare system, namely the quality of care and the congestion of hospitals resulting in long queues, insurance companies have to develop two types of services:

- *Physically located healthcare facilities:* insurance companies have to make connections with public hospitals in addition to setting up private healthcare facilities;
- *Virtual healthcare providers:* we will see below the development of digital healthcare in liaison with insurance companies. The online insurance market is still largely geared to property and automobile insurance, but life and health insurance are likely to follow.

The Revolution

The internet is now changing the very nature of the insurance market.

Distribution network: With more than 500 million connected consumers and 300 million users of social networks, there is a huge potential for online distribution channels. So far, one identified obstacle to the development of private healthcare insurance is the amount of broker commission. With virtual platforms, insurers can directly reach their customers without intermediaries.

Insurance and connected mobile health devices: It has now become very common that, in order to define the premium to pay, insurance companies ask individuals to wear a mobile health device for a determined period of time. This device allows them to measure the physical activity of the future policyholder, as an element of the health status condition assessment.

Legal Context: In July 2015, the China Insurance Regulation Commission (CIRC) announced that it would approve online insurance companies that could offer insurance services through self-operated or third-party-operated insurance sales platforms.

As a consequence, companies are investing heavily to take advantage of this new regulation. For instance, German insurer Allianz recently joined with Baidu and Hillhouse Capital to create an online insurance company.

In addition, online services with added value can easily be bundled with the healthcare insurance package, be it from the insurer itself or from a third party. As a case in point, AliHealth has signed a memorandum of understanding with CPIC Allianz Health Insurance, a subsidiary of China

Pacific Life Insurance, in order to explore new online health insurance services. This service should tap into the Cloud set up by AliHealth, regrouping the full patient database of participating hospitals.

Innovative services also aim at bypassing long waiting times, but for the moment this is at the experimental stage. Other services include getting a second opinion online regarding diagnosis and procedures to be carried out.

Obviously, billing and reimbursement will also be key to the appeal of such schemes for customers. In a very near future, Alipay should establish operations linked to insurers that would enable patients to access their medical history and prescriptions on a digital platform and obtain real-time medical expense reimbursement. Another example is Zhongshan Hospital in Shanghai that is partnering with UnionPay to implement the "Modern Hospital" programme, which includes payment and reimbursement services.

As we see, the use of the internet will improve both health and healthcare information. It allows a more targeted insurance package at an adjusted premium but this mass of information will allow a more accurate DRG-fee to be calculated. So far, the pilot programme for a DRG-based payment system for hospital has delivered mixed results. One reason is the lack of relevant information for setting up the DRG classification and associated fees. With the development of health and healthcare databases such as the EMR (electronic medical record) and EHR (electronic health record), the availability of accurate information to establish a DRG classification and consistent associated fee may change the hospitals' reimbursement rules in the near future. For instance, private insurance companies will contract with the hospital for a pre-paid package covering a number of defined DRGs.

For Whom?

The management of the patient journey by insurance companies makes it possible to address the issue of referral, avoiding systematically using resources from Level 3 or 3A hospitals. In addition, the recent conversion of insurance companies to e-health may give birth to an array of services with added value, be it to reduce queues or to enable direct billing.

Nonetheless, these services are only offered to the part of the population that can afford the insurance premium, basically the urban population that has reached a significant level of income.

A Model Run by Internet Companies

As we have already seen, the three main internet companies, Alibaba, Baidu and Tencent are all becoming, in their own way, big players in the health market.

One of the key advantage they have over insurance companies is their knowledge of patient data. Even though the use of these data is limited by law, it still makes it possible to screen patients or even the population as a whole, which insurance companies are not able to do at present.

The pilot trial rolled out in 2014 by Alibaba offers a good example of a model run by an internet company. "Future hospital", as it is called, is an integrated model of online–offline services. First the patient needs to set up a bank account with the banking arm of Alibaba. This makes it possible to ensure his or her solvency. Then, e-services are offered to this patient, while storing his or her medical records online for any medical staff involved to be able to access the full medical history of this patient.

The three internet giants have become key links in the value chain of health, in particular for telemedicine, hospital appointment management, teleconsultation, medical record management and medicine sales.

Telemedicine: As explained in Chap. 9, Alibaba group has implemented a pilot programme providing telemedicine to a fishing village in Hubei province. Remote healthcare is provided by a physician from a very high-tech hospital (Level 3 or above). The aim is to develop an offer for remote areas where healthcare facilities are not easily accessible and where the population cannot easily travel to access them. The advantages of this offer are as follows:

- A higher standard of healthcare quality is provided than would be physically available in the area;
- An offer at an affordable cost is provided;
- Healthcare providers can consult without actually travelling to remote places;
- All medical information on the patient can be shared between all healthcare medical staff;
- Remote follow-up after performing the medical acts.

Another advantage of this offer is that it is bundled with the banking and pharmacy services of the Alibaba group. The patient can get the appropriate drugs from the Alibaba pharmacy subsidiary. The drugs can be sent to remote places through postal services. The solvency of the patient is ensured by his or her account at an Alibaba financial subsidiary. This kind of service is aimed at an audience that can afford to spend money on healthcare but cannot afford access to physically located high-level health-care facilities (i.e. basically the middle-income class located in rural areas).

Hospital appointment registration systems: In some provinces such as the municipality province of Beijing, to get an appointment in Level 3 and Level 3A hospitals, patients are now obliged to get an online appointment registration. This service can be provided by some apps, including the most popular app in China, WeChat from Tencent group. In Chap. 9, we saw the necessity for public authorities to outsource to major internet companies the implementation of such complicated online systems, given their skill and technological advance.

These online registration systems make it possible to avoid the long lines of people queuing for a doctor's consultation. It leads to a change in the climate inside the hospital by reducing the noise nuisance for medical staff, and it also reduces the risk of contamination by minimizing the close proximity to those suffering from different diseases. However, it does not reduce the waiting time to get to visit a doctor.

In order to avoid fake online appointments or the trafficking of appointment registrations, the identity of the individual is required. As a consequence, the company managing the system gets access to a lot of information concerning the patient and his or her pathology. This information can be used to screen the population and assess the risk of disease according to the individual's characteristics.

Virtual information platform: To store medical information at the individual level, virtual platforms are used. As for the hospital appointment registration systems, even if local public systems are involved, the set-up and management of such systems is often outsourced to specialized commercial companies, to maximize efficiency. For instance, the Beijing municipal government has launched a health iCloud platform with partial delegation to the Baidu group. As a consequence, a massive stock of historical health and healthcare information, at the individual level, is managed by a commercial company, which may then use it, under the constraint of legal regulation, to propose tailored services to the population.

Online drug sale: To complete the offer, the model is also based on online drug sales. So far, only non-prescription drugs can be sold online. These are split into two lists with one involving specific authorization. As presented earlier, the online sale of prescription drugs is still not fully authorized.

For Whom?

We have seen that this model can target quite diverse audiences. It is perfectly suited to well-off, urban, digital natives, but can also be directed to less affluent groups. In particular, the online aspect makes it attractive for a rural population previously quite isolated from many medical resources.

A MODEL RUN BY PUBLIC AUTHORITIES AT A LOCAL LEVEL

As explained earlier, Level 3 and Level 3A hospitals are in the inner center of the healthcare organization in China. The limitations of this system are the over-crowded conditions of these facilities and the extreme tension between patients and medical staff. To solve these issues, a set of measures aims to bring about a new healthcare system model involving:

- An online booking system;
- The development of a healthcare centre network in the rural areas;
- Family doctors;
- Consultations and drug prescriptions: from the virtual to the physical location.

The context: Currently, it is fair to say that public hospitals cover the vast majority of medical outpatient consultations and hospital inpatient admissions. This situation has dramatic consequences for healthcare spending. It is estimated that 30% of admissions are medically unjustified. The cost of an admission is calculated to be 37 times more than that of a consultation. Furthermore, in China the length of a hospital stay is twice as long as the average time recorded among OECD nations.[11]

Online booking system: People usually consider it better to queue up in a hospital that can provide quality healthcare rather than visiting a more local centre, which is more accessible but is not considered able to offer the desired quality of treatment. In any case, Level 3 hospitals provide an "all-in-one" option that Community Healthcare Centres (CHCs) and Level 1 hospitals cannot offer, due to their fragmented nature. As a consequence, the first priority is to provide a more efficient booking system. Today, the one adopted is the online booking system. To help those less familiar with virtual tools, a phone service is offered as well as the possibility of going in person to a physically located centre. This service is an improvement on both sides: demand and offer. For patients, it avoids waiting hours standing in the hallway of the healthcare centre/hospital.

For hospitals, it creates a more peaceful climate for medical staff without the over-crowded noisy patients waiting to be seen.

As we saw earlier, internet grant companies pre-empt this system. However, the key question is: who takes advantage of the information contained in the database set up from the online booking system? If the public authorities at a local level are able to use the data, they may adapt their offer to the demand. As a result, a more efficient public model could emerge.

Development of a network of healthcare centres in rural locations: Online booking systems do not solve the fundamental issue of congestion in Level 3 and 3A hospitals; they just make it more tolerable. Chinese authorities are currently attempting to modify the patient journey by creating a network of local healthcare centres. Their main advantages are:

- Their proximity;
- The availability of the supply without the nuisance of queues.

Still, they have to overcome some shortcomings:

- They do not have the "all-in-one" option that is a strong advantage of hospitals at Level 2/Level 3 and above;
- The level of qualification and training of doctors is not equivalent to what is offered in hospitals at Level 2/Level 3 and above;
- So far, there is little incentive for patient to modify their healthcare access patterns. Given the low level of reimbursement from public insurance for outpatient consultations, the difference in out-of-pocket payments between the patients following the new recommended journey and those still keeping to their previous habits is minimal.

Family doctor or general practitioner (GP): The incredibly long waiting times are in conjunction with very short consultations with doctors, often lasting less than 3 minutes, eventually causing stress and tension between medical personnel and patients and their families. The implementation of a family doctor system is at the heart of this new system. It is supposed to both:

- Improve communication between patients and medical staff, as well as obtaining better knowledge over time of the patient's medical history; and
- Shift the focus of hospitals to inpatient care.

As of today, the main obstacle to the implementation of family doctors resides in training, as it did not exist as such until recently. Young students must be confident in the commitment of authorities to this drastic shift in the system before choosing this career path. As far as patients are concerned, they have yet to overcome their prejudices against what they still see as insufficiently trained physicians.

Consultations and drug prescription: from the virtual to the physical location: To get around this lack of trust in local physicians, who are often considered to be insufficiently qualified, public hospitals also provide remote consultations from seasoned professionals. This system makes it possible to reduce the waiting time while monitoring any complication that may occur and require admission. Local health centres are involved in the process, functioning in parallel with hospitals. This makes it possible for the patient to be rapidly taken care of while benefiting to some extent from the quality of a bigger hospital. For both sides, it saves a lot of time, but hospitals must control the information within their networks, preventing its dissemination, which is a source of concern today.

Another point relates to the expenses associated with being treated. A first series of reforms to deal with this issue concerned the zero mark-up policy mainly targeting the drug's price when sold in hospital. A DRG-based payment is also a way to deal with healthcare expenses. To each DRG is associated a fee. These fees are defined *ex-ante*, before any hospital activity. Then, during the activity's period, each stay is associated with a DRG according to the pathology, co-morbidity and diagnoses of the patient, and for some cases, the procedures performed during the stay. At discharge, the hospital is reimbursed for the stay according to the DRG associated with this stay. This reimbursement is then disconnected from all additional procedures carried out on the patient. This type of payment limits the incentive to over-diagnose.

As explained before, a DRG-based payment is conditional on health and healthcare database implementation (including Electronic Medical Record (EMR) and Electronic Health Record (EHR)).

For Whom?

This organization of the healthcare system is suitable for any patient, even though it does not offer tailored care. In practice, it is probably most suited to patients with lower incomes, while patients who can choose their supplier might turn away from it, in order to consult the best-skilled doctors.

COMMONALITIES BETWEEN THE THREE MODELS

As a conclusion, whatever the model described, some general points appear. All three have in common:

- A transfer of consultations out of the hospital. First, because care in hospitals is very expensive. Then because hospitals are increasingly turning into high-tech centres, with low human interaction between patients and physicians. There is a growing consensus, globally and not just in China, that the actual time spent in hospital needs to be minimized while developing centres dedicated to recovery;
- An increase in the time doctors spend with patients. A genuine relationship needs to be built through this improved consultation time, be it online or elsewhere;
- A wide use of digital devices to improve communication between patients and doctors, but also between physicians. Connected devices enable medical staff to have accurate information regarding the patient's health status in real time. This information at the individual level, with very precise time sequences, generates an important mass of data making Cloud computing essential.

The Chinese healthcare system is in the midst of a transition. It has to transform to address its own specific issues, but the solutions that are implemented could inspire many other countries. So far, there are very few studies on this system and on the digital revolution that is happening there. There is probably material for many researchers to study, in a context where China is leading the pack in terms of digitalization of healthcare.

NOTES

1. Jeffrey Moe, Shu Chen, and Andrea Taylor, "Initial Findings in a Landscaping Study of Healthcare Delivery Innovation in China," IPIHD (International Partnership for Innovative Healthcare Delivery) Research Report 14-01, 2014; Xuezheng Qin, Lixing Li, and Chee-Ruey Hsieh, "Too Few Doctors or Too Low Wages? Labor Supply of Healthcare Professionals in China," China Economic Review, Vol. 24, No. 1, 2013.
2. "Industry Report, Healthcare: China," The Economist Intelligence Unit, August 2014.
3. The proportion of GDP spent on healthcare was 4% in 1990. It is 17% in the United States.

4. "600,000 Chinese Doctors Sign Petition against Hospital Violence," China Daily, 19 July 2015. www.chinadaily.com.cn/china/2015-07/19/content_21326495.htm. Accessed September 2017.
5. During my multiple visits to Tie III hospitals in Beijing and Shanghai, I also observed that police were routinely stationed at the entrance of every hospital complex.
6. To some observers, the turning point for the reforms incorporating more aspects of social security was the 2006 speech by Party General Secretary Hu Jintao, where he introduced the notion of a "harmonious society". Joe C.B. Leung and Yuebin Xi, China's Social Welfare, Cambridge, UK; Malden, MA: Polity Press, 2015.
7. W. Yip, W. Hsiao, W. Chen, S. Hu, J. Ma, and A. Maynard, "Early Appraisal of China's Huge and Complex Health-care Reforms," Lancet, Vol. 379, No. 9818, 2012, pp. 833–842.
8. W. Yip, W. Hsiao, W. Chen, S. Hu, J. Ma, and A. Maynard, "Early Appraisal of China's Huge and Complex Health-care Reforms," Lancet, Vol. 379, No. 9818, 2012, pp. 833–842.
9. J.L. Hougaard, L.P. Osterdal, and Y. Yu, "The Chinese Healthcare System: Structure, Problems and Challenges," Applied Health Economics and Health Policy, Vol. 9, No. 1, 2011, pp. 1–13.
10. Q. Long, L. Xu, H. Bekedam, and S. Tang, "Changes in Health Expenditures in China in 2000s: Has the Health System Reform Improved Affordability?" International Journal for Equity in Health, Vol. 12, 2013, p. 40.
11. World Bank, "Urban China: Toward Efficient, Inclusive, and Sustainable Urbanization," Development Research Centre of the State Council, Source MoH, 2011.

BIBLIOGRAPHY

Hougaard, J.L., L.P. Osterdal, and Y. Yu, "The Chinese Healthcare System: Structure, Problems and Challenges," Applied Health Economics and Health Policy, Vol. 9, No. 1, 2011, pp. 1–13.

"Industry Report, Healthcare: China," The Economist Intelligence Unit, August 2014.

Long, Q., L. Xu, H. Bekedam, and S. Tang, "Changes in Health Expenditures in China in 2000s: Has the Health System Reform Improved Affordability?" International Journal for Equity in Health, Vol. 12, 2013, p. 40.

Moe, Jeffrey, Shu Chen, and Andrea Taylor, "Initial Findings in a Landscaping Study of Healthcare Delivery Innovation in China," IPIHD (International Partnership for Innovative Healthcare Delivery) Research Report 14-01, 2014.

Qin, Xuezheng, Lixing Li, and Chee-Ruey Hsieh, "Too Few Doctors or Too Low Wages? Labor Supply of Healthcare Professionals in China," China Economic Review, Vol. 24, No. 1, 2013.

World Bank, "Urban China: Toward Efficient, Inclusive, and Sustainable Urbanization," Development Research Centre of the State Council, Source MoH, 2011.

Yip, W., W. Hsiao, W. Chen, S. Hu, J. Ma, and A. Maynard, "Early Appraisal of China's Huge and Complex Health-care Reforms," Lancet, Vol. 379, No. 9818, 2012, pp. 833–842.

Index[1]

[1] Note: Page numbers followed by 'n' refer to notes.

© The Author(s) 2018
C. Milcent, *Healthcare Reform in China*,
https://doi.org/10.1007/978-3-319-69736-9